Advance Praise for
Transforming Space Over Time

"I have found Beowulf to be a marvelous colleague, even (or especially) on challenging and complex projects. His creativity, ability to solve problems, and collaborative spirit are all in evidence in this useful, entertaining, and inspiring book that is both practical and personal. It is so like him to offer not only his own wisdom but that of his most experienced and articulate co-conspirators. I'm proud to be one of them."
~James Lapine, writer/director of *Into the Woods* and *Sunday in the Park with George*

"Beowulf Boritt is one of Broadway's brightest set designers. His work on my play *Meteor Shower* deftly expressed the complexities of the play and its demands for instant set changes. The play could not have been done without his incredible gifts."
~Steve Martin, writer/actor/banjo player

"Beowulf Boritt is one of the most exciting set designers to come along in the last decade. His attention to detail is evident in all of his productions—he becomes a master storyteller through his designs. The same dedication he brings to his glorious work, he also brings to this book. It's a completely engaging and insightful read."
~Susan Stroman, director/choreographer of *Contact* and *The Producers*

"In addition to Wulfie's enormous talents as a designer and craftsman, he is almost uniquely gifted with a sense of what a piece 'really is.' Every idea of his seems to amplify the initial intention. It's kind of uncanny!" ~John Kander, composer of *Chicago* and *Cabaret*

"Working with Beowulf on our modern-day *Much Ado about Nothing* was indeed one of the great joys of my professional life. To feature a brick home set in Atlanta, Georgia, draped with a political banner bearing the name of Stacey Abrams and the year 2020 set the scene perfectly for patrons to sit in Central Park and embrace this masterpiece written in 1585." ~Kenny Leon, director of acclaimed Broadway revivals of *Fences* and *Raisin in the Sun*

"If you love theater, either as a theater maker or as a theater appreciator or both, you should read Beowulf Boritt's book. He brilliantly and meticulously takes apart the process of creating a production. He is an immensely talented designer who understands both the plumbing and the poetry involved in making a show." ~Jerry Zaks, director of acclaimed Broadway revivals of *Guys and Dolls* and *Hello, Dolly!*

"Beowulf Boritt has an eye and a gift for storytelling, he marries the playwright's words to the images that create the world we live in onstage, he is a master, he knows never to overwhelm the story with a heavy hand of design, allowing every touch to illuminate the tale we're trying to tell. He's a master who studies the masters. In *Sunday in the Park with George*, the words 'look' and 'see' appear often. If I may borrow the words that Sondheim and Lapine gave Seurat to say: 'Give us more to see.'" ~Mandy Patinkin, George in the original Broadway production of *Sunday in the Park with George*

"This book is a must-read for anyone interested in the art of stage design. Beowulf is a mad genius. He brings ideas on paper to life on stage—and he does it brilliantly." ~Mel Brooks, writer of *The Producers* and *Young Frankenstein*

"Beowulf provides consistently clear-eyed insight into the process of creating theater—both straight plays and musicals. He complements the story of how the show was made with deeply engaging interviews with each show's director. Longtime theater-makers and fans of theater will be delighted by this book." ~Thomas Kail, director of *Hamilton*

"I love theater for the magic it can create and not just for audiences willing to suspend their disbelief but for the actors as well. That magic happened for me when I stepped onto Beowulf's stunning set of *The Seven Deadly Sins* at Lincoln Center's State Theater. I was transported by Beowulf's imagination, wit, and elegance, which allowed Wendy Whelan, the New York City Ballet dancers, and me to soar in safety and in inspiration. That is a feat. That is a great designer. That is Beowulf. The insights and stories in this book will be of great value to young directors and designers." ~Patti LuPone, Eva Perón in the original Broadway production of *Evita*

"Most of the design books I have read have been very technical and dry. Beowulf takes you on a journey. This book tells a story, actually several well-told stories. Stories about the people behind some of the best shows in theater and how those stories are in every fiber of his theatrical designs, and isn't telling well-told stories what theater is all about? I loved this book." ~James Monroe Iglehart, Genie in the original Broadway production of *Aladdin*

"From Cher's yellow plaid to Christian's convertible, design helps define stories. Beowulf is one of Broadway's best (and coolest) designers. This invitation to peek backstage with him is a treat for anyone who loves the theater." ~Amy Heckerling, writer/director of *Clueless*

"As both an audience member and a collaborator, I have literally had a front-row seat to the magic and artistry of Beowulf Boritt's scenic design. His knowledge, ingenuity, and creativity serve as an inspiration to all theater makers, and now, how fortunate we are to have this entertaining, informative, and enlightening book showing us Beowulf's process in motion. For anyone looking to expand their skill set and educate themselves about this important art form, this is a must read." ~Tom Kitt, composer of *Next to Normal* and *Flying over Sunset*

"When I go to a show designed by Beowulf Boritt, I have something special to look forward to: Where will he take me next? How will he realize his sense of 'where'? With abstraction, naturalism, romanticism, or some new way? I'm always captivated; I'm always surprised. In *Transforming Space Over Time*, Beowulf shows how he develops, inspires, and expands audiences' ideas of how a set can function and tell story in the theater." ~Jeffrey Seller, producer of *Hamilton* and *Rent*

"I couldn't put it down and read it straight through. I learned a LOT and had a ball reading it. Something VERY special and valuable here. Bravo." ~Thomas Schumacher, producer of *The Lion King*

"Working with Beowulf was a joy, and I felt held onstage by his design choices. Raising the stakes and pride of our entire production." ~Amy Schumer, actor/comedian

"Playing on Beowulf Boritt's sly and minimalist set established the tone for subversive play in the *Scottsboro Boys* musical, which was a deconstructed minstrel show. It had all the trappings of a glitzy yet makeshift world in which you could do anything, play anything, and be anything. It put the demands on the audience goer to let their imagination soar high and deep. A play space that was off-kilter set up by the beams that framed our space that gave dimension and depth to the stage but immediately you would know that something was awry. I loved playing on Wulfie's sets in New York, Minneapolis, and London. A designer who truly loves actors and trusts that he and his director would invite the artists into a play space in which they can have full agency as creators and interrupters of the space." ~Colman Domingo, Mr. Bones in the original Broadway production of *The Scottsboro Boys*

"I have always had great affinity for designers and have had such good luck in my work in the theater. Our design meetings about the Yiddish *Fiddler on the Roof* were magical and the result, perfection. I'm so grateful." ~Joel Grey, actor/director, Emcee in the original Broadway production of *Cabaret*

TRANSFORMING SPACE OVER TIME

SET DESIGN AND VISUAL STORYTELLING WITH BROADWAY'S LEGENDARY DIRECTORS

BEOWULF BORITT

APPLAUSE
THEATRE & CINEMA BOOKS

Essex, Connecticut

APPLAUSE
THEATRE & CINEMA BOOKS

An imprint of Globe Pequot, the trade division of
The Rowman & Littlefield Publishing Group, Inc.
4501 Forbes Blvd., Ste. 200
Lanham, MD 20706
www.rowman.com

Distributed by NATIONAL BOOK NETWORK

Library of Congress Cataloging-in-Publication Data

Names: Boritt, Beowulf, author.
Title: Transforming space over time : set design and visual storytelling
   with Broadway's legendary directors / Beowulf Boritt.
Description: Guilford, Connecticut : Applause, [2022] | Includes index.
Identifiers: LCCN 2021054407 (print) | LCCN 2021054408 (ebook) | ISBN
   9781493064847 (cloth) | ISBN 9781493064854 (epub)
Subjects: LCSH: Boritt, Beowulf—Anecdotes. | Theaters—Stage-setting and
   scenery—United States. | Set designers—United States. | Theatrical
   producers and directors—Interviews.
Classification: LCC PN2091.S8 B643 2022 (print) | LCC PN2091.S8 (ebook) |
   DDC 792.02/50973—dc23/eng/20220213
LC record available at https://lccn.loc.gov/2021054407
LC ebook record available at https://lccn.loc.gov/2021054408

For Mimi
You were born in
a merry hour.
Was a star danced, and under that were you born.
I love you with so much of my heart that none is
left to protest.

Contents

Foreword

How Does He Do It?

In the course of examining any artist's body of work, inevitably I begin to notice recurring motifs: a use of a particular material, a certain color, a specific harmony, a characteristic turn of phrase. Those repetitions, whether they're conscious on the artist's part or not, are guideposts to what an artist is really saying, what that oeuvre is really "about." I fell in love with Beowulf Boritt's work over twenty years ago, and I have been watching avidly since then, trying to articulate some essential quality of his set designs that makes them so clearly identifiable, so utterly his. But Beowulf doesn't make it easy.

My problem stems from the fact that what really draws me into Beowulf's work is the sheer "differentness," the chameleonic versatility of his designs. It's not just that one set looks different from another; what's remarkable about Beowulf's theatrical vision is that each set *thinks* differently. Not only does the visual aesthetic change but so does the mechanism that drives it. If one stage picture indulges in bold theatrical metaphor, another is realistic to the most quotidian detail. If the show you're seeing tonight feels natural, organic, earthen, then the show you see next week will almost certainly be industrial, cold, electronic. Sure, there are characteristics that define a Boritt set—most particularly his gentle but pointed humor—but at a glance, his twenty-five Broadway set designs (to say nothing of what must be upward of four hundred international, regional, and off-Broadway productions) don't seem to add up to a single statement. And yet I'm convinced that there is a big story being told over the course of Beowulf's career.

Set design is always a collaboration—primarily between the director, the writer, and the designer—but it is also a summation. What the set designer must do is make the writing, the direction, the size of the theater, the way an actor moves through space, even the very neighborhood where a play is being performed, all merge into a single physical representation of what this piece of theater has to say about the world we live in. Beowulf is not the kind of designer who imposes a point of view onto the work; rather, he creates a space where that point of view has room to announce itself. That gift is at the heart of Beowulf's magic, and this book is a key to understanding how he does it.

This is a book about how collaboration drives the artistic process, and as such, it's hardly just a book about set design or about theater. What comes out again and again in Beowulf's conversations with some of the greatest directors in the American theater is the relentless challenge of simply communicating. How can the art communicate the story, the emotion, the idea? This isn't a purely philosophical exercise. In order for the art to communicate, everyone has to be clear about what exactly they're trying to say, and as a rule, anyone who is unshakably clear about what they want to say is not to be trusted. So the process is about exploring the ambiguity in the idea, turning over both sides, trying the thing you know for sure is wrong so that you can see if maybe it's right. And to pull that off, you need both extraordinary technical skill and, even rarer, the ability to negotiate the impossible politics of ego and economics that are at the heart of theater making in the twenty-first century.

I've known Beowulf since his first big off-Broadway design, which was for my show, *The Last Five Years*, in 2001, and in these two decades, I've watched him guide audiences through stories of every possible genre and provide settings for every imaginable emotion. He's still got a long way to go before he's finished, but if I were basing my theory on the work I've seen so far, I think what Beowulf is trying to say is that the theater—with its skewed and forced perspectives, its endless limitations, its essential unrepeatability—is the place where we come to understand our lives. Some artists insist on telling the story; some move mountains so that there is space for the story to be told.

—Jason Robert Brown, April 2021

Prologue

I've designed 25 shows on Broadway in the past fifteen years. I've designed more than 450 across the globe in the course of my career. Yet when I'm asked what my design process is, it's difficult to answer. I start by reading the script and discussing it with the director, and I communicate the finished design by building a very detailed scale model. In between those two points, the process is as varied as the shows I've designed.

Collaboration between a designer and a director sparks creativity in both directions—and everyone's work is better for it. I've had the astounding good luck to have worked with some contemporary giants of the American theater, including James Lapine, Kenny Leon, Hal Prince, Susan Stroman, and Jerry Zaks. Each is a unique artist, and each resulting production was very different. The six shows included here were chosen to illustrate approaches to visual storytelling as different as these five directors are from one another.

The sixth interview is with a writer, Stephen Sondheim. His work is intrinsically tied to two of the directors I've included: Hal Prince and James Lapine. Reading and listening to Steve and James's musical *Sunday in the Park with George* was my gateway to a life in serious musical theater. I never had the good fortune to meet the other American literary giant who opened my eyes to what great modern theater could be, with *Fences*: the late August Wilson. But I'm lucky to have had the opportunity to work with Kenny Leon, one of his disciples.

Although my focus is on visual storytelling, I included a writer because I think of theater as essentially a literary form. In film the primary communication is visual: motion pictures. In dance the visual is paramount, usually in conversation with music. Music *is* the form of communication in opera; the words are secondary. But in theater—at least the kind of theater I tend to work on—the primary communication is literary: words.

That literature—the words of the script—is conveyed by actors to the audience. All the rest, including the design, is frosting. Design enhances the experience, focusing the audience's attention and enhancing the meaning of the words, but it's not strictly needed. Still, I prefer my cake with frosting.

Communicating place and time period can be an important part of set design, but I'd equate it to an actor being able to do a variety of accents. You ought to be able to do it, but it's not what makes your work great. Establishing time and place is neither the most important nor most interesting aspect of the work. Visually representing the themes of the story is. My goal is to couple thematically evocative visuals with a considered transformation of the physical space as the story plays out. Set design is a kinetic sculpture that is constantly being manipulated to enhance the emotions and narrative of the story: transforming space over time.

Thematic evocation and spatial transformation are my tools to create an intellectual concept to guide the scenery and support the story. Once that concept is clear in my mind, I can envision the style of the set: literally, what it will look like. When the process goes well, the frosting really does enhance the cake.

For each of the six shows I've chosen, I have mapped out my process from the very first glimmer of a concept, through its various permutations, all the way to the finished design the audience sees. Integral to that process is my collaboration with the other artists on the team—particularly the director, but also my fellow designers and production technicians. And perhaps equally critical are the business realities, the showbiz, associated with mounting a production, whether it is a star-powered show headed directly to Broadway (*Meteor Shower*) or a tortured, five-year marathon journey (*Prince of Broadway*).

I hope this book is entertaining for theater fans and theater veterans alike. My experiences on these shows, and the accompanying interviews with their directors, are meant to provide aspiring theater practitioners with practical tools and examples as well as an inspiring window into the art and craft of stage design. And because I clearly remember the challenges of being a young designer myself, I hope they provide encouragement to all who are just beginning their adventure.

—Beowulf Boritt, November 2021

ONE

Fairy Tale

Designing *Act One* for James Lapine

Once Upon a Time

In early January 2013, my phone rang. The caller ID said James Lapine.

"Beowulf, how are you? I've got a job for you, and I think it's a peach. But it's going to be very, very hard. I'm adapting Moss Hart's *Act One*."

"I'm in," I said.

A little history. The writer/director James Lapine created the Pulitzer Prize-winning *Sunday in the Park with George* with Stephen Sondheim. Sondheim has written in his book, *Look, I Made a Hat*, "James was . . . the first (and only) writer I've worked with who thinks like a director. His first impulse is visual." James also wrote and directed *Into the Woods*, *Passion*, and William Finn's *Falsettos*, among many others. And, most important to me, he directed *The 25th Annual Putnam County Spelling Bee*.

In 2004, as a young designer, I was interviewed by the director Michael Unger to design the first production of *Spelling Bee*, by William Finn and Rachel Sheinkin, at Barrington Stage, a small summer-stock theater. I was offered the job . . . and then I read it. It was a terrible idea for a show. It featured adult actors playing children; there was audience participation; and the music seemed inane to me. (Of course, I was too unsophisticated to consider the fact that I was listening to a rough "scratch tape" of the musical director playing and singing it.)

I told my agent, Ron Gwiazda, that I was busy and thought I should pass on the job. "I really think you ought to do this one," he suggested. "It has potential. David Stone [the producer of *Wicked*] is interested in it."

Ever the obedient client, I listened to him. Lucky break number one.

Parenthetically, about ten years later, I was offered another project that seemed profoundly uncommercial—a musical about 9/11. Who would want to see that, no matter how good it was? My new agent, Seth Glewen, said, "I really think you ought to do this one." Again, I listened. It turned into *Come from Away*, which, as I write this, has five companies playing. Suffice it to say, these experiences taught me that I need expert help in determining what's commercial!

Back to *Spelling Bee*. It went through several iterations in the year that followed. The tech process at Barrington was rough. Michael Unger couldn't seem to make Bill Finn happy no matter what he tried. After the Barrington production, Michael was fired, and Finn's old friend and collaborator, James Lapine, took on the project. Some members of the creative team were let go but, after an interview, James asked me to continue with the project. Lucky break number two.

The show opened off Broadway to great reviews, and David Stone decided to move it to the Circle in the Square Theatre. It was my first Broadway show. It ended up running for three years, and nothing opens professional doors in the theater like a hit Broadway show. Lucky break number three.

I designed several other shows for James in the succeeding years and didn't design several I thought he should have asked me to!

Bespectacled and bald, James is probably the least overtly dramatic personality featured in this book. But that quiet exterior belongs to a director who is exacting, difficult, and time-consuming to work for—and it's all worth it. The results are always exciting, because he's incredibly smart, and I know that all his pushing will stimulate me to design something more interesting than I would have come up with on my own. My work with James is "collaboration" in the best sense of the word. And as I've gotten to know him, I've found him to be a warm and caring guy under that cool exterior and biting wit. So when he called in 2013, I was thrilled.

Act One is the autobiography of Moss Hart, a titan of early twentieth-century American theater. Hart wrote nine plays—six with George Kaufman, including *Merrily We Roll Along* and *You Can't Take It with You*. In later years, he directed the classic musicals *My Fair Lady* and *Camelot*. *Act One* is arguably the theater's most famous and beloved rags-to-riches memoir. I gather it offers a very liberal version of the truth, but it perfectly captures the spirit of life in show business to this day. Call it a fairy tale of the theater.

The 400-page book covers a lot of ground, and James's adaptation is pretty faithful. The draft I first read was 160 pages long (about 50 pages longer than most scripts) and passed through about fifty locations. For perspective, Shakespeare's plays often have many locations, but he usually establishes each new place by having a character walk in and say something to the effect of, "Forsooth, what a nice castle this is, and it sure is dark tonight!" You seldom need more than a door, a balcony, and a bench to ensure that the audience at a Shakespeare play understands where they are. Modern playwriting, influenced by film, similarly tends to cover many locations but often with a minimalist design aesthetic in mind, so those locations can be boiled down to a table, a bed, a door. James's *Act One* called for the realism of a classic Moss Hart play. The kitchen needed to be a kitchen, with an icebox, a working sink, and a stove. The producer's office needed a desk, a typewriter, and a door, plus a door to an inner office that also needed a desk and chair. The mansion needed a desk, a typewriter, a daybed, a table to serve tea on, and so on . . . through fifty locations. It was important to embody Moss's rise in the world from the squalid and cramped tenement where his story began to the grand home of George S. Kaufman, where he ended up.

This wasn't a play; it was a movie.

I read the script first, then the book. With the flavor fresh in my mind, I made a chart breaking the play into locations, noting the duration of each scene by number of pages and physical needs, such as doors, windows, props, and so forth. Because of the complexity of the play, this document grew to the size of a small book—but it provided structure and organization.

While some scenes went on for many pages and would take up five or ten minutes of stage time, many ran less than a page before the location changed. The set would need to be fluid enough to carry the action from point A, to point B, to point Z swiftly and easily, without slowing down the storytelling. To further complicate matters, most of the scenes involved just two or three people; they needed to be played intimately. We couldn't risk the characters disappearing within a cavernous set.

When I sat down with James for an initial discussion, he had a vague idea that the show should play out on a multilevel structure that sounded a bit like Shakespeare's Globe Theatre. But the thing that really stuck in my mind from that first conversation was his desire to capture the excitement and energy of youth. Moss Hart is a young man in the story, ambitious and frenetic, and James wanted to show that. "I see him madly dashing up and down lots of stairs and banging on closed doors," he told me.

Lincoln Center's Vivian Beaumont Theater is a wonderful "thrust" stage, my favorite kind to work on. But it's huge. The proscenium portion is about sixty feet wide while a typical Broadway proscenium is less than forty. I had never designed for the Beaumont before, although I'd seen many shows there, so I spent some time sitting in the house, trying to get a sense of the space and imagining different ways to fit *Act One* into it. Fortuitously, on one of these visits, I ran into the brilliant set designer John Lee Beatty and asked if he had any advice about the space.

"Remember that it's enormous," he said. "It takes a long, long time for scenery to travel from the wings to center stage."

What constitutes a long, long time? In a show with just a few scene changes, twenty seconds may not seem very long. But if you have fifty locations and it takes twenty seconds to change each set, that amounts to more than fifteen minutes of scene changes in the course of an evening! That can absolutely kill the pace of a play, especially one that is three and a half hours long to begin with.

The concern that scene changes would weigh down the story led me toward an idea that the action could all play continuously in an abstract space. Usually, less is more onstage, so I started working on a set representing an empty theater seen from the side, perhaps with an onstage auditorium visible. The scenes would play out with minimal furniture used flexibly; for instance, the kitchen table might become the producer's desk just because the actors treated it as such.

This was hardly a new idea. I'd designed this sort of "backstage" set before, and other set designers have too. But it seemed right for a story about life in the theater and would also allow me to mask the depth of the huge stage so it wouldn't overwhelm the intimate scenes. I had a nagging feeling that the idea was not grand enough for the scope of the play, but I made an appointment to show it to James and get his reaction.

After six minutes of showing and explaining this "backstage" idea, I could tell that James thought it was a cliché. Stifling a yawn, he said, "You got anything else?" Luckily, I did.

The night before our meeting the nagging voice in my head had told me I needed a better idea—and I'd had a eureka moment. An idea had popped into my head almost fully worked out. It felt like divine intervention, but I guess it was my subconscious. My only tool to encourage these epiphanies is to spend time thoroughly reading and discussing a show and then to leave it alone for a few weeks without attempting to nail the design. My subconscious seems to keep working even when I'm not, occasionally with exciting results. This kind of inspiration doesn't always hit, but in this case, at zero hour, it did.

I could use the Beaumont's huge size to my advantage rather than fighting against it. I'd make a three-story-tall structure out of massive, raw wooden beams, like the skeleton of a turn-of-the-century tenement. The beams would define many, many small rooms in which the story took place, all packed and stacked together around a turntable. This way, each of the locations could be fully realized. If I could work out the location of each room in the scenic structure to mirror the play's written structure, actors could simply step from one location to the next as the turntable carried it to center stage. Each space would have to be relatively small—and that would help focus the audience on the tight, two-person scenes. Small spaces would also lend a note of realism; we were, after all, talking about cramped tenements and tiny producers' offices.

Once I had the idea, I realized I had better find a way to show it to James the next day. So I stayed up all night madly building a rough model with matchsticks, balsa wood, old popsicle sticks, and whatever else was handy to create the structure. Then I tore through my shoe box of leftover model pieces, doors, windows, and architectural details scavenged from earlier sets to flesh out the idea. By the wee hours of the morning, I had a model pulled together—quite rough but conceptually clear. In fact, its very crudeness seemed to speak to the play, which is all about the boundless energy and messy exuberance of youth. Its messiness also seemed to reflect the visual disorder of New York City, a place that's constantly rebuilding and reinventing itself, continually piling new structures over and around old ones. The exuberance of the model was exciting; I'd need to translate that into the final set.

I pulled this second model out and walked James through it. He thought for a moment and then said, "Yes. That's it." The whole thing, from idea to approval, had unfolded in about twelve hours. I'd spend the next six months sorting out the details and the six months after that realizing them.

Planning the Quest

As I worked, James developed the script. He reduced the required locations to maybe thirty-five instead of fifty. I broke the set into six pie wedges to organize it. The important locations that characters returned to multiple times would be more fully realized, while the sites visited only once or twice would share more neutral parts of the set that could be redressed between scenes to define new places.

The tenement that Moss Hart grew up in would be a full three stories, complete with an upstairs neighbor's apartment and a rooftop, all evoking the crowded living conditions. A stage with a proscenium, a working curtain, box seats, and a second upper balcony (important to the story) became another permanent part of the set. With few changes, this could serve as the seven different theaters needed over the course of the story.

George Kaufman's grand East Side town house, with an upstairs study, adjacent bathroom, grand entry hall, and downstairs living room, was another permanent structure. Connecting these three areas were three neutral spaces that could be transformed into all of the minor locations. An Escher-esque maze of stairs would connect the various levels to facilitate movement and provide additional playing spaces.

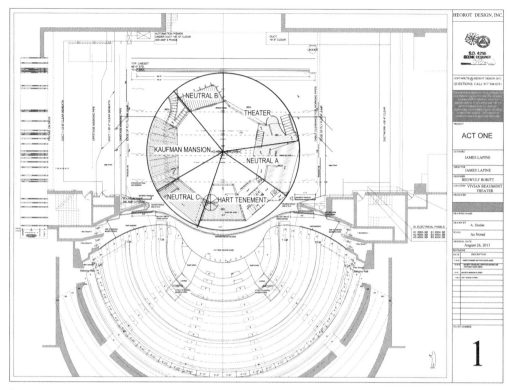

Ground plan of *Act One*

The set was designed to sit on an expansive donut turntable 75 feet in diameter. (For perspective, typical Broadway turntables are 20 to 25 feet in diameter.) Once the multistory structure was built on top of it, it would be downright huge. Almost from the start, I'd had the costs of the set hovering in the back of my mind, so I decided on the donut (a moving outer ring with a stationary center), thinking it would be a little cheaper to build if the entire 4,500 square feet didn't need to move. Sometimes producers insist that they don't want to shackle the designer's imagination with budgetary concerns, but the reality is that scenery costs money. If the budget is going to be fifty cents, there's no point in pursuing a brilliant idea that costs a hundred dollars.

For a set like this, I knew money would be a challenge. My budget was on the low side for a Broadway set in 2013. I had more money than I would for a single-location straight play but only about half what I would have expected for a musical—and *Act One* was like a musical in its requirements.

There's an old but valid cliché: "Fast, cheap, good—pick two." One reason Broadway sets are so expensive is that producers often have to wait to find out what theater will be available to them, and, with just a few months before the show opens, they have to scramble to build everything and rush it into the theater. Construction becomes extra expensive because of overtime premiums and rush orders on materials. I realized that in this case, because we knew we were going into the Beaumont and I could fully design the set well ahead of time, the shop would have longer than normal to engineer and build it.

To address the money crunch, James and I went to André Bishop, the artistic director of Lincoln Center Theater, and Jeff Hamlin, the production manager. We explained our idea for the set and showed them the rough model and some sketches. I think André was worried that the giant set might overwhelm the play, but, to his credit, he told us to move forward if we were confident about it.

Once I design a set, my assistant creates the technical drafting. Then I typically bid out the work to multiple scenery shops to see who comes back with the best and most economical plan. In this case, however, Jeff suggested that in light of our (too) modest budget, we approach a single scene shop and work with it to figure out the best way to build what we wanted within our means. He suggested a shop in Connecticut called ShowMotion, headed by Bill Mensching, a jolly bear of a man who is a perfect combination of artist and engineer. Bill always seems to know, or is curious enough to figure out, the right technical solution to the weirdest artistic challenge. Lincoln Center has had a long, solid relationship with ShowMotion.

Over the next few months, I worked with Bill to figure out how we could make our idea more affordable. One of the first things he suggested was to reduce the overall scale of the set to fit onto a sixty-foot turntable rather than the seventy-five-foot one I'd had in mind. It would still be pretty huge, apparently the largest turntable in Broadway history, but considerably less expensive. Bill also suggested we forget the idea of the donut. He had a thirty-foot turntable in stock, and it would be cheaper to enlarge it than to build a whole new donut. So much for my original cost-saving notion!

Working with the shops, painters, and technicians to build a set is every bit as much a collaboration as that with the director and other designers. If I listen to what they say and encourage them to bring their own creativity to bear, it almost always turns out better than if I keep a tight rein on every detail.

Having signed off on the smaller turntable, I began rethinking how the set could function within these new constraints. Don't misunderstand: I don't think of "constraints" as a negative word. There are always constraints, and sometimes they inspire good new ideas. In this case, the full turntable would allow me to expand some of the set structure inward. Moss's tenement could now be several rooms deep. Upstage of the kitchen would be more rooms, creating a warren of humanity all crammed

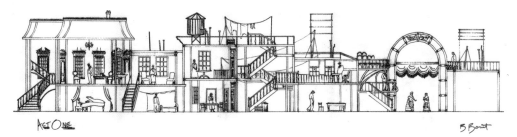

Initial and final sketch elevations of *Act One*

together. The added depth would also allow me to add interior catwalks and stair-cases, so actors could move through the middle of the space and appear in unex-pected places on the second level.

I read and reread the script. I drew and redrew a flattened-out elevation of the entire set, trying to work out where each scene would take place so the action could flow seamlessly. I began to think of the set as a line drawing of New York, sketched in wooden beams.

The massive wooden posts would be the outlines of the various locations and define their salient features but would define those spaces impressionistically, with-out including every detail. I had stumbled onto the etchings of Martin Lewis, a bril-liant early twentieth-century artist, and was using them as inspiration for minimal but specific detailing.

My crude first model was a starting point, but I'd need to build a more finished model in order to work out the details in three dimensions. I knew this was a physi-cally complex idea, and the model would be crucial in explaining various aspects of the set to James, the actors, and the shop. And it would be handled a lot, so it needed to be really sturdy.

I bought a bundle of square brass rods at the scale of the beams I envisioned and fired up my soldering iron. Throughout the swelteringly hot summer of 2013, I soldered and soldered and soldered. I built parts, stared at them for a day, and then tore them apart and rebuilt them. As fate would have it, my wife, actress Mimi Bilinski, was out of town doing a show, but I had other distractions to worry about:

Glow of the City by Martin Lewis, 1929

major construction going on next door to my apartment meant a literal jackhammer pounding in my ears. As I worked day after day, week after week, I became so focused on tuning out the noise and building the model that I stopped putting away my laundry or cleaning the apartment.

After a few weeks, I was living in tenement conditions myself, but I had a brass model of a set that would fit in the available space and serve the needs of the scenes. I added a bit of white paint and made it look like it was made of bleached, weathered wood. I decided to paint the surface of the turntable bright red to heighten the set's theatricality.

I'd "finished the hat" and was ready to show it to James. I was thrilled with the details and scope of what I'd done. Now to get the apartment cleaned up before Mimi returned.

James was away for the month and invited me to come up to his summer place on Martha's Vineyard to show him the set. I'm not ordinarily a fan of trekking out of town for design meetings, but a summer weekend on an island beach was appealing!

Model for *Act One*

After an endless drive through summer traffic and a relaxing ferry ride, I found myself sitting on James's deck, stepping through the model scene by scene to explain how the action would move from one location to the next.

James wanted even more stairways and doors, pointing out places where they would give him added flexibility in staging. But, on the whole, he loved the structure and the way it allowed the story to flow from scene to scene. We discussed the three neutral pie wedges as potential locations for new scenes he might write—an inevitability with a new play. These spaces could remain adaptable as the script changed.

But he hated the white set against the red floor. I had been trying to create tension between the rough, wooden beams of the structure, the modern cleanliness of the whitewash, and the red, but James felt it looked too modern. In tone, the play was meant to hark back to the early twentieth-century works of Kaufman and Hart. I promised to repaint everything in darker, more traditional wood tones so we could look at it that way.

By late summer, the model was finished. The tenement was a multiroom rabbit warren. On the deck level was the family kitchen with a working sink, an old gas stove, a pantry, and a kitchen table where Moss would write his plays. Next to it was a tiny bedroom for his aunt Kate. Upstage, stretching toward the middle of the turntable, was the rest of the apartment, with a living room sofa where Moss's parents would sleep and a bedroom for the boarders who supplemented the family's meager income. All these spaces were separated by sheer scrim sheets hung on clotheslines. This enhanced the patched-together, claustrophobic feel of a space that had been divided and subdivided in an attempt to give its inhabitants a little privacy.

Out the front door of the apartment was the common front hall with a three-story stairway leading upward. One level up was a public hallway with a telephone where Moss would receive an important call at the end of the first act. An apartment occupied by the Harts' nosy neighbor was directly above theirs. Finally, the stairway led up to the tenement roof where Moss would retreat for a little peace and quiet. The entire structure of the tenement section of the set was painted nearly black, like old wood layered with a hundred years' worth of black soot and grime.

Stage left of the tenement was a neutral area. A low-ceilinged lower level would be re-dressed from scene to scene to be a fur-coat factory, a rehearsal room, a diner, and a hotel bar. Above it was a room with windows facing into the turntable. This would function as three successive producers' offices, each one better appointed than the last as Moss climbed his professional ladder. New window dressings and show posters would indicate the change. In the second act, this space would be George Kaufman's dressing room.

Continuing stage left down a flight of stairs was the theater. I made a proscenium arch with a few working curtains. There were box seats and a second balcony—the

Act One model: Tenement and three-story stairwell

"cheap seats" from which Moss would see his first play. Through the proscenium arch, when the curtains were raised, was a view into the center of the turntable that would prove useful down the road. Next came another neutral space, a high-ceilinged open area that would become a theater manager's office, a crappy dressing room, and an all-purpose backstage room full of old flats and props. In the theater section of the set, the beams were painted to look like well-worn mahogany, the rich red tone reminiscent of the paneled interiors of traditional theaters rubbed to a warm patina by countless passing audiences.

Next was George Kaufman's town house, a version of the real one that still exists on East Sixty-Third Street. Kaufman's daughter, Ann, still lived there when I visited, and it's lovely, but I felt the theatrical representation needed to be grander. Kaufman provided Moss's entrée into theater work, and the house had to exude glamour and success.

I made a three-story front hall with a grand, sweeping staircase leading to Kaufman's upper-level study. Below the study was a twenty-five-foot-wide living room with a grand piano, sofas, bookshelves, and a dining table. A lavish party scene would occur here, where Moss would meet many of Manhattan's luminaries of the twenties, from Dorothy Parker to Langston Hughes to Edna Ferber. The party scene is a theatrical-memoir trope where a young up-and-comer meets and is awed by establishment bigwigs—and anyone who has worked in the theater can attest to its basis in reality. For me, this scene played out when I received my first invitation to Hal Prince's annual Christmas party at his Fifth Avenue duplex overlooking Central Park. Mimi and I huddled in a corner, happily overwhelmed, listening to Jason Robert Brown on the piano while Joan Rivers chatted with Lauren Bacall and Elaine Strich. On our way out the door, we literally bumped into Stephen Sondheim coming off the elevator. On my set, I wanted to create a room that might hold such an experience.

On the second level of the town house was Kaufman's office, the locus of the longest and most essential scenes at the heart of the play. It's the place where Moss becomes a playwright as he learns from and collaborates with Kaufman. These scenes are a window into how a playwright works and seemed to me a window into James's collaborations with Sondheim too. I would come to discover that the published version of James's *Act One* is dedicated to Sondheim—thus confirming my suspicion.

I made the office big and wide, with an oriental rug and nice though not ostentatious furniture. Three twelve-foot-tall windows opened to upstage. This was the "castle" of the fairy tale, the visual representation of a star playwright's success. To

Act One model: George Kaufman's mansion

the left of the office was an elegant little bathroom with a working sink, because Kaufman was obsessed with washing his hands. The entire town house, made of beams like the rest of the set, would be painted a bright white, so that Moss would journey from the grimy, sooty, filth of his impoverished roots to the bright cleanliness of Kaufman's affluence.

A final neutral space fit between the mansion and the tenement, serving as a hotel room in act 1 where Moss would encounter a crazy, stark-naked producer. In act 2, with new curtains and furniture, it would be a hotel room where Kaufman and Moss would work on endless rewrites. Below this space, reached by a steep, straight stair that Santino Fontana, the actor who would play Moss Hart, would dub the "suicide stair," was the small tenement bedroom mentioned earlier, re-dressed later to serve as a hotel lobby.

That was 90 percent of the set, but there were a few bits of scenery not connected to the main sculptural structure. Throughout the show, a massive red scrim curtain could travel, closed or partially closed, in front of the turntable to hide portions of the set and focus the audience's attention. There were several important scenes set in the back row of the theater, where Hart and Kaufman watched their plays in previews. In one scene, Moss watched his play descend into disaster, causing him to throw up into a trash can. A couple of metal back-row railings moved by actors into place in front of the theater balcony would represent this location. The scrim would partially obscure the trash can and the more graphic aspects of Moss's upset stomach.

Finally, I imagined ten light-up 1920s theater marquees that would fly in at the end of act 1, as Moss feels the door to Broadway opening to him. For this detail, I got lucky: Lincoln Center had made similar signs for an earlier production and had them in storage. I would probably have had to forgo this bit of frosting otherwise. Mirroring these signs, at the end of act 2, a huge marquee for *Once in a Lifetime* with Kaufman's and Hart's names emblazoned on it would fly in—visual evidence that Moss had indeed made it to Broadway.

Upstage of all of this was an enormous white cyclorama with a black scrim in front of it. Since the set was so massive, a sense of openness was crucial to keeping it from feeling heavy and crude. Lighting the cyc would reveal the open filigree of the set and make it feel light despite its size.

It was time to set the gears in motion and realize my design, so I handed the model over to Alexis Distler to do the technical drafting. I'd first hired Alexis in 2008 as an assistant on a small project. Within five years, she had become my most trusted associate. Alexis is a calm, sophisticated woman and an incredibly reliable associate whom I trust to make tasteful artistic choices when I'm not in the room. She has a great rapport with carpenters and painters, who always seem happy to do what she asks, and she's never shy about diving in and helping them do it. The first time I saw her, in three-inch heels, doing paint touch-ups on a set, I knew her elegance wasn't a barrier to getting the job done. She has been by my side through most of the experiences I recount in this book. My trust in her when we're working on a show makes her almost an extension of myself—and if I don't mention her that often, it is because we function so seamlessly as a team.

Act One was the most complex show Alexis and I had ever worked on together. It was such a maze of spaces and stairs and beams that it was tricky to flatten into two-dimensional drawings. Soon after this show, we would switch to virtual modeling in three dimensions—which, in retrospect, would probably have made the process easier here—but at the time we were still confined to a two-dimensional format.

After a few tough weeks and, I suspect, many sleepless nights, Alexis completed the detailed technical drawings for ShowMotion. In early September 2013, the shop had a go-ahead on a set we didn't need delivered until February 2014. Fast, cheap, or good? We had time on our side and the cost under control, so the only wild card was whether my work would prove to be *good*.

Before the set could be built, we had to figure out how it could be lit. This was trickier than usual because it was two and three stories tall, which meant that many of the locations had ceilings.

Ken Billington, the show's lighting designer, is a tall, elegant, white-haired man, always a gentleman and a consummate professional. Ken has more technical knowledge in his head than fills many textbooks, and he is a brilliant artist. We've worked together many times, but even on *Sondheim on Sondheim*—our first collaboration, when this Broadway legend found himself lighting for a novice set designer—he always treated me respectfully and kindly. Ken spent several days with the model, figuring out where he could hide tiny lights under the ceilings. While he was doing that, I laid out a plan for incorporating practical lights into the set: wall sconces, chandeliers, hanging light bulbs, you name it. By the time we were finished, there were so many individually controlled lights on the set that it was impractical to run individual control cables. Instead, Ken put six stacks of dimmer packs on the set itself, and I promised to find a way to hide them with steamer trunks or old tarps or fancy tablecloths. Ultimately, we had 126 individually controlled electric channels built into the moving set.

Next, I turned my attention to the hundreds of props the story required. My longtime collaborator Buist Bickley was on board as properties supervisor. Buist is six-foot-five and thin as a rail. He has a charming South Carolina accent and is brilliantly creative—one of the best prop supervisors in the world. As for his name

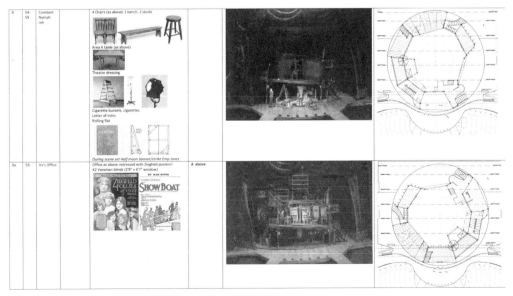

One page of the *Act One* scenery/props tracking chart

(and mine), Patti LuPone once quipped, "Beowulf Boritt and Buist Bickley? You sound like a vaudeville act."

I had been steadily expanding my tracking charts with details of how the set would rotate and what the props and dressing should look like. By the time I started working with Buist, I had thirty-six pages of information, including my notes on the re-dressing of spaces that had to be transformed, often in a matter of seconds.

Picking the props was crucial because they would have to do a lot of the work of defining and differentiating the many spaces within the vast set. We looked at varieties of furniture for Kaufman's study that might suggest refinement and wealth. At an antique store in my neighborhood, I found the perfect writing desk, but it cost $75,000! That's the danger of shopping in Midtown Manhattan. Buist found some furniture that looked downright tacky up close. Its upholstery was woven through with gold threads, and the finish was clearly cheap faux mahogany—perfect for a Real Housewife of New Jersey. But it looked great from twenty feet away. Buist was experienced enough to recognize what would work beautifully for our purposes—stage purposes.

We wrestled with each space, trying to come up with a limited number of props that would define the location clearly. The multiple dressing rooms were a big challenge. Generic theater dressing rooms, when not decorated by the actors inhabiting them, are blank, uninteresting spaces. Their only real defining characteristic is a wall mirror flanked by light bulbs—and we had a set with no walls. Buist found several freestanding Depression-era mirrors we could place on tables, and he built vertical banks of bare, period light bulbs protected by classic wire cages. He wired these to batteries and wireless dimmers so they could function wherever we placed them. This meant that a table serving as an accountant's desk in one scene could become an actor's dressing table seconds later.

In one scene, young Moss works briefly as an actor in a low-budget production of O'Neill's *The Emperor Jones*. We planned to place this on the theater section of the set, but I had to find the particular bit of added scenery that would define the scene. I looked at Jo Mielziner's original set for the opera version of *The Emperor Jones* and devised a cheap interpretation of it that looked particularly sad on an otherwise empty stage.

A particularly difficult scene to be staged on the theater set was a production of *The Beloved Bandit*, Moss Hart's very first play. In the book, Moss describes it as having the "ugliest green set you ever saw." James dutifully noted that description in the script, and he pronounced too tasteful every version I showed him. Finally, in frustration, I bought a set of children's poster paint and painted a saloon drop on cheap

Jo Mielziner's sketch for an opera version of *The Emperor Jones*, 1932–1933 (Museum of the City of New York)
Jo Mielziner

canvas—with my left hand. The thing would hang in my little proscenium and shiver, shake, and wrinkle whenever an actor walked near it.

Several cherished scenes in the book had to be included, and we had to figure out how the set might accommodate them. Late in the story, Moss has an epiphany and bursts in on George Kaufman, who is taking a bath, to tell him about it. Not surprisingly, James and I agreed it should be played in the bathroom that adjoined Kaufman's second-floor hotel room. The problem was that the prime downstage spot was needed for the sink for Kaufman's many hand-washing scenes. So, late in the show, I was going to need to swap out that working sink for a full-size bathtub. Karl Rausenberger, Lincoln Center's clever head prop man, managed to concoct a little internal pump, which we hid among towels under the sink so that water could run from the taps—yet the whole unit was self-contained and could be picked up and moved. I'd hide the bathtub (a lightweight, fiberglass clawfoot) nearby, under a table-cloth in the tenement's upstairs apartment, until crew could move it into the bath-room. It was a complicated switch, but the scheme for the set was full of these sort of prop changes to define locations.

Early and final versions of *The Beloved Bandit* set

The second important-but-difficult scene comes at the very end of the story. Moss's play is a hit on Broadway, and he can finally move his family out of their squalid quarters. As he leaves the tenement behind, it's raining, and he pauses to open a window, as if symbolically washing away his unhappy past. The only window in my tenement set was far upstage, and even with all our careful economies, the budget wouldn't cover the expense of making real rain on a three-story moving set! James and I discussed the issue several times. I always felt this was a weak ending. What kind of person floods an apartment, even a crappy one, that is no longer his? James kept insisting that it provided Moss a sense of release—that it showed him striking a physical blow against the world of poverty he was escaping. We decided to table the whole problem and hope a solution would present itself later.

This sort of detailed work continued until we had dressing for every location on the set. By the time we were done, we'd filled one of Lincoln Center's large rehearsal rooms with furniture. One day, John Lee Beatty happened by again and it was his turn to ask me a question. "How many shows are all of these props for?" he wondered.

"Oh, this just for act 1 of *Act One*," I replied.

Slaying the Dragon

There was no rehearsal space at Lincoln Center large enough for a sixty-foot set to be taped out. Instead, James opted to have a small upper platform with stairs built so he could get a sense of actors on multiple levels. He would have to track the actual locations of scenes in his head, using the model to help him, while our crack stage management team, led by Rick Steiger, shuttled props on and off as needed. I continually updated my tracking chart with the required props and furniture and began noting when I thought the props crew would have to come in to change set dressings as spaces transformed. The skeletal nature of the set meant there were only brief moments where the various spaces would be hidden from view so the crew could access them. The props shifts would have to be carefully choreographed.

Meanwhile, the set was nearing completion at the shop. Although it was meant to look as if it had been fashioned from big wooden beams, it was actually made of five-inch-square box steel painted by scenic artists to look like wood. Ironically, on our "wooden" set made of steel, the only real wood was some pieces painted to look like steel plates with rivets.

Because the set's structure was a giant ring, each piece of it helped support the rest, making it very solid. The shop had come up with some clever engineering choices to help with stability: For starters, all the banisters on the set, which I had initially specified to be wood, were built from steel rails and custom-fabricated steel balusters. Those railings became structural trusses to diagonally brace the set and keep it from shaking. Bill Mensching estimated that the set would weigh about a hundred thousand pounds when it was finished, and Lincoln Center hired an engineer to make sure their stage could support the weight; luckily, it could.

Even with our generous schedule and careful planning, set construction went down to the wire. The massive turntable was the first part transported to the theater for installation. The three-story structure had been assembled on top of it in the shop in order to test its movement, but the scenic painters hadn't finished their work on it when the turntable needed to be disassembled for shipping. So, one snowy February day, I walked into ShowMotion to see the entire three-story, sixty-foot set hanging by chains three feet in the air as the turntable was taken apart beneath it. As the set swayed on its chain hoists, thirty-five painters sent from Joe Forbes's Scenic Art Studios climbed around on it, painstakingly finishing all that steel to look like wood.

Over the next few weeks, the set was finished, moved, and reassembled on the Vivian Beaumont stage and then filled with props and dressing. After a year of preparation, we were ready to add the actors and see if our ambitious idea would pay off.

Whenever a story is about to play out on one of my sets for the first time, I'm both excited and scared. In this case, our physical idea was so massive and so relatively inflexible that it was especially terrifying. I could alter the set dressing and had made some parts of the set neutral enough to allow us some wiggle room in staging, but if, for example, we discovered that the long scenes in Kaufman's office felt too remote

The set suspended in the air at ShowMotion

up on the second level, I couldn't bring it closer to the audience. And—speaking of fear—the actors were experiencing their own kind of terror as they faced the prospect of learning their way around the giant moving structure.

About halfway through our first day on the set, James came up to me and said, "Thank you." He's frequently sarcastic, so I took a nervous step backward, wondering what scene or scenes I might have ruined. "No, truly, thank you. It's perfect," he reiterated.

After a few days, the cast had oriented themselves and were moving comfortably through the space—but an unanticipated problem arose. The enormous set moved so smoothly that even when they were standing on the turntable, they were unaware of its motion. Consequently, when they exited, they had no idea which direction they were facing. They might think they were exiting stage right but in fact were headed directly toward the audience. They kept getting lost.

Enter Lincoln Center's associate production manager Paul Smithyman, with side-burns and accent right out of a Dickens's story. He bought yards and yards of red and green rope light that we hung in the wings—red for stage right, green for stage left. It wasn't visible to the audience but provided the directional cues the cast needed.

Over several weeks of exhausting sixteen-hour days, we teched the show and continued to finesse the set. Alexis and Buist powered through with me, exhausted. On many meal breaks, we used the three "bedrooms" in the set for naps. The biggest challenge turned out to be executing all the prop switches involved in transforming the individual spaces. The play ran swiftly, which was good, but that made the quick changes *very* quick, which was hard. In one eleven-minute section of the first act, while the action alternated between the office set and the stage set, there were nine scene changes. The four props men would silently slip around inside the set to change one location while a scene took place just a few feet away—with very little internal masking to cover their activities. Watching from the house, we found ourselves much too aware of their activity.

I solved this in two ways. First, we added an eight-foot-tall masking curtain just downstage of the cyc. Without compromising the feel of sky and air in the distance, this created a shadowed bottom area that obscured the crew on the deck. And then, when the masking was removed for act 2, the set felt even more open and airy—a serendipitous correspondence to the arc of the story, as Moss began to escape the squalor of his childhood.

The second thing I did—reluctantly—was to sneak some masking into the dark corners of the main set structure. I didn't want to compromise the feeling of openness, but working judiciously, we were able to hang masking in a few key places without calling attention to it. Rather than black velour, which we feared might show against the open wooden set, Buist suggested we get some samples of less typical masking materials. We looked at various fabrics under different light cues and, much to my surprise, a forest-green synthetic chenille—something I'd never before even thought of using—seemed to blend in and disappear best. This was a great lesson in testing material under light whenever possible.

But even these alterations didn't solve all of our quick-change problems. The props men were working hard to stay hidden, but we kept catching glimpses of them. I simplified some dressing, and we spent several mornings rehearsing all the shifts with a stop watch. As we began the final dress rehearsal, I was hopeful we'd cracked the difficult section of the first act, but in the run-through, the changes remained a bit of a mess. We saw crew onstage, and when we couldn't see them, we could hear them thumping around. At one point I turned to James, ashen-faced, and, referencing a scene from the play, said, "I'm going to the lobby to throw up." He glared and shot back, "*You* don't have that luxury."

The morning of our first public preview, we rehearsed the difficult prop changes yet again, and I simplified some of the looks even further. I got rid of a difficult switch in the second act where we had to strike a producer's desk and replace it with a dressing room table. Instead, we re-dressed the desk, put one of our freestanding dressing room mirrors on it, and hid the producer's ornate chair behind a folding screen. One advantage of the fact that most scenes were short was that the audience didn't have time to scrutinize the locations too thoroughly. A few bold changes were all we really needed in order to transform the space.

Before the preview, I was a wreck—too anxious even to let Mimi come. Buist and Alexis insisted that I needed to have a drink before the show. I'm a lousy drunk and don't drink often, but they were right: A couple of margaritas helped calm me down. And miraculously, the show ran smoothly, as is often the case under the sudden pressure of having a live audience. The simplified prop changes had helped with the shifts, but mostly the crew had had one more day to practice their moves.

In previews, we discovered a potential masking concern in the theater set, too. Bill Nagle, the Beaumont's splendid head carpenter, had overseen the massive load-in and had been a rock through the long tech process. For the run of the show, he would be on deck, helping with scenery changes and operating the working curtains and drops in the theater proscenium. He came to me after a few previews and said, "Are you really sure you want me doing this? The entire audience can see me." I made a note of how exposed he was and wrote down the changes he was particularly worried about.

That evening, I sat in the fourth row and really looked for Bill. The truth was, I could barely see him. Although there was nothing physically masking him, Ken had lit the show so specifically that I simply couldn't see him. This was one way that the Beaumont's vast size worked in our favor. Far downstage, Bill felt exposed—but he was still a good twenty-five feet from the front row of the audience. That's far enough that the ambient light emanating from the scene being played even farther downstage didn't reach him; he disappeared into the midstage gloom. We could never have gotten away with that in a smaller theater.

A final difficult prop switch came with the appearance of Kaufman in the bathtub. We had figured out a way to get our lightweight bathtub into place in the bathroom for the famous scene, but there was no way to get water into it. And even if we could solve that issue, there was no time for Tony Shalhoub, who played Kaufman, to shuck his clothes and get in the tub, then get out of it, dry off, and dress for his next scene.

Buist came up with a clever solution. He made a sheet out of a clear, rubbery Bubble Wrap that looked sort of like a bubble bath. Tony would strip to the waist and pull this "water sheet" over his lower body. Because the tub was on the second level, only those audience members in the high seats would see the "water," and they'd be far enough away for the illusion to work. It sounded like the answer but, despite rehearsing it a couple times, we could not make the timing work in our fast-paced production. James could have lengthened the scenes before and after to provide more time, but he felt that the play needed to move at top speed as it neared its conclusion. With regret, we abandoned the bathtub—but that didn't mean it wasn't there. For the rest of the run, it sat disguised as a side table in the neighbor's home. The whole episode taught me not to get too tied to the source material. The bathtub scene was something people remembered fondly from the book, but it didn't fit well into our telling of the story. James was smart to let it go.

And then there was our rain problem. Once we were on the set, it was clear that opening the tenement window and cueing the sound of rain would not be an effective dramatic gesture. James suggested that instead of Moss throwing open the window to "destroy" his past, he could make a mess of the place by tearing down the sheets that had divided the tenement's rooms. We spent a morning installing some quick release catches on the ropes that held the sheets, and voilà, we had a nice punctuation mark for the scene. The gesture was simple but had a dramatic finality to it that made the point.

At the first preview, the play ran three and a half hours. James diligently refined the story, cutting a sentence here and there and carefully chiseling away at unneeded language. I don't think he ever cut a whole scene, yet he managed to make the show a full hour shorter. I've never seen anything like it.

The actors tightened their performances, and the action of the set got tighter as well. Bursts of short, staccato scenes progressed seamlessly from one location to the next as the turntable shifted the audience's view. Moss dashed up flights of stairs and through doors. When he hit his first major setback—the failure of his first play—the set mirrored his dejection as he took a long, slow, silent walk through half the moving set, back to the filthy tenement where he had started out. This was my favorite moment in the show. The scenic structure was seamlessly melding with the writing structure. The space was transforming over time to help tell the story.

At the end of the first act, the glowing Broadway marquees slowly appeared, transforming the space in a new way—literally lighting the way toward Moss's future. In act 2, James's writing changed to allow for longer, calmer scenes, which I mirrored in the appearance of Kaufman's massive, immaculate mansion. At the same time, we revealed more of the cyc, making the entire giant sculpture feel lighter and airier. The set still revolved, but less frequently and more slowly, as Moss matured and grew. Finally, the appearance of the *Once in a Lifetime* marquee announced the fact that Moss Hart was now a bona fide member of the Broadway elite as a final set-revolve carried off his tenement forever.

Happily Ever After

After five weeks of previews, we opened. I loved the project, and I've become accustomed to shows I love being destroyed in the press, so I was fully prepared for bad reviews. During an elegant opening night party at the Plaza Hotel, Jane Greenwood, our brilliant costume designer who looks and sounds like a diminutive English elf, came up to me and said, "The *Times* is out. And it's good!" In fact, most of the press was quite generous. It seemed that all our hard work was being appreciated by both the press and the public.

Normally, once a show opens, I'm done. Often, I don't even see it again. But it was late April, and that's awards season in the New York theater.

I want to digress for a moment here and talk about theater awards. They have always seemed like a popularity contest to me—like voting for homecoming king and queen. How do you determine the best actor or play or set or whatever among a field of diverse shows? "Best" is subjective—not quantifiable. If we gave awards for highest-grossing show or largest audience, that could be measured. But "best" play?

Having said all that, winning awards leads to more and better opportunities—more chances to design sets for exciting shows. And perhaps more important, a vote of approval from a group of peers feels good! It's nice to know that people you've worked with or may work with in the future like what you've done.

Of course, it stings a little to do good work and get passed over. Chalk the whole thing up to a very human impulse to give and receive recognition and to the more mercenary impulse of calling attention to shows that need audiences to keep running. From Student of the Month to the Nobel Prize, awards aren't going away . . . so I have tried to make peace with the whole process. I try to stay unaware of when the nominations are going to be announced—which isn't easy, since the theater press makes a big deal out of it. Toward the end of every April, I give myself a mini news blackout. I figure that if I'm not nominated, I'll notice eventually; and if I am, someone will let me know.

On a Tuesday morning in early May, my phone buzzed, and there was a text from Buist saying, "AAAAAAAAAHHHHHHHHHHH!" I figured that was good news. As it turned out, *Act One* was nominated for quite a few awards, including best set design.

I had been nominated for a Tony once before, for *The Scottsboro Boys*. But that show had closed months before the nominations, so many voters never saw it. And the set, though clever and effective, was very, very simple and highly unlikely to win a Tony. *Act One* was a different story. As we'd loaded it into the theater, Alexis had said to me, "I think this is your Tony." I told her to shut her mouth and not jinx me. But people kept saying it, and that's hard to ignore.

Maybe some people truly love the excitement of the awards process, but it makes me completely neurotic. When you get a Tony nomination, literally everyone you've ever met, everyone your parents have ever met, and some people you've never met, call, text, or email. It's very, very nice, but it's overwhelming. The weeks between the nomination announcement and the actual awards are a marathon of cocktail parties and press events; it's like living in a movie montage. That has its enjoyable moments, but it's completely divorced from real life and it's exhausting. Keep in mind that I'm only a designer, and most of the world doesn't even care about theater design. I can only imagine the pressure on actors, directors, and writers, who are squarely in the spotlight throughout. I know . . . poor me.

To further ratchet things up, *Live from Lincoln Center* announced that they were going to film *Act One* for telecast on PBS. I was thrilled that the production would be recorded for posterity, a rarity in the ephemeral theater. But it didn't do much to calm my frayed nerves.

By the time we reached Tony night, I was a nervous wreck. Over and over, I had heard, "You're going to win!"—which made me think, *And if I don't? Does that mean I'm letting my friends down?* Sitting there while your name is *not* called is a very public letdown in front of your peers.

On the night of the Tonys, Mimi and I had pre-show drinks with Jess Niebanck and her husband, Paul. Jess is the general manager of Lincoln Center Theater and one of my oldest, dearest friends. The point was to try to calm down. That mission was not accomplished.

The Lincoln Center press office had requested I walk the red carpet, so I did—with Jane Greenwood and Dan Moses Schreier, my fellow nominated designers for *Act*

One. In a way, walking the carpet put the whole hullabaloo in perspective, because, as designers, we were one step above invisible. The press wanted a picture of James Earl Jones, who was to my left, and Patti LaBelle, to my right. I was just some guy in the way of their shot. I made it to the entrance with my ego only slightly bruised.

You probably know that the Tonys are televised. But designers have been deemed uninteresting to the general public, so the design awards are given during the commercial breaks or—in this case—before the telecast even began. Billy Porter and Karen Ziemba read out the names of the nominees, and then I heard, "The 2014 Tony Award for Best Scenic Design of a Play goes to Beowulf Boritt for *Act One*."

For all my attempts to downplay awards, there's really no way to describe the rush of emotion and adrenaline at a moment like that. I kissed Mimi and ran onto the stage. If they hadn't neatly stepped back, I think I would have kissed Billy Porter and

With Mimi outside Radio City Music Hall

Karen Ziemba. Mimi had insisted I write down a thank-you list (despite my insistence that it would jinx me!), and thank God she did because, there I was, staring out at five thousand people packed into Radio City Music Hall, and my mind was a blank. I stammered out my gratitude and escaped to the wings—the world beyond the spotlight where I've made my life.

James had invited me to help tell a story. I had a lucky flash of visual inspiration a year before. That idea had journeyed through sketches and models, survived through budget constraints and engineering challenges, and helped tell the sprawling tale it was designed to accompany. Most improbably of all, I was being rewarded with a trophy acknowledging all that. It was the perfect ending to my fairy tale.

And we all lived happily ever after. I wish.

TWO

Deceptive Perspective
A Conversation with James Lapine

Setting: *James Lapine's office is a spacious studio apartment on Manhattan's West Side in a condominium famous for housing Broadway folk. Minimalist midcentury modern furniture makes a comfortable, casual sitting area. James's desk sits at the far end of the room, backed by a wall of posters from his many shows, from* Sunday in the Park with George *to* The 25th Annual Putnam County Spelling Bee. *Framed design renderings offer the tiniest hint of the director's focus on visual storytelling, but on the whole, the space is a deceptively conventional-looking base of operations for a man whose approach to Broadway is very un-Broadway.*

BEOWULF BORITT: James, let's start at the beginning. How did you become a director? You trained to be a graphic designer, yes?

JAMES LAPINE: I went to grad school for photography at Cal Arts, and while getting my master's, I took a couple of graphic design courses. After graduating, I made money doing freelance photography work for journals and magazines. I found it incredibly stressful. I really wanted to be a fine-art photographer. So I switched over to making my living through graphic design, because it was a craft and I knew how to do it. To make a long story short, I ended up getting a graphic design job at the Yale School of Drama, designing their theater magazine. As part of my job at Yale, I also had to teach an advertising class to the management program. My students encouraged me to direct a play because they knew that although I didn't go to a lot of theater, I was interested in avant-garde, Richard Foreman kind of stuff, which they weren't doing at Yale at the time. I said, "Give me a play," so they found this Gertrude Stein play called *Photograph*. The title alone got me. It was five acts but only three pages long. "Perfect," I said.

I did about an hour-and-fifteen-minute production, which was about sixteen variations on the play, using different images, different photographs and paintings, as the inspiration for each variation. One of them was *A Sunday Afternoon on the Island of La Grande Jatte.*

The local paper came and reviewed it and loved it. My girlfriend was a stage manager, and she said we should do it in New York. She found a loft for us to do it in, but we didn't have any money. Another friend of mine was doing her doctoral dissertation on Jasper Johns, and she said, "Jasper Johns loves Gertrude Stein." I wrote him a letter, and he sent us $2,500, and we put up the play. It was so, you know, "Hey kids, let's put on a show." I literally put up posters all around Soho saying, "Anybody want to be in a play?" And whoever showed up—

BB: —was in the play?

JL: Mostly! Another friend of mine said we needed to get reviewers in. She was a kind of sexy, persuasive woman, and she picked up the phone and called the lead critic of the *New York Times* and talked him into coming, and he gave us a half-page rave review. So that's how I started in the theater.

BB: I call my chapter about *Act One* "Fairy Tale." Your start sounds like a fairy tale, a bunch of amazing happy accidents. One of your early shows got an Obie Award, didn't it?

JL: It was *Photograph*. Because of my design background, I think one of my favorite parts of every show is designing it, working with the designers to figure out the look. I just fell into directing.

BB: When did that turn into writing?

JL: Pretty much right away. Designing the magazine for all those years, I was reading plays all the time. The first one I wrote was called *Twelve Dreams*, based on a Jungian case history that included strange dream images: dancing on the moon, birds emerging from a girl's skin, weird things like that. I "wrote a play," but it was really about setting these visual images that interested me.

BB: It was very visually oriented?

JL: Yeah. It was skeletal. It wasn't a great play. I've never really had a block about just trying things to see if they work: I just give it a go. I discovered that I liked writing.

BB: My whole career I've thought, *Try it.* Plenty of people will tell you what you can't do; you don't need to tell yourself no. Although . . . I find the older I get, the harder it is to follow that advice.

JL: When you're young and stupid, it's great. You have free rein to do anything.

BB: You have nothing to lose financially. You have no reputation to lose. You're fearless.

JL: You haven't done much, so you're freer. Once you've done a lot, you start repeating yourself.

BB: I'm very aware of this. Mimi came to see one of my shows, *Superhero*, and said, "The set's good, but it looks a bit like *The Scottsboro Boys*." She was right.

JL: If you talk to Sondheim, he'll tell you the same thing. He'll be writing a song and suddenly it feels like a song he's already written. I think anyone who works long enough finds they start repeating themselves.

BB: Speaking of Sondheim, let's start with *Sunday in the Park with George.* How did that show come about?

Sunday in the Park with George by Stephen Sondheim and James Lapine tells the story of pointillist painter Georges Seurat, creator of the painting *A Sunday Afternoon on the Island of La Grande Jatte.* The figures in the painting are characters in the story, which revolves around the love affair between George and his model, Dot, a love doomed by his devotion to his art. In the stunning finale of the first act, the actors (and a few life-size cutouts to complete the illusion) compose the painting live onstage. The second act presents a different George—great-grandson of the painter and a modern conceptual artist in the 1980s. He is guided by his grandmother, Marie, the child of Dot and Seurat, to a stop questioning himself and create. Lapine and Sondheim won the Pulitzer Prize for Drama for *Sunday,* and James's words for George at the beginning and end of the show are a touchstone for me: "White: a blank page or canvas. His favorite—so many possibilities." James directed the original production with a set by Tony Straiges, costumes by Patricia Zipprodt and Ann Hould-Ward, lighting by Richard Nelson, and sound by Tom Morse. Sam Buntrock directed the 2008 revival with musical staging by Christopher Gattelli, set and costumes by David Farley, lighting by Ken Billington, projections by Timothy Bird and the Knifedge Creative Network, and sound by Sebastian Frost. Sarna Lapine directed and Ann Yee choreographed the 2017 revival, which I designed, with costumes by Clint Ramos, lighting again by Ken Billington, projections by Tal Yarden and Christopher Ash, and sound by Kai Harada.

JL: As I mentioned, I loved the painting. I'd already done a variation on it in *Photograph*. In terms of a design, it's easy talking about *Sunday* because it's driven by the image. You're working backward, which dictates certain decisions. There are a lot of things about the painting that are screwy in terms of its perspective. We couldn't create the deceptively weird perspective of the painting.

Tony Straiges, born in Minersville, Pennsylvania, in 1942, designed his first Broadway show, *Timbuktu*, in 1978. Sixteen more would follow, including *Into the Woods*, *Golden Child*, *Rumors*, *I Hate Hamlet*, *Harold and Maude*, and *Enchanted April*. Although my only experience of his design for the original production of *Sunday in the Park with George* is seeing it on video and studying the model, I find it so spot-on brilliant that I never wanted to design the show. There seemed simply no way to improve upon his design or even come up with a different way to approach it.

BB: To quote your show back to you, the people are "out of all proportion." Had you worked with Tony Straiges, who designed your set, before *Sunday*?

JL: No, although I knew Tony's work from Yale. I just felt he was the right guy because he's a literal designer in a way. Do you know what I mean? It's not quite fair to say "literal"—but he loves painted sets.

BB: I think I do know what you mean.

JL: He's old school. He has no assistants. He hand paints all of his models. He builds them himself. He's a very nineteenth-century kind of guy to this day. He just recently learned to do email and has no cell phone. That's probably why he doesn't have much of a career—he's a Luddite. But brilliant.

JL: One of the ways we created the painting was with cutouts of people and animals, which we used to fill out the image. It was a vocabulary that went through the second act too.

BB: One of the soldiers is a flat cutout, as are the dog and the monkey. In the second act, George leaves cutouts of himself at a cocktail party "chatting" with tedious art patrons. Was that always the way you planned to present some characters?

(Clockwise) Mandy Patinkin, Bernadette Peters, and company on Tony Straiges's set for the original Broadway production of *Sunday in the Park with George*. The monkey and the dog are two-dimensional cutouts; Mandy Patinkin as George with a cutout of himself; Jake Gyllenhaal, Analeigh Ashford, and company in the 2017 revival of *Sunday in the Park with George*; Daniel Evans, Jenna Russell, and company on David Farley's set for the 2008 revival of *Sunday in the Park with George*. Top images: Martha Swope, © Billy Rose Theatre Division, The New York Public Library for the Performing Arts; Bottom left: Joan Marcus; Bottom right: Matthew Murphy

JL: Yes, we were trying to make it about the power of George's imagination.

BB: He was able to literally grab a piece of the visual composition and move it to a different position.

JL: The biggest challenge, one of the biggest design choices, was pointillism.* How do you do that onstage?

BB: In reality the dots that make a pointillist painting are tiny; you can only see the individual points of color when you're right on top of it.

JL: The theater audience is so far back that if you really want to portray pointillism, you need pretty big dots, which would make it a different-looking kind of set. David

---

*Pointillism is a technique of neo-Impressionist painting using tiny dots of various pure colors, which become blended in the viewer's eye. *Oxford Languages Dictionary*.

Hockney came and saw it and stormed out at intermission saying, "Where are the fucking dots?"

BB: If you made them large enough to see from the back row it would have looked like a nursery school or children's theater.

JL: We decided not to do that in the set itself, but to do it in the canvases that were onstage.

BB: You didn't emphasize the pointillism in the set, but it's very evident in the music and the structure of the music. You can hear George's brush dotting the canvas in the quick notes in "Color and Light." Did you guys talk about how you could express visuals musically?

JL: No, and Steve really didn't weigh in much on the visuals. I would describe this and that to him and he would just say, "I don't know how visual dynamics work." Of course, the minute I showed design ideas to him, he'd have many interesting things to say. I don't want to psychoanalyze it, but I was the first person to work with him after all those years with Hal, so I think we were just finding our own way of working together.

BB: Was *Sunday* the first time Sondheim worked with a cowriter who was also directing the show?

JL: Definitely, yeah.

BB: That must have been different, though, having worked with Hal myself, I know he's intrinsically involved in the writing of his shows.

JL: When Steve and Hal did a show, they had a team that included a book writer, composer/lyricist, and a director, and now suddenly, Steve just had me. I prefer to work that way.

BB: You created an arc for the show that involved starting with a blank canvas and ending with a full painting. Was that always the plan?

JL: Yes, that was the starting point. I wrote the first act before Steve wrote anything. We'd talk endlessly about the show. He'd talk about lyrics and sometimes read me some quatrains, but he never really wrote anything except the opening arpeggios. That was nerve-racking, because I thought, *This guy's never going to write a song. This will never happen*. But, in fact, he was thinking all along. He doesn't like to write until he knows exactly what he's doing.

BB: That makes sense; his words and music are always so intricately, carefully structured and balanced.

JL: That's why he is who he is. Nobody else approaches the work with such care and detail.

BB: Approaching a set, I think of it as a whole. All of the parts of a set, even if they're not seen together, are interconnected. They balance each other visually over the time the audience is watching the show. A big flashy scene at one point in the story can be balanced by a minimal set later. If a scene is cut in previews so its scenery is gone, I find it really jarring—like a house of cards that might collapse. When I get upset about this, people look at me like I'm crazy. Maybe it's only a problem in my head!

JL: No, I get it. It's how you've conceived it. It happens in writing too.

BB: You workshopped *Sunday* at Playwrights Horizons and then immediately moved to Broadway?

JL: Yes—which was insane because we didn't even have a finished second act! What can I tell you . . . it was a different time. That whole process of creating and mounting the show took only two years, from the day I met Steve to opening on Broadway. And keep in mind that Steve didn't write any music for the first six months—so it was really a year and a half. Of course . . . he was used to writing shows even faster than that.

BB: Steve and Hal created a lot of those shows very quickly.

JL: Yes! Steve says some of the early ones, like *West Side Story*, were crazy fast because Bernstein had so many other commitments. They just *did* it.

BB: Sometimes "fast" works. You don't overthink it, and you get it right.

JL: Exactly. But . . . we had a tortured preview period for *Sunday*.

BB: On Broadway, you mean?

JL: Yeah. Off Broadway, everyone thinks everything is great. They make all sorts of allowances because we're still working on it, putting in new songs, changing things, and so they love it. The things they don't love they think, *Oh, they'll fix that*. But even as we workshopped it, from that very first moment where the tree flies out as he's erasing it from his pad, we were establishing the language of the show. Audiences started laughing at that moment, and when Steve heard that, he grabbed me and said, "They get it!" So we knew it was a good idea for George to be in control of the design in that way.

BB: Because you approach theater so visually, and you were writing and directing the show, you could really drive the storytelling with the images. The abstraction possible in theater allows two separate worlds to coexist easily: a person and the representation of what that person is imagining. That visual conceit is baked into the writing of *Sunday*.

That visual representation of George's thought is what I loved about Sam Buntrock's use of projections in his revival. I often don't like projections, because they can be too literal, too obvious. But in Sam's version, I felt I was watching George think.

JL: It worked really well.

BB: You and Steve were not involved with that revival, right? Other than seeing it and saying, "Yeah, this can come to Broadway"?

JL: I think Steve said, "It *should* come to Broadway." So I agreed! It was exciting to see these young people with a new take on it.

BB: *Sunday* is one of my favorite shows ever, though I didn't see the original. But when I was in high school in Gettysburg, I took a dramatic literature class at the local college. I first read *Fences* and *Sunday* in that class. So I knew the show as literature, and I'd seen the video of the Broadway production. It was so wonderfully, meticulously designed that I never wanted to attempt it because I didn't have any new or different idea about how to do it. Then Sam's version came along, and it was very different—really smart and took advantage of new technology. That confirmed that I didn't want to do it. I still didn't think I'd have a new idea. So there's an irony that I ended up doing the most recent Broadway revival. I honestly don't know that I designed it very well.

JL: Well, it was a concert version, a glorified concert. You were stuck with the orchestra onstage.

BB: Yes, which limited the design possibilities in a show *about design*.

JL: I think you did an absolutely fine job with it. And in some ways, maybe the show worked better, because if you take the visual elements out a little bit, it makes the audience fill them in.

BB: In general, I love stripping things down. I did the Yiddish *Fiddler on the Roof* that's running right now, and it's really stripped down. That can be exciting, especially on a show that people know well. It makes everyone hear it in a different way. Of course . . . sometimes it works, and sometimes it doesn't.

JL: It must be hard for a designer, because you don't get to show off. But if you do it right, the show is the star.

BB: You once told me that in one of your early shows in New York, someone wore a costume made out of paint chips—those color samples you get on cards at the paint store—and that was part of the impetus for *Sunday*.

JL: That was designed by this brilliant woman, Maureen Connor, who was a sculptor. I did two shows with her before she said, "Forget this theater thing." She didn't want to work with actors anymore. She had an incredible imagination. The brilliant paint-chip costume was for the *Sunday* section of *Photograph*. We had no money, so Maureen went to all these paint stores, took paint chips, and made a costume out of them. It was brilliant. She made a cravat out of plastic into which she put crayons, so there were all these colors of crayons—it was extraordinary. Maureen made really magical things. For *March of the Falsettos*, she put the actors into . . . what's it called . . . buckram?

BB: Scrim-like fabric, but stiff?

JL: Yeah, totally stiff. The actors came out and the light shone through it—it was brilliant. A lot of her sculpture was clothing-related.

BB: Did she make it all herself?

JL: Yeah.

BB: One of the things that frustrates me about commercial theater is that you have to function in the *business* of it to make a living. I used to build more of my designs myself, but that takes so long that I really have no choice but to turn it over to shops to build it all for me if I want to survive.

JL: I hear what you're saying. When we were first putting together the workshop of *Sunday*, Tony Straiges would stay at Playwrights after we all left and work all night painting the set himself. And once we got to Broadway, despite the union restrictions, he somehow managed to keep doing it.

BB: I don't really know Tony, but the story is famous: They would lock him in the theater at the end of the night, and he'd do whatever he needed to do.

JL: Yeah.

BB: It's a constant issue for me, wanting to put my personal touch onto the show. I find that as long as I'm respectful of the union crew—and my associates are respectful—they'll usually let us pick up paintbrushes and work a bit. But working on enough shows to make a living doesn't leave a lot of time to make or paint scenery.

JL: The economics for designers are terrible, I know, though you seem to be managing to make a living. I do believe your work can suffer from doing too much.

BB: It can. Absolutely.

JL: I've been pretty lucky in my career to be able to do just one show at a time. But I have had to take other jobs to make money. I've directed movies and a couple of plays that were really just for the money. You have to balance it.

BB: Learning how to do that is part of growing into a career in the theater, isn't it?

JL: What's been interesting to me about my own growth as a director working with designers is trying to find collaborators who can give me something with flexibility, who don't stick me with something immutable. I was a neophyte when I did *Into the Woods*, so maybe I didn't know how to demand this. Tony designed a set with a kind of sweep in the deck.

BB: It was a raked turntable in the middle of the set, yes?

JL: Yes. It never went away. I was stuck with it for the entire show. It worked great sometimes, but not always, and I couldn't get rid of it.

BB: It's so important that the space be able to transform over the time of the play. When you and I work together, it's one of the challenges. You're always pushing me for something visually interesting, but we're both aware of needing flexibility too. It's hard to create both at the same time.

Into the Woods was either the first or second Broadway show I ever saw. I remember reading a *New Yorker* review of it beforehand and thinking, "That sounds so cool." I didn't know who Stephen Sondheim was. I thought you were James Levine of the Metropolitan Opera, which I knew about from their Saturday afternoon radio shows. My parents and I were coming into New York for a weekend and I said, "I want to see *Into the Woods*." I also saw *Phantom of the Opera* on a rush ticket the same weekend. It's poetic that years later I ended up designing for both you and Hal.

I also saw your *Into the Woods* revival thirteen years later. The two productions offered very different takes on the design, but let's talk about the original one. Can you tell me a little about how you developed the first design with Tony Straiges?

JL: Tony designed these sliders made up of tree branches—really beautiful—and we had this turntable-rake idea. Tony does very exacting drawings, so the show looked

Into the Woods, Sondheim and Lapine's second musical, weaves characters from multiple fairy tales into a single story. The first act tells the tales as we know them, in a series of overlapping adventures (including that of Jack and the beanstalk and his beloved cow) leading to happy endings. In the second act, the wife of the giant Jack killed in act 1 descends to wreak vengeance on the kingdom as the various characters (Rapunzel, Cinderella, Little Red Riding Hood) begin to explore the consequences of their actions. James directed and Lar Lubovitch choreographed the original production with a set by Tony Straiges, costumes by Ann Hould-Ward, lighting by Richard Nelson, and sound by Alan Stieb and James Brousseau. He also directed the 2002 revival with choreography by John Carrafa, a set by Douglas W. Schmidt, costumes by Susan Hilferty, lighting by Brian MacDevitt, projections by Elaine J. McCarthy, and sound by Dan Moses Schreier.

great as renderings. As a relatively inexperienced director, I didn't really know enough to think about beyond those moments. Cinderella's song looked great, and the Baker's song looked great, but we hadn't really thought through how to go from A to B to C.

BB: It's one of the dangers of beautiful renderings and models, they can be so seductive that you forget they're just a tool to get to the design onstage. When I storyboard a show, I draw every transition, with lots of notes and arrows indicating what's moving. Robin Wagner says, "Designing a musical is about designing the transitions."

JL: Yeah, and I really learned that the hard way on *Into the Woods*, because it has a lot of little scenes. One reason we revived it thirteen years later was that I felt I hadn't fully cracked it. I thought I could improve it as a writer as well as refining the design. What I discovered was, I couldn't. It had been just fine the way it was. My so-called improvements didn't have a big impact.

BB: It's a really solid story, but less reliant on design than *Sunday*, so a different set didn't radically change the experience.

JL: The second time, I worked with Doug Schmidt, who designed a much more literal kind of woods. The set was beautiful.

BB: Doug's set could more fully transform from one location to the next; you avoided the immovable center stage rake. I remember it being beautiful and very storybook, literal *storybook*, with big books onstage.

JL: Yeah, it was literal.

BB: Whenever you and I work together, we have endless discussions of "That's too literal" or "That's not literal enough." The woods are both literally part of the story and a metaphor for life, so I guess you can choose to represent them literally or not. Both of your versions of *Into the Woods* had literal woods scenery, but I could see it working well without a single tree.

JL: I've seen lots of different productions over the years, and it's a show that seems to be able to sustain a lot of different interpretations. Once you're doing a show that's become iconic in its way, you don't have to do as much. But when you're launching something—

BB: When I'm doing the first production of anything, I feel I owe it to the writer to stick closer to what they've written. When you're doing *Hamlet,* you can set it anywhere and no one is going to be confused.

JL: That's true.

BB: In Doug Schmidt's set, the books opened to become houses and Rapunzel's tower. Was that a starting point or did that come later?

JL: That was the initial concept—that the books would be there from the beginning of the story.

BB: Another design change for the revival was the cow. In the first version, the cow was a toy, basically.

JL: That they carried like a suitcase! The challenge was how to make it fall over dead.

BB: It was a costumed actor for the revival.

JL: Susan Hilferty designed that great cow costume for the revival. It was originally played by an actress, but she couldn't physically do it.

BB: Because you need a lot of upper body strength to wear a costume like that? You're supporting your whole upper body with your arms, your arms on stilts.

JL: The cow understudy took over and was brilliant. I had to yell at him because he was always stealing focus. He could steal any scene just by batting those cow eyes.

BB: The danger of animals, even fake ones, onstage! Between your original and your revival, I did a production in summer stock. I wanted to create the giant as a shadow somehow. Everyone in theater has had the experience where you're standing onstage and something moves in front of a light and makes an enormous moving shadow. Everybody jumps because they think something's falling. I thought that was how to make the giant—but we never quite made it work. What Elaine McCarthy did in your revival, creating the giant as a projected shadow, was wonderful, really effective. Literal, but it made the giant a presence in an exciting way.

JL: That's always the challenge.

Sondheim and Lapine's *Passion* unfolds in nineteenth-century Italy and concerns a handsome soldier engaged to a lovely woman. His colonel's unattractive and awkward cousin, Fosca, falls obsessively in love with him, and ultimately—surprisingly—her relentless adoration wins his love in return. James directed, with choreography by Jane Comfort, set by Adrianne Lobel, costumes by Jane Greenwood, lighting by Beverly Emmons, and sound by Otts Munderloh.

BB: Speaking of challenging shows, your third musical with Sondheim was *Passion*—in 1994.

JL: Adrianne Lobel designed it.

BB: I saw it on Broadway.

JL: We made a big booboo on that one, which, in retrospect, was totally solvable: that dining table, that big thing lumbering on and off. Now, I would have said, "Cut it in half! Bring it on as two pieces! Make it more manageable." I didn't have a great choreographer on that one. She's a great choreographer, Jane Comfort, but she's not a staging problem-solver.

BB: It's important to have a choreographer who understands musical staging, directing traffic. Often in musicals, that means the choreographer is responsible for dragging scenery on and offstage to maintain the rhythm of the show, but I'm sure it's not any choreographer's favorite part of the job.

JL: You have to make the transitions work.

BB: I remember the set design as quite simple, a big sliding wall painted in the style of J. M. W. Turner.

One of Adrianne Lobel's early sketches for *Passion*
Adrianne Lobel (courtesy of Douglas Colby)

JL: Very simple. Adrianne is an abstract designer. There was a big staircase and scrims.

JL: We worked hard on it, but we had a lot of problems with *Passion*. We did a simple workshop, and everybody just thought it was the best thing that had ever happened. And it *was* pretty great with nothing—which is probably why I went the abstract route. When we got to Broadway, I don't think people understood they were in nineteenth-century Italy where, for example, if you loved someone, you cut your hair off and gave him a braid. I found that fascinating and put it in the script, but audiences just roared with laughter. They thought the character was an idiot for doing that.

BB: You think the abstraction of the set meant it wasn't providing enough historical context?

Adrianne Lobel was born in Brooklyn in 1955. Her first Broadway design was for Tommy Tune's 1983 production of *My One and Only*. She designed the scenery for the Broadway productions of *Passion*, James's 1997 production of *The Diary of Anne Frank*, the 1998 revival of *On the Town*, and *A Year with Frog and Toad*, which she also produced. Off Broadway, she designed James's 1995 revival of *Twelve Dreams*. Other notable productions include the Peter Sellers production of John Adams's opera *Nixon in China*, and Mark Morris's *The Hard Nut*.

JL: I saw Eric Schaeffer's revival of it in Washington, designed by Derek McLane. I thought that they got it right. It wasn't abstract; it was literal—but interesting. They just used architecture. It was forced perspective in a tiny space, but it worked. The bed kind of slid out from the architecture. The set had a period background to it; it could be the city, the barracks, anything. And it helped the audience know where they were.

BB: My instinct is for abstraction and simplicity, but there are times when a show needs you to provide specific visual information about time and place, or it confuses the story.

JL: It's a tricky piece, but I love it. It's one of my favorite things I've done. I had wanted *Passion* to be sung through—no spoken dialogue—which we tried at a workshop. Steve got very hot under the collar and I asked him why. He said, "Because my music sounds like shit. You need a rest from the music. It's not opera." He's so smart. Once I set up the songs with dialogue, everything had more cohesion—even though it's not a show with big musical numbers per se.

BB: That interplay between the dialogue and the music creates the rhythm of the show. The rhythm of shifts in the physical space shapes the storytelling similarly. If you screw up that rhythm, it creates speed bumps that disrupt the flow of the story.

JL: I assume you listen to the music while you're designing a musical?

BB: If it's been recorded, I listen to it a lot. The truth is, I'm musically incompetent. I played the violin—badly—for eight years, so I can read music a little, but I am basically ignorant about music. Of course, hearing the music of a show gives me a feel for the mood, emotion, and pace of it.

JL: I'm stupid about music, too, but I'm musical. You respond to it or you don't. I think a director has to be musical.

BB: I suppose to direct any theater piece, but certainly a musical. Or something like *Act One—*

JL: That was a musical in disguise.

BB: Those are the kind of plays I tend to design, plays that function like musicals—meaning they have lots of locations, just no song and dance. That's really what got me studying how the rhythm of the spatial transformations has to be in sync with the rhythm of the writing.

JL: Well, the writing of *Act One* was musical—maybe because it was inspired by the book, which has a musical drive and energy to it.

BB: When we were designing *Act One,* we talked endlessly about the structure of the scenes and using the physical presentation to tie everything together. We wanted the short, staccato scenes to flow together within the physical structure of the set, and find the places where we could do a big scenic revolve that rhythmically worked with the show.

JL: That was a brilliant set. You got your Tony, but I don't think people appreciated how complicated that set was. We had a huge, long first act, and even though you'd created one big set for the whole show, you managed to keep the second-act surprise—the Kaufman mansion—hidden. It was brilliant. It was there all along, and nobody knew it.

BB: My favorite response was from [set designer] Tony Walton, who emailed that he had loved it but wondered how we were able to add the big Kaufman set in at intermission. I told him he was looking at it the whole time! It was all about how we angled the turntable.

JL: That was a coup, even if audiences didn't realize it. But we discovered it was tricky when I pulled out a scene. It had all been beautifully laid out, and suddenly we had to punt to get the action from here *way* over to the other side of the set.

BB: We had enough neutral areas on the set to change things as you adjusted the script. It's always the same issue on new musicals: the written structure is invariably going to change. You get it on its feet, and you find out that some scene doesn't work and has to be cut. This is one of the reasons I love working on revivals. When I designed *On the Town*, I knew what the show structure was; I knew scene 4 would always follow scene 3 and wouldn't get cut! There's a different kind of fun in those situations. I think this is a good segue to a musical where the structure remained in flux well into previews: *Sondheim on Sondheim*.

JL: That set was great.

BB: I loved it because it was so abstract and so endlessly flexible. But it took us a long time to figure out that set—largely because we didn't know exactly what the show was.

JL: Yeah.

BB: I don't tend to like video in shows, because it can easily rely on uninspired realism: this is the park scene so here's a background of a pretty park. I don't think that serves theater well. But the video we ended up with in *Sondheim on Sondheim* was very abstract even when the footage was literal. It filled out the shape of the televisions as we moved them into different compositions. It became the surface of the sculpture and at the same time relayed information. I'm actually including a whole chapter on that show.

JL: What was brilliant about it is that it *was* Steve. The set *became* Sondheim. His mind is a puzzle, and you made a puzzle set that mirrored how he constructs shows.

BB: We kept pulling the set apart and reconfiguring it.

JL: It was very cool but I have to say, I was a nervous wreck thinking the whole thing was an accident waiting to happen: all those TVs flying through the air . . . we've all seen scenery crash into itself so many times.

BB: The fact that the worst never happened is a testament to a great technical director. I think ours was excited by the challenge, even if he didn't show it! We talk about this as a collaborative art form, and that extends to everyone on the production. In the scenery world, it's the painters, the props people, the carpenters, and the technical director.

JL: What about the playwrights? Do you think of them as part of the collaboration?

BB: Honestly, I seldom have much close contact with the writers on my shows. You're the exception because you write and direct. Writing is the map for what I'm designing, but the director is the driver. I find that, in general, theater works well with the director as dictator. Ideally, it's a benevolent dictatorship, but the director has to be in charge—especially on a musical.

JL: It makes me crazy when a director complains about the writing. It's the director's job to make the material work. You chose to direct it; make it work!

BB: Speaking of how directors tell stories, are there any other shows in which you specifically used the design to further the storytelling? You talked a little bit about the buckram costumes for the original *March of the Falsettos*, but are there other examples?

JL: Well, we haven't talked at all about our collaboration on *Little Miss Sunshine*. I think what you did was extraordinary and really furthered the storytelling.

BB: I think creating the VW bus out of rolling chairs was crucial because it allowed the actors to expand and break it apart as needed; they weren't trapped in a static piece of scenery. I loved the surround of that set. It was a simple idea of a Google map of the Southwest, but it was massive and immersive.

JL: It was fantastic. It created the road in a way I haven't seen before. That was a very difficult show to design.

Rory O'Malley and David Rasche in the 2013 off-Broadway production of *Little Miss Sunshine*

Little Miss Sunshine, by William Finn and James Lapine, tells the story of an awkward young girl named Olive who needs to get from her home in Albuquerque, New Mexico, to the "Little Miss Sunshine" beauty pageant in Southern California. Her outlandish family turns the task into a road trip in an ancient VW bus across the American Southwest that is beset by misadventures. Although Olive does not win the pageant, she learns a valuable lesson about self-worth and teaches the others a few things along the way. James directed the 2013 off-Broadway production, and Michele Lynch choreographed it. I designed the set and projections, with costumes by Jennifer Caprio, lighting by Ken Billington, and sound by Jon Weston.

Heidi Ettinger (also known by her married name, Landesman) was born in San Mateo, California, in 1951. She designed scenery and costumes for her first Broadway show, Marsha Norman's *'Night, Mother*, in 1983. Her ten additional Broadway credits include *Big River*, *The Secret Garden* (which she also produced), *The Red Shoes*, *Smokey Joe's Café*, *Moon over Buffalo* (also a producer), *The Adventures of Tom Sawyer*, and a 2005 adaptation of *Dracula*. She was a producer of the original production of *Into the Woods*. Her off-Broadway designs for James Lapine include his original production of *Twelve Dreams*, *A Midsummer Night's Dream*, in Central Park in 1982, and a 2007 production of *King Lear*.

JL: As a director, what I want in a designer is someone very stimulating who can think outside the box. I need someone who understands how a show moves, especially if it's a musical. I learned from Heidi Ettinger that you need some gags. She always called them gags.

BB: Some "showbiz."

JL: Something that's surprising. Something that turns into something else.

BB: Something theatrical.

JL: I worked a lot with Heidi early in my career. She had a really theatrical way of doing things. Every designer brings their own point of view, and they're all different.

BB: That's why I asked about your background. You started in graphic design. Hal was a stage manager. Susan Stroman was a dancer. Kenny Leon and Jerry Zaks were actors. Everyone comes at it in a different way because of their particular skills.

JL: That's really interesting. Everyone brings different strengths to their approaches to directing.

BB: Knowing where they come from—what they've done besides directing—helps me focus on what's important to whoever I'm working with.

JL: It's interesting that you bring it up. There are shows that I'm offered and turn down that end up being great successes. But I can't say yes to something when I read it and feel I'm not the right guy for it. I couldn't do *Hello, Dolly!* I mean, that's a Jerry Zaks show. He's masterful at that kind of show. I've tried to do all kinds of different shows because that's fun—but in hindsight, I realize that some of them weren't what I do best. There were people who could have done them better.

BB: As long as I've known you, you've said that. I've seen you turn down shows because of that. Ten years ago, that way of thinking confused me. I thought, *I can take on anything and figure it out.* As I've gotten older, though—and maybe in part because I have enough financial security that I don't have to take on everything—I will turn things down. If I really don't begin to see how to do it, I take it as a sign that maybe I shouldn't try.

JL: I did some movies even though my heart really wasn't in them. The first one, *Impromptu*, I was excited about. After that, I found movies more of a craft. In theater, I always want to be emotionally connected to the piece. On every show I do, I have to stop and remind myself why I'm doing it. What was my intention with the show? On something like *Annie*, halfway through, I asked myself, *Why am I doing this?* I was trying to do some things differently on that show, and it just didn't turn out the way I hoped it would. That's the way it is. You learn from everything, and often more from the things that don't work.

BB: When I tell people who aren't in the theater what I do for a living they look at me like, *That's a job?* It doesn't occur to them that someone is working their ass off to figure out what the set should look like. Do you have a first memory of stage design—a moment when you were first aware of it as a distinct part of the storytelling?

JL: Well, the first show I ever saw was *Bye Bye Birdie*. I grew up in Mansfield, Ohio, and the most famous guy from our town was Lee Adams, who wrote the lyrics. We literally drove from Mansfield to New York to see the show. In the scene where the kids are all on the phone, there was a set piece built of cubes, and each cube had a kid on the telephone in it. I remember being wowed by that.

BB: The "Telephone Hour" song—it's a famous set! I've never seen the show, but I know the scene. It's an unconventional bit of staging within what I think is a fairly conventional musical.

JL: I also remember seeing the original *Sound of Music*. A little knoll covered in grass came out with Maria sitting on it. Even then I thought, *That's so dopey.*

BB: I try to remind myself constantly of the things in shows that I thought were stupid when I was a kid—things that pulled me out of the show. Stupid stuff like being aware of guide tracks in the floor or seeing the wires holding someone when they're flying. I hated that stuff; it felt false to me, though I wouldn't have articulated it that way. In my own work, I do my best to disguise those things and not just accept that they're there and I can't do anything about it. I mean, often I can't do anything about them, but I try to at least be aware. I don't want to just ignore a problem because I can't yet figure out how to solve it.

JL: You know what I really remember loving? *Sweeney Todd*. It was the first Sondheim show I ever saw. I went back a few times, feeling like it was just the perfect piece of theater. Hal's work was amazing, and yet it looked so simple. It was minimalist. I thought it was so cool that you could do that.

And I loved Robert Wilson's *Einstein on the Beach*. And Richard Foreman's stuff, and his great visuals. Those productions really made big impressions on me.

BB: I guess that encapsulates your approach. You've done a lot of Broadway musicals, with Sondheim, Bill Finn, and others, that employ unconventional visual approaches to the storytelling. When you're trying out a less conventional way of presenting a show, you just can't know ahead of time if it's going to work or not. Sometimes it doesn't, but I think your career shows that more often than not, for you, it does!

Robert Wilson's *Einstein on the Beach*
Lucie Jansch

Rendering of *Act One*

Santino Fontana, Bob Stillman, Mimi Lieber, and company in the tenement

Santino Fontana, Andrea Martin, and Tony Shalhoub in Kaufman's house

The tenement stairwell

Joan Marcus

The Broadway marquees

Chuck Cooper and Santino Fontana on the theater set for *The Emperor Jones*

Matt Saldivar, Tony Shalhoub, and company on the theater set for *The Beloved Bandit*

The same space re-dressed as three different offices and a dressing room

Rendering of *The Scottsboro Boys*

Rodney Hicks (standing CL) and company in the boxcar

Brandon Victor Dixon (sitting center) and company in the jail cell

The finale

The company performs "Electric Chair"

The original Broadway company

THREE

Heartbreaker

Designing *The Scottsboro Boys* for Susan Stroman

Fall in Love

In the summer of 2009, I got an email from Susan Stroman inviting me to a reading of a new Kander and Ebb musical she was directing called *The Scottsboro Boys*. I knew "Stro"—the director/choreographer of *The Producers* and *Contact*—by reputation but in real life only slightly. She is a beautiful woman with a mane of thick blond hair and a smile that could light up Times Square. We were both working on an upcoming musical called *Paradise Found* with Hal Prince but so far had only met briefly.

I was happy to be invited to the Vineyard Theater for the reading. What I didn't know at the time was that Stro's invitation meant I was being asked to design the show.

I also knew of *The Scottsboro Boys*. John Kander and Fred Ebb—the legendary writing team behind *Cabaret* and *Chicago,* among many others—had had four new projects in the works when Ebb died in 2004. *The Scottsboro Boys* was one of them, developed with Stro and the librettist David Thompson. I had heard it referred to as "the minstrel show."

Maybe you're aware of the awful history of the minstrel show, but if not, here's a little background. It was the most popular form of entertainment in the United States from 1850 to 1950—and it was deplorable. Usually white but sometimes Black performers did skits and songs in blackface and embodied buffoonish, racist caricatures of Black persons. Ultimately outlawed in many places, the form died out and has largely been forgotten—so I had no idea what to expect when I went to the reading.

The show turned out to be a postmodern take on the minstrel show that flipped the form on its head by using its conventions to tell a true story of racial oppression. The Scottsboro boys were a group of nine Black youths who were dragged off a train in Scottsboro, Alabama, in 1933 and accused of a gang rape of two white women. Everyone involved—accused and accusers—knew the young men were innocent, but that didn't stop their being put on trial for their lives. Their case was taken up by members of the fledgling civil rights movement, including a young Rosa Parks, and became one of the most nationally celebrated trials of the decade.

In the musical version of this tragic tale, Black actors played all but one of the roles, portraying the white characters as absurd stereotypes—reversing the conventions of the traditional minstrel show.

I was deeply moved by the reading of a show that had that rare mix of intellect and heart—bold concept and deep meaning—that had made me fall in love with musical theater in the first place. I quickly emailed Stro to say that I hoped she'd consider me as a designer if it were produced, and soon after that she officially invited me to join the team. *The Scottsboro Boys* would be produced off Broadway, at the Vineyard.

I was ecstatic—until I discovered that the proposed dates of the production conflicted with the Broadway tech for *Sondheim on Sondheim*, a new revue I was designing for James Lapine. I asked Stro if I could have an assistant cover any aspects of the tech work on *Scottsboro* that I couldn't be present for. She very reasonably said, "No, it's the first production of a new musical; I need my set designer there."

So that was that—until it wasn't. In one of those strokes of luck I seem to experience more than my share of, the *Scottsboro* dates changed by a few weeks and I could handle both—saving me from endless regret over a great show that got away.

Stro had done a huge amount of research on minstrel shows and the historical Scottsboro boys, so I had to rush to catch up. I read gut-wrenching, first-person accounts of the events by two of the accused men, Haywood Patterson and Clarence Norris. Then I tackled a minstrel show handbook from the early twentieth century that Stro gave me, written as a guide for community theaters who wanted to mount their own such entertainments. That was a tough read as well. The cruelty humans are capable of never fails to shock me; even now, ten years later, I'm uncomfortable thinking and writing about this material. But I knew that if I was going to help tell this story, I needed to learn about its context.

A typical minstrel show featured a semicircle of chairs onstage in which the performers sat throughout. An "interlocuter," or master of ceremonies (who would be the sole white actor in our version), sat at the center and managed the show. "End men" with featured roles sat at the outer ends. Stro's idea was that we'd tell the story with little more than those chairs. She wanted me to provide all the locations called for in the story using twelve chairs and as little else as possible. Of course, there needed to be some sort of surrounding scenic environment; Stro's guidance on that was to make it "modern."

Even if it was going to be modern, I felt I needed to evoke the period somehow—so I looked at images of minstrel shows and vaudeville acts for ideas.

Minstrel show illustration from the *Witmark Amateur Minstrel Guide*, 1899

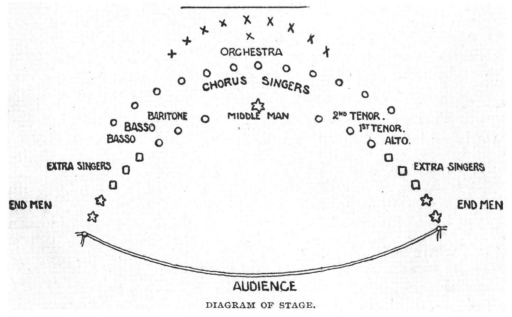

Minstrel show plan showing the semicircle of chairs, the "end men," and the interlocuter, called the "middle man" here, from the *Witmark Amateur Minstrel Guide*, 1899

A world constructed out of chairs is clearly an abstract theatrical world. That's what Stro wanted, and it is always my inclination to push in that direction anyway, so we were on the same page. Film does realism well, and theater does abstract suggestion well. If you lay down the ground rules clearly and stick to them, an audience will happily believe a chair is a train or a door or whatever you pretend that it is.

I've occasionally run into less sophisticated directors who want to change the rules of the game midshow. I did a Shakespeare play once where we presented the world minimally but realistically. A chair was a chair and a trumpet was a trumpet—until we got to a moment when the trumpet was supposed to be a camera. The choreographer had insisted on it with no explanation and simply directed the actor who had been playing the instrument to suddenly "take a picture" with it. It was a challenge to me, and to the audience, to make any sense of that trumpet camera. As I said, I'm all for abstraction but within consistent rules that you establish. For *The Scottsboro Boys*, I was excited by the idea of making a whole world out of chairs, but that kind of abstract presentation would have to be thoughtfully and consistently built into the production.

The show felt like a ghost story. Once, as a teenager, I stumbled across the ribs of a mostly decayed deer half submerged in the ground in the woods near my parents' farm. *The Scottsboro Boys* story reminded me of the revulsion I felt when I came upon those bones, a scary but fascinating presence rising up from the ground.

I'm not particularly religious, but my thoughts about the show came out in religious terms. The set should be a spiritual purgatory caging the souls of these young men much as their physical bodies were trapped in a legal purgatory. Was there a way to make a minstrel stage that conjured up both a cage and that buried skeleton emerging from the ground? I could see a visual parallel between the bones of a skeleton and the "bones" of a 1930s architectural structure of beams and lath. Could all of that be envisioned as a sculptural cage to surround the story?

Simultaneously, I started researching chairs that would evoke the 1930s and help me create the locations in the story, which included a boxcar on a train, a prison bus, several courtrooms, and many prison cells. I was hoping to find existing chairs we could purchase so that I could spend more of my small budget on whatever surround I created.

Let me digress for a moment about budgets. Broadway scenery budgets can be huge—in excess of a million dollars. It might seem crazy to spend that much on an imaginary place when you can buy a comfortable house (or several) for that money in most of the world. Theater scenery is like a custom-built house—but a bespoke

Research for *The Scottsboro Boys*
Alan Curtis/Alamy Stock Photo

Research for *The Scottsboro Boys*, including lath used to build the armature for the Statue of Liberty

Research for *The Scottsboro Boys*

house which is built in one location and then pulled apart and packed in a truck to go to another location, where it is rapidly reassembled. In most cases, it must be able to slide around or fly above or disappear below a stage eight times a week. Sets are custom-built sculptures designed to do a lot of tricks quickly, consistently, and safely. That's why they cost a lot of money to make.

Part of what I love about working on Broadway is that I typically have more money, and that allows for grander execution: a river of real water or a sixty-foot turntable, for example. But I firmly believe that a strong idea can be executed as a hundred-dollar set or a million-dollar set. Let's say I want to depict "justice overturned." If I have just a little bit of money, I may create smashed scales of justice. But, let's say I have an extravagant budget. Perhaps I'll decide to create a life-size Statue of Liberty, clad in genuine oxidized copper, smashed through the wall of the theater.

The Scottsboro Boys came with a small, off-Broadway budget, and my challenge was to settle on a strong, clear idea and an economical way to create it.

I imagined a decrepit vaudeville proscenium with fragments of Victorian filigree still visible but with much of its "skin" worn away to reveal the bones beneath. I was worried about effectively describing a proscenium/skeleton, so, to help get my idea across to the rest of the creative team, I built a very finished model of what I had in mind and painted it white to emphasize its skeletal nature. I felt there was something potent about young Black men trapped in a literally white world.

I finished the model in time for our first production meeting. It was the first time I met the "book writer," David "Tommy" Thompson (who at first glance seems more like a college professor than the successful Broadway librettist that he is), and the costume designer, Toni Leslie James (whose shaved mahogany head, piercing eyes, and sharp tongue make her seem exactly the ace costume designer she is). We were joined by our lighting designer, Kevin Adams (who I can only describe as looking

First model for *The Scottsboro Boys*

like a cowboy from some alternate-universe Texas). I had worked with Kevin many times and was excited to collaborate with him again.

That meeting is not one of my favorite memories. Although I was armed with my detailed model of the surround, I'd given very little thought to how the minstrel chairs might work. Stro remained polite as ever, but it was clear she wasn't impressed with the proscenium I'd made. She was concerned that it would take up too much space on the small Vineyard stage and get in the way of the choreography she had in mind. It's important to note that Stro started as a choreographer, and her approach to any show is informed by how she envisions the performers moving through space. In the projects we've done together since *Scottsboro Boys*, I've learned to start out by determining what type of dance or movement she intends to deploy. Sometimes her vision necessitates wide-open space and sometimes it doesn't, but open space is a good place to start on a Stro show.

In 2009, I didn't know that. She very kindly suggested that maybe we could start with what I had designed, but perhaps it could quickly be pulled into the wings and out of the way. I got the message; it really wasn't what she wanted. Kevin, who's never shy about his opinions, chimed in with other ideas for the set. Because I was the "kid" in the room, I felt uncomfortable, and I left in a cold sweat, wondering if I'd be replaced.

Stro called me the next day "to say hi" and ask if I was OK. It was a very sweet and reassuring gesture—exactly the type of behavior I've come to understand makes her who she is. I went back to the drawing board. I realized (belatedly—it should have been obvious) that the chairs and how they were used were integral to how the show moved and functioned. I needed to figure that out and worry about the surround later. I began to explore all of the ways the chairs could be stacked, configured, and reconfigured to create abstract locations. Of course, using them as building blocks meant that I'd need to make them from scratch, even if it consumed most of my budget. How quickly and fluidly the chairs could be transformed would drive the pace of the story. They'd need to interlock like Legos, be strong enough to dance on, and light enough to dance *with*.

I decided I'd make the seats flat and square and position them on a cube-like base of legs so they'd be extremely stable. The backs would be straight and exactly the same height as the legs, so that two chairs stacked seat to seat (configuration A below) would make a strong pedestal. We could then lay a plank across two pedestals to make a sturdy raised surface. This simple design would allow for a variety of configurations; with some creativity, we could create all of the locations required.

Once I was satisfied with the basic design and function of the chairs, I'd add decorative metal elements for the sake of variety and to make them feel more "period." Finally, I'd paint them shiny ebony. I figured that black chairs against an all-white set would reinforce the idea of Black men trapped within a white power structure.

Stro liked the basic approach and we agreed to build a few chairs and test them out with dancers during preproduction the following month. Then I turned back to figuring out the surround.

I still liked my notion of men trapped in a version of purgatory. I imagined them falling slowly through a twisting vortex and made a model consisting of a series of three simple white frames that twisted off-kilter as they moved upstage. In a much simpler way, these frames recalled the proscenium of my first design. They suggested

CONFIGURATION A "BOXCAR"   CONFIGURATION B "JAIL WINDOW"   CONFIGURATION C "THE BOX"

Ideas for how the chairs could be used

my original image of a bleached rib cage emerging from the ground and also invoked the gibbet that literally and metaphorically hung over the characters in the story. The truth is, the set design I'd arrived at was very simple—which is exactly why it could be invested with so many meanings. It was open-ended in a way that would encourage audiences to see in it what they would—to participate in the storytelling.

I finished the frames with a rough wood texture and covered them with chipped and flaking white paint, as if they'd been exposed to the wind and the rain for many years. Then I made a worn, whitewashed plank floor to match; and finally, I added a row of sad, mismatched footlights to the front of the stage, providing a simple representation of a vaudeville theater.

Once the footlights were in, I got the idea that the three frames could hide additional vaudeville light bulbs. Each frame would have a hidden flipper panel that would pop open for the show's finale to reveal a surround of chasing light bulbs. I wanted these to be in visible porcelain sockets and be wired together with 1930s-era, cloth-covered, twisted electrical cord. I hoped that these very realistic period details would create an interesting tension with the minimalism of the basic set.

I designed an upstage olio* drop that said "The Scottsboro Boys" in old-fashioned, cheerful lettering—like many of the musical's songs, a stark tonal contrast to the

Second model for *The Scottsboro Boys*

---

*"Olio" is a vaudeville term for a curtain that rolls up onto a tube—a technique used when there's no fly space, as at the Vineyard. The necessity of a rollup drop had the added thematic benefit of being a vaudeville technique. It's said that the term derives from the fact that once upon a time, many of these drops were painted on oilcloth.

Research example of vaudeville lightbulbs with exposed wires

events of the show. I added a tattered black scrim that could slide into frame and focus the darker scenes in courtrooms and prisons, and a worn and stained white cyclorama upstage that could be altered by lighting to provide a bright background for happier moments and exteriors.

Stro and the rest of the team liked what I presented. At the same meeting, Toni brought in images she'd found of the real Scottsboro boys in all-white prison uniforms that were nothing like the striped prison clothes of popular imagination. What was emerging was a very stark, monochrome production that seemed perfectly appropriate to the story we were telling.

Even my seemingly simple set was more than we could afford, until my excellent tech director, Ben Morris, agreed to build it himself on the stage for much less than it would cost to have a shop do it. The specialty chairs would be built very reasonably by Tom Carroll Scenery, with whom I had worked for years.

By the time of Stro's preproduction workshop several weeks later, I had the first few chairs ready. I'd specified that they were to be sturdy enough to hold a dancing man while weighing less than twenty pounds each, and they came in at fifteen—made of aluminum and very manageable.

Over the course of two weeks of experimentation, Stro found a wide variety of ways to use the chairs. We took notes, and every few days brought in some new chairs made with slight variations. Thinking of them as an odd set of Tinker Toys, we narrowed the seats of some so that the legs of others could sit around them snugly. We developed a set of steel pins that could be fitted into Teflon receivers on the chairs' backs to connect one chair to another. By the end of preproduction, we had a full set of nine metal chairs with myriad function, all safe and ready for rehearsal.

We filled out the set with three antique wooden chairs, an armchair for the white interlocuter, and two delicate wooden side chairs for the two end men. We wanted to differentiate these performers, who mostly played the tormentors, from the nine actors playing the Scottsboro boys. I also made two sturdy "wood planks"— actually narrow, shallow, very strong aluminum-framed slabs painted to look like wood. These could be laid across the chairs to create raised surfaces representing boxcars or benches. With the information I'd gathered during preproduction, I was able to storyboard the major scenes using photos of the model.

The preproduction process yielded an important style discovery. The workshop prototypes of the chairs were a metallic silver color, but I'd always intended to paint the final pieces ebony black. As we worked with them, I realized that their blocky shapes meant they'd never truly look like antique chairs. I suggested to Stro that leaving them silver might be interesting. There was a beauty in the raw aluminum finish and a simplicity in not trying to force them to masquerade as something different. It seems like a small detail, but the chairs were so important to the show that it was a big change. Just as the show blended an old broken-down theatrical form with a modern

Opening look, a boxcar, a bus, and a jail cell

interpretation, the sleek modernity of the untreated metal chairs was a strong contrast to the worn wood finishes on the rest of the set.

I had the full set of chairs ready when the show began rehearsal in January 2010. We quickly discovered that, although chairs were exciting as a simple storytelling device, they were tricky to keep track of through the show. For example, chair 7 had to move from position A to position B to position C and so on until, ten scenes later, it would match up to chair 5—which was its mate for position M. Multiply all that by nine chairs moved by thirteen actors over many, many transitions. Because of the various ways they fit together, the chairs weren't identical, but they were hard to tell apart. A chair out of place could create a big problem, even a safety issue when in a stack with someone standing on it.

We solved this problem fairly easily, by numbering each chair in silver paint, in a spot that the actors could see but the audience could not. Even so, each actor had dozens of chair configurations to memorize, and drilling them fell to Stro's capable assistants, Jeff Whiting and Eric Santagata.

Keeping track of the blocking chart was a full-time job for those two; it had to be updated constantly as the show developed and changed, resulting in endless paperwork. The challenge inspired Jeff to begin work on an app to make and manipulate complicated blocking charts. Ten years later, that app—Stage Write—is the industry standard.

As rehearsals progressed, the design idea held up well. Stro and the cast began filling in new areas of the story, and that inspired us to enhance the design in exciting ways. In a song called "Friends with the Truth," a young man named Billy commits a series of small crimes until he is lynched and goes to heaven where, in a final indignity, he is forced by Saint Peter to enter through the back door. The song wasn't directly related to the story of the Scottsboro boys, but unrelated novelty songs are part of the minstrel show tradition, and its dark-humored indictment of racism was certainly in the flavor of the show. We decided to step out of our basic staging mode, hang up a sheet, and enact Billy's story as a shadow play on it.

Simple shadow play, a genuine element of traditional minstrel shows, is remarkably interesting to watch onstage. We based our imagery for the sequence on the work of the artist Kara Walker, who has created beautiful yet grotesque silhouette images depicting the abuses of American racism and slavery. Walker's beautiful and seductive images—which, on closer inspection, are stomach-churningly horrible—matched the tone of the musical and of this number in particular. As Stro began rehearsing the number, she asked for specific cutouts that would help tell the story, and I did my best to create them in Walker's style.

SHADOW PANTOMIMES AT HOME.

Shadow play illustration from the *Witmark Amateur Minstrel Guide*, 1899

Minstrel show illustration from the *Witmark Amateur Minstrel Guide,* 1899

At the end of the song, Billy would ascend to heaven on a high pyramid of stacked chairs. In rehearsal one day, the pile collapsed, and Julius Thomas III, the actor playing Billy, could have been badly injured. We decided to sneak several chairs onstage already welded into part of the pyramid. In one sense it felt like cheating, because our aim had been to do the whole show with nine simple chairs—but I don't think audiences were aware of the swap. Our illusion remained intact, and so did our actor. At the end of the song, the shadow-sheet on two sticks would become Saint Peter's wings.

Props for "Friends with the Truth" using Kara Walker's imagery as inspiration.

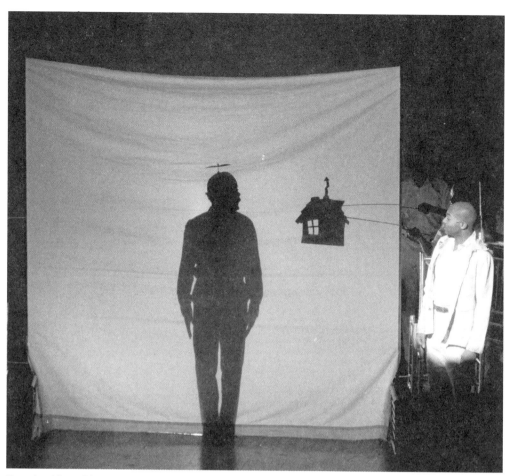

Brandon Victor Dixon and Julius Thomas III

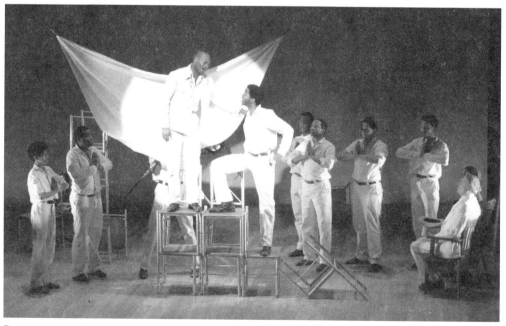

Brandon Victor Dixon, Julius Thomas III, and company

Rehearsals progressed until we were ready to tech. I was nervous because it was my first tech with Stro and I didn't want to disappoint her, but I needn't have worried. The choreography had been developed using the actual chairs, and actors had rehearsed with them, so they knew how to use them. The rest of the set tricks were minimal and simple. That said, there were some things we couldn't control. About halfway through tech, a blizzard bore down on New York. At midnight, as we were finishing for the day, Stro called the whole company together. I thought she was going to say something like, "The weather outside is frightful, so be careful, be safe, and if you can't make it in tomorrow, that's OK." I was half right. She said, "The weather is going to be bad tomorrow, so be careful, be safe, but we need you all here. Plan ahead and do what you have to so you're here on time!" That is Stro: kind and understanding but all business when it counts. She plans thoroughly, works herself hard, and expects the same of everyone involved.

Through rehearsals and previews, the show came together beautifully. To this day, I remain astounded by the simple transitions. Stro engineered moments where, in twenty seconds of dance, the chairs seemed to rearrange themselves magically, creating a location and then re-forming to establish the next. Only after watching the show many times was I able to discern the subtle stagecraft she'd employed so

Colman Domingo, Forrest McClendon, and company in a transitional moment

that while you were occupied by watching a virtuoso dance step here or a bit of comic buffoonery there, the remainder of the cast seamlessly moved the chairs to a new configuration.

For the train scene, all nine of the guys stood on planks meant to suggest the tops of boxcars. Stro had us hang tambourines (another minstrel show convention) on tiny hooks to form the wheels of the train. The music of the song established the clackety-clack of a moving train, and the cast mimed the appropriate movement. Kevin Adams projected subtle moving light onto them and the cyc behind them. Although each element was simple, they added up to create the illusion of a moving train in an extraordinary way. That said, my heart leapt into my throat when that number began, as the whole cast bounced on the planks. Theoretically, they'd been engineered to hold the weight, but as I watched them bounce and the planks flex, I couldn't help being terrified one of them would buckle. I should have trusted in the materials. In the ensuing years, I remounted the show nine times in a variety of the-aters all over the world, and the planks always held up.

These same planks were flipped onto lower chairs to form prison benches in the jail scenes. Chairs with slatted backs became the barred prison windows. We used our trick of stacking chairs upside down on each other to create barred walls.

In a sequence in the middle of the show, the principal character, Haywood Pat-terson (played at the Vineyard by Brandon Victor Dixon), is thrown into a small solitary confinement cell called "the box." Stro had found a gruesome image from the 1930s of imprisoned Black men in an underground cell, their hands reaching up through the bars. We re-created a version of it, shoving Brandon into a tiny space created by the chairs.

The finale of the show was an all-out showbiz song-and-dance number. Having changed out of their white prison uniforms, the cast reappeared in Fred Astaire–style top hats and tails, wearing traditional minstrel blackface for the first time. I always found the moment terribly chilling yet grotesquely beautiful. I think some Black people (and probably some others) found it offensive, and I'm sorry for that. We understood we were treading into deeply sensitive cultural territory but believed— hoped—the grotesque power of the image and the actor's ultimate rejection of it onstage would communicate a strong, ultimately uplifting message.

To support the showbiz finale scenically, I unfurled the Scottsboro Boys olio again and we flipped open the panels in the three frames to reveal their hidden light bulbs. Although it wasn't an enormous gesture, in a show where all the scenic moves had been simple, the appearance of chasing, flashing light bulbs was a big surprise.

Convict camp in Greene County, Georgia, 1941
Jack Delano/Library of Congress

Brandon Victor Dixon and Julius Thomas III in the "box" scene.

There were changes as we previewed the show, but nothing major. One night, John Kander walked into the green room musing about the song "Financial Advice," which we all called "Jew Money" because that was a repeated lyric. John, who is Jewish, said to the room, "That song needs to be nastier. What rhymes with 'kike'?"

Despite—and because—of its minimalism, the physical production was exhilarating. It opened on a bare stage and some chairs as if declaring, "We have nothing to hide." Those chairs transformed into every location the show required because every design element worked seamlessly to tell the story.

My favorite spatial transformation took us almost instantly from the row of boxcars on a sunny, Southern afternoon into a dank jail cell. I've already described Stro's ability to entertainingly misdirect attention as a scene is reshaped. The audience didn't see the actors resetting chairs to form a cell until she wanted them to—so it seemed like stage magic. The lights carved a bright square into the darkness, containing and constraining the space. The sound of a steel cell door slamming as the final chair was set in place created an undeniable sonic reality. The prison guard jackets and hats slipped on by the end men helped describe the location. All of it was just enough to trigger the infinite imagination of the audience and make them see, hear, and feel the most cramped, awful prison cell ever.

The energy in the tiny Vineyard Theatre was electric. Audiences were blown away by the show. Word of mouth spread quickly, and we were soon sold out for the entire run. I had to miss the opening-night performance because I was teching *Sondheim on Sondheim*, but I made it to the party, where Mimi snapped this happy picture of me with Stro.

Opening night at the Vineyard Theatre
Mimi Bilinski

Everything was magical. Then the *New York Times* review came out.

Rebound

Ben Brantley, the *New York Times* critic, offered some grudging respect for the show but basically hated it. It wasn't the first time a show I loved had been savaged by a critic, and it wouldn't be the last. Ultimately, a review is just one opinion—though theoretically an informed one. But when you've poured your heart and soul into a project only to see it dismissed in nine paragraphs in the "paper of record," it's disheartening to say the least.

I figured our off-Broadway run was probably the end of it but, much to my surprise, commercial producers Barry and Fran Weissler said they believed in the show and wanted to transfer it to Broadway—*Times* review be damned. For a few days, there seemed to be a chance we would try to rush the show in as part of the 2009–2010 season. Fewer new musicals than usual had opened that year, which would give *The Scottsboro Boys* a good shot at a Tony. But in the end, there wasn't time to retool and transfer it before the Tony cutoff.

To help us rethink the show for Broadway, the Weisslers arranged for us to remount it over the summer of 2010 at the Guthrie Theater in Minneapolis. I was excited to do a show at the famous Guthrie but a tad apprehensive about working with the Weisslers. I hadn't known the husband-and-wife team prior to working for them on *The Scottsboro Boys*, but at the Tony ceremony one year, Rosie O'Donnell had famously described them as "the cheapest people in the free world." Granted, it's a producer's job to watch the bottom line, and when artists don't get everything they want, it's often because of necessary financial constraints imposed from on high. I've watched undisciplined producers sink a show by allowing it to get too expensive to survive: the artistic freedom feels great—until it doesn't. I could only hope that the Weisslers' reputation for cheapness was overblown as I excitedly dove into the next phase of the project.

We didn't plan to make big changes to the set, although Kevin Adams argued for a show curtain for the Broadway version. I feel strongly that a show curtain is exciting if it rises to reveal something fantastic. The strength of the *Scottsboro* design was its simplicity—the fact that we were creating so much from so little. An audience walking in to see a nearly empty stage is very different from raising a curtain to reveal a nearly empty stage. We didn't add a curtain.

Since we were moving from the tiny Vineyard to considerably larger theaters, I would need to enlarge the set a little, but not massively—just about 25 percent.

This would allow the actors a little more room to move and dance, and provide me more air around the set to highlight the off-angles of the portals. I spent many days tweaking the exact angles for the new space and found the larger canvas beneficial to the design.

Early in the transfer process, Barry Weissler invited me to come by his office. He said he didn't know my designs, wanted to meet me, and asked if I could send him a copy of my résumé so he could familiarize himself with my work. I retain only a vague impression of his office, but I remember some striped wallpaper that gave off a *Waiting for Guffman* vibe—like something an unsophisticated person would consider "fancy." *Whatever*, I thought. Barry had certainly proved his ability to produce hits, so who cared about his taste in wallpaper?

We had a nice chat, and he assured me he always took good care of his designers. I said I would try to be very economical on the project and thought I could manage the entire Guthrie-to-Broadway process with just six paid weeks for an assistant. (Unionized design assistants are usually paid by the week, and six weeks for a musical was an absurdly low request. But I had calculated that I could make that work and hoped it would impress my new boss.) He said it sounded reasonable, and I went on my way.

Contracts are a headache. I wish I didn't have to deal with them. I'm including a discussion of my contract here because, as an artist, the amount you are paid affects the quality of the work. If I need ten dollars to cover my personal expenses for a year and I'm paid a dollar per show, I have to do ten shows that year to make a living. If I make fifty cents per show, I have to design twenty shows—which means spending half as much time and energy on each. The point is, the better I'm paid per show, the fewer shows I have to do—and the more work and creativity I can put into each one. Similarly, the money I'm allotted to hire an assistant can have a serious effect on the overall quality of the design.

Ron Gwiazda, my agent at that point, handled the negotiations, but it was up to me whether I would or wouldn't accept the final terms. Through Ron, who was dealing with Barry's general manager David Richards, I agreed to a relatively small fee for a Broadway musical. I was young, the design was simple, and I was trying to be accommodating. David said the Guthrie would pay for the first three weeks of assistant work and asked that we table the discussion of the other three weeks I'd requested until closer to the Broadway dates. You can probably see what's coming; naïve and trusting young Beowulf didn't. But I'm getting ahead of myself.

Based on the absurdly low fees we were being offered, Kevin Adams decided to withdraw from the show. The Weisslers' go-to lighting designer was Ken Billington

The Broadway model for *The Scottsboro Boys* finale sign

(whom you met in the *Act One* chapter), and they suggested him for the project. I had just done *Sondheim on Sondheim* with him and was pleased when he joined the team.

The enlarged set retained the same quality as the smaller one. We added a huge sign covered with light bulbs that said "The Scottsboro Boys" to replace the canvas olio in the minstrel finale when the portal light bulbs were revealed. Its hundreds of flashing, chasing lights gave us a little more showbiz razzmatazz. While I was designing it, Stro asked me to make the light bulbs inside the letters individually controllable so the sign would be able to flicker out bit by bit, as if the power were slowly draining from it. In tech, I realized that as the letters went out a few at a time, for a split second the lit letters said "S . . . t . . . ro." At first, I thought it was a happy accident, but of course it was planned. After one run-through, Stro cut it, thinking better of this little Easter egg of a signature. She didn't want to distract any audience members who might notice it.

Another small but important design improvement really did come about by accident. At the Vineyard, the frames' fronts had flipped open to reveal the light bulbs. On the larger set, the panels got too big to operate reliably, so we opted for several smaller pivoting panels. I underestimated how visible the edges of these panels would be. I've made this kind of mistake many times: I hope that something won't be detectable from the house but find it ends up being all too visible and sloppy-looking. There's nothing worse than a stage surprise that everyone sees coming an hour before it occurs. If I wanted the portals to stay hidden until their big moment, I'd have to figure something out. I had the idea of adding some hardware, big metal plates with bolts in them, lined up with the edges of the flipper panels. It's a simple trick in set

Plate and bolt details on the Broadway set for *The Scottsboro Boys*

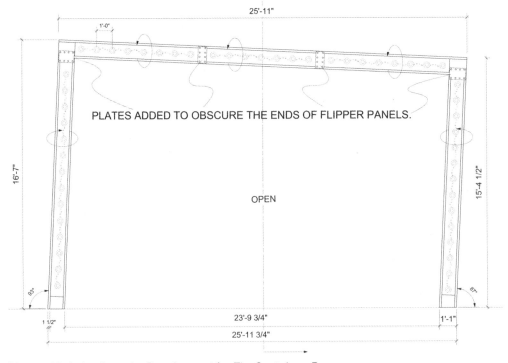

Plate and bolt details on the Broadway set for *The Scottsboro Boys*

design: If there's a line you want to hide—a break between flats or a secret panel—put a more prominent line next to it, and the subtler break disappears. It worked, and what's more, it gave the portals a nice solid architectural quality.

There were some cast changes. Brandon Victor Dixon, who had played Haywood Patterson, was unavailable, so Joshua Henry stepped into the role. Each was brilliant in his own way. James T. Lane came aboard as Ozzie/Ruby, as the dance requirements for this role got more complex and called for a stronger dancer. Cast changes in a close-knit ensemble can be difficult, but in this case, the changes only seemed to bring the cast closer.

There were some rewrites and a lot of little fixes. At Ken Billington's request, I darkened the deck. Making the floor a little grungier on a grungy set was fine—and it allowed Ken to isolate actors in pools of light more effectively. The relative lightness or darkness of a set, especially when lighting actors with darker skin, is crucial to good set design. The lighting designer must be able to make the actors pop out of the stage image. This particular principle comes up over and over in this book, and it highlights one of the set designer's most important responsibilities. In this case, the fix was easy and didn't compromise the integrity of the design.

Happily, we were a big hit for the Guthrie and very well received. The chance to redo the show out of the New York spotlight was valuable and made the whole thing

Light defining space in *The Scottsboro Boys*

tighter and cleaner. It gave us a chance to tech the show slowly and carefully, which was particularly significant, as we were planning to load the show into its Broadway house, tech, and start previews very quickly.

I mean *very* quickly. The plan was to start tech on a Monday morning and have the first preview Thursday night. I've teched faster in summer stock many times, but this was a Broadway musical with a lot of complicated choreography and detailed light cues. Because of our time at the Guthrie and the team's ability to work fast and cleanly, we made it through. There was a pent-up demand to see the show, and the first-preview audience exuded an excitement and adrenaline I've seldom experienced since.

Contract problems marred the excitement for me. David and Barry couldn't understand why I might need an assistant during previews and refused to continue to pay Alexis after tech was finished. As I sat despondently on the steps of the Lyceum stage door trying to figure out how I was going to get the show through previews with no help, Stro walked up and asked what was wrong. I told her, and without a pause, she said, "You need an assistant. I'll pay for her." This is Stro's hallmark. If you work hard, she'll support you. To this day, I get a warm feeling remembering her generosity in that moment.

While I'm complaining about our management, I'll reiterate that controlling costs is their job—I understand that. But I felt shackled on *Scottsboro* to a degree I've never encountered before or since. I angrily pleaded my case to David Richards during previews, to no avail. In fact, every time I've done a Broadway show with David, we've found ourselves in a shouting match. Somehow, though, we've managed to keep our professional arguments out of the personal sphere and have remained friends. The Weisslers, on the other hand, have never called on me to do another show. That's OK too.

I was nursing my anger about the whole financial situation when Ken Billington pulled me aside. "I know you're frustrated by the lack of money," he said, "but this is a risky commercial venture. They're tough businesspeople; they're keeping costs down. That will allow them to keep the show running for a long time." Ken had designed the Weisslers' revival of Kander and Ebb's *Chicago*, then in its fourteenth year on Broadway. I clung to that as we fought our way through previews.

We had three weeks to clean up any outstanding issues before we opened officially. In retrospect, our set challenges seem small, but they were all-consuming at the time! We had a series of confetti-drop machines that sprinkled gold and silver mylar disks—a rain of coins—during the song we all called "Jew Money." Colman Domingo, playing the Alabama prosecutor, accuses the defense of being financed by

Colman Domingo catching falling coins in the "Jew Money" sequence as Sean Bradford watches. This photo is from the off-Broadway production; during the Broadway run, I was far too busy trying to corral stray confetti to snap photos!

New York Jews trying to defy Southern justice. The effect worked well, but invariably a few coins would get stuck in the machines and later, at some deeply inappropriate moment, they'd come floating down, sparkling in the light. It drove Stro crazy. It became my mission to try to make sure not a single piece of confetti ever showed up when we didn't want it to.

We created fabric flaps I called "confetti diapers" that could be pulled under the confetti tumblers to catch any stray mylar. Still, errant coins fell when they were least welcome. Ken added a couple fans aimed at the top of the nearby portal and turned them on full blast at the button* of the confetti sequence to dislodge any mylar that had gotten stuck during the drop. Still, we had stray confetti!

In desperation, I asked my prop master, Chris Pantuso, to buy a leaf blower. Chris is a big Italian American guy with waist-length black hair he wears in a long braid. He looks like someone you wouldn't want to meet in a dark alley, though he's so kindhearted, I doubt he'd kill a fly. Before every show, Chris would send gales of wind up into the flies to try to blow loose any lurking confetti from the night before. Our various efforts were 99 percent successful, but occasionally a coin would elude us and come sparkling through the air during a solemn moment. Confetti, like glitter, sand, or water, can never fully be contained.

My next problem was that the stage floor was taking a beating from a heavy tap dance sequence called "Electric Chair"—a grotesquely beautiful powerhouse number in which Jeremy Gumbs, as the youngest of the Scottsboro Boys, has a nightmare about being executed. Two brilliant tap dancers, Julius Thomas III and Kendrick Jones, tore up the stage as dancing electrocution victims. Unfortunately for me, they literally tore up the stage.

We had built the floor from extra-sturdy marine plywood that I had been advised would withstand tap dancing. But over the course of previews, the wood got so pounded that big chunks of it started coming up, and patches of the white floor turned black from the taps. Paying for union painters to do touch-ups is expensive, and our producers were averse to spending money. Since union designers are sometimes allowed by the theater staff to do a tiny bit of painting, Alexis managed to charm her way into the privilege of doing some quick touch-ups each day. With a combination of paint and Bondo (a very durable, very smelly, automotive patching putty), she kept the deck looking good and safe to dance on.

---

*A button is the final moment of many musical theater songs which, in a variety of ways, punctuates and defines the end of the song and tells the audience, "It's over; time to applaud."

Throughout previews, we kept getting messages from people who thought our show was one of the best they'd ever seen. There was also a contingent of mostly Black people who felt it was racist and set up a protest outside. My friends and acquaintances who saw the show, both Black and white, came down on both sides of our frankly provocative show. It is a fact that, with the exception of Toni Leslie James, we were a team of white creatives telling a story about a group of Black people. I don't think that would happen in 2020. John Kander recently said, "I think we were probably kind of naïve about being white writers telling a Black story, because we thought we were all on the same side."* But, except for John Cullum, the performers were all Black and, to my knowledge, all believed deeply in the message of the show.

Because I collaborate mainly with director and designers, writers tend to make only cameo appearances in these accounts—but I want to momentarily shine a spotlight on John Kander, the show's legendary composer. In his mideighties at the time of our production, John was hale and sturdy, with a gentle, kind presence. He's been called "the nicest man in show business." I ended up spending a lot of time with him over the three initial mountings of the show. We seldom talked about the show—artistic discussions went through Stro—but that didn't stop John and me from chatting during the long afternoons of rehearsals and previews. One day, he asked me what I was doing next. I told him and then complained that it was a dumb job that I was doing primarily for the paycheck. "In theater," he replied, "there are the jobs we do for love and the jobs we do for money. Both are honest work."

There's great freedom in that idea. I repeat it to myself often.

Three weeks of leaf blowing, paint touch-ups, and previews slipped past, and our opening night arrived. It had been a stressful and exhausting few weeks, but we knew we had a great show. The audiences had continued to be electric, and it was thrilling to be in the theater every night.

The opening-night party was at the smallest restaurant I've ever been in—to save money, I supposed. It was as crowded as a rush-hour subway car, and I'm not being hyperbolic. At one point I found a little uncrowded corner roped off with a sign saying "creatives only." I sat down with Mimi so we could catch our collective breath. But barely had we settled onto a banquette than a representative of the producers strode over and announced that "creatives" didn't refer to me and I'd need to vacate the VIP area. I'd had it. We went home.

---

*https://www.playbill.com/article/the-oral-history-of-the-scottsboro-boys.

The next day, Charles Isherwood's review appeared in the *New York Times*. Like Brantley's had been, it was grudgingly respectful but largely negative. We'd been punched again.

Then the Weisslers decided to cut their losses and close the show.

If They Remember

In high school, where I did two plays a year, each one was the most important, most wonderful that I'd ever done. But the more shows one works on, the less special each one becomes. That said, I do fall in love with some projects. My first off-Broadway show, *In-Betweens*, by Bryan Goluboff, was directed by my friend Dante Albertie. We slaved over it and knew how good it was. Peter Marks (who, years later, would become a cordial acquaintance) bashed it in the *Times*, and it closed quickly. To this day, I can conjure up the feelings of heartbreak and utter disbelief I experienced when reading that review. My mind could barely accept it as reality. I kept rereading it, thinking he must be talking about some other show. That one hurt as much as when an adored girlfriend broke up with me without warning.

But over the years, I've hardened to the caprices of show business. I find myself less surprised and damaged by bad reviews. As of this writing, I've designed more than 450 shows and have tried to find something to love in each of them—something about them that excites me enough to come up with a great set—but the truth is that many come and go without leaving a significant mark on me. *The Scottsboro Boys* was not one of those. It was special for me and for everyone involved. It was a passionate labor of love. To this day, when members of that company run into one another, a shared affection for the show and for each other instantly resurfaces.

It was one of my sadder closing nights. The show had burned brightly, but its Broadway life had been brief, and suddenly it was over. Life moved on, and so did we.

Five months later, I was having a breakfast meeting at the Westway Diner on Ninth Avenue when my phone rang. It was a friend telling me I'd just been nominated for a Tony Award for my *Scottsboro* set—my first nomination. While I was talking to her, three voice messages came in from people telling me the same thing. My social media was swamped. I was flabbergasted. Despite my aforementioned habit of ignoring the nominations as best I can, I had read that they were going to be announced and thought, *There's no way I'm getting nominated for a show with almost no set.* Wrong, and happily so! In fact, *Scottsboro* got twelve Tony nominations, a lovely affirmation for a work of art we thought was dead and buried.

Bizarrely and unjustly, Toni Leslie James—the sole Black member of the creative team—was the only one of us *not* nominated. Her costumes had been every bit as exciting as my scenery. They had told the story with visual economy interspersed with bursts of showbiz flare. I never discussed it with Toni, but I have no doubt the irony wasn't lost on her.

In the end, our company didn't win any awards—not even John Kander, whom I thought might win for his final score with his legendary partner. Or Stro, whom I thought might be recognized for her brilliant choreography. I knew I had little chance of winning for a simple set on a long-closed show, but as the announcement approached, I couldn't help thinking, *What if . . . ?*

The absence of trophies didn't change the fact the theater community had said, "Good job. This show was of the highest calibre."

We went on to remount the show across the country at a variety of nonprofit theaters. It was a hit in Philadelphia, San Diego, San Francisco, and Los Angeles. Then we were asked to remount the show at the Young Vic, in London. In the small South London venue known for adventurous theater, once again the show was rapturously received. Catherine Schreiber, who had been an investor in the Broadway production, decided to transfer the show to the West End (London's version of Broadway), where it ran for a year.

The London run was gratifying and would make a nice end to this chapter. But in 2017 we got a request from the Smithsonian Institution's American History Museum in Washington, DC, for any artifacts of the show we could provide. I still had the original Vineyard set model, and I happened to know where a couple *Scottsboro* chairs were hiding. During Broadway previews, Chris Pantuso had ordered some backup chairs from Tom Carroll Scenery. The show was very physical, and it seemed wise to have some backups in case a chair broke. True to form, our producers refused to pay for the backups, so they were never delivered. A couple of them were still sitting in Tom Carroll's shop in Jersey City eight years later. One of those chairs and the model are now at the Smithsonian.

Repeatedly during my involvement with *The Scottsboro Boys*, I thought the project was over, only to see it come back to life. The power of the story and the storytelling continue to shine in people's memories and in subsequent productions. Sadly, its message is no less relevant today than it was ten years ago.

When I wrote on social media about the pieces going to the Smithsonian, Brandon Victor Dixon sent me a note quoting one of his last lines in the show: "If they remember. . . ."

They remember.

FOUR

Clear Floor

A Conversation with Susan Stroman

Setting: *Susan Stroman's office is a large one-bedroom apartment on Manhattan's West Side, in the same Broadway-friendly condominium that houses James Lapine's office. She lives in the penthouse a few floors above, so getting to work couldn't be easier. The office is painted white and so spare that on first visit, it looks as if someone is just moving in or out. A couple of pieces of modern art, including a Jeff Koons puppy, punctuate the large main room, but there are none of the show posters or Broadway memorabilia that typify most show-folks' work spaces. In the big open area is a grand piano and a folding table with chairs to host meetings, but it could all be swept aside in an instant to make a clear floor for dance.*

Tucked in one corner is a small built-in desk used by both Stroman and her longtime assistant, Scott Bishop. Shelves above it hold books related to current projects, and a small kitchenette remains stocked with a supply of snacks, drinks, and often full meals for visitors. What feels impermanent at first glance soon reveals itself to be a clean, ever-blank canvas awaiting the creation of stories.

BEOWULF BORITT: You started as a performer. Did you always want to be a director?

SUSAN STROMAN: It was the first thing I wanted. I know how difficult it is to achieve that on a big scale, how fortunate I am. I am very grateful—I love what I do.

Music has always been part of my life. I was surrounded by it from an early age because my father was a wonderful piano player. I would dance around the living room while he played the old standards. He played some rock and roll and classical, but it was mainly those old standards connected to Broadway shows and the Great

American Songbook. I knew all those songs and would create numbers and scenes as he played.

I was in a dancing school from age five, but I have always *visualized* music. To this day, I play all sorts of music—I particularly love jazz—but while I listen, hordes of people dance through my head. I think I was meant to do what I'm doing now or I'd have probably gone crazy! No matter what type of music it is, I imagine full scenes in costume with sets. So listening to music is not a relaxing experience for me.

BB: I guess not.

SS: I studied all forms of dance: tap, jazz, ballet . . . and as I got older, ballroom. I started to become a big fish in a little pond in Delaware, choreographing for the local community theaters and the halftime shows at the high school. I loved it so much. I knew this was what I wanted to do, but I also knew I couldn't just come to New York as a director or choreographer. So I came and worked as a song-and-dance gal to make a living. But even though I worked as a performer, my plan was always to get onto the other side of the table.

BB: Performing was your "day job."

SS: Yes, because I didn't enjoy singing and dancing as much as *creating.* I wanted to create for the theater. So I started to direct industrial shows, commercials, and people's club acts. It was a beginning for me. I learned how to create scenarios, songs, and scenes, and arrange music with dance arrangers. It was a chance for me to learn how to create something that mattered to an audience.

BB: Something the audience would respond to.

SS: Yes. And then I was in a Broadway show called *Musical Chairs.* I was also assistant to the director. One day, Scott Ellis [now a very successful Broadway and television director] and I were out on the stoop in front of the theater lamenting how we wanted to be on the other side of the table. I had done the national tour of *Chicago* with Kander and Ebb, and Scott had done *The Rink* with them. We decided, *What if we went to see Kander and Ebb, just knocked on their door and said, "We'd like to do one of your shows off Broadway?" The worst that could happen is they'd say no.* So we did it! We went to them and asked if we could do *Flora the Red Menace* off Broadway—and they said yes!

We couldn't believe it. We hadn't directed or produced anything in New York before. We did the show down at the Vineyard Theatre in a kind of WPA theater style, because it's about Communists, and that aesthetic worked really well off Broadway.

BB: You bring up such an important lesson—that you can't say no to yourself. Let someone else say it to you; plenty of people will. And you can't let the inevitable rejections destroy you. You have to keep reaching for anything and everything. Clearly, you had that instinct. Anybody coming into the business needs to know how important it is not to be terrified or undone by rejection.

SS: Right. But you need to go in prepared too. I don't think you can just knock on someone's door and say, "Hey, it's me!" You have to have an idea and a plan. Once we did *Flora*, Scott and I never went back onstage. I think we made $200 for doing it and ate very little that summer. But Hal Prince saw it; Liza Minnelli saw it. We became best friends with Kander and Ebb, and we all went on to create *The World Goes 'Round* and *Steel Pier* together. I ended up choreographing Liza's big show at Radio City Music Hall, directed by Fred, and then *Showboat*, with Hal Prince. Looking back, taking that one chance—and starving for a little bit—changed our lives.

BB: Years ago, I started a chart. I wrote down the names of every show I'd designed, year by year, and then drew lines showing how they were all connected. Every show connected back to another somehow, though there were plenty of dead ends too. I think all of show business is interconnected. A career is built because of all the people you meet and work with. You have to keep trying things, doing things, because you never know what is going to end up opening a lot of doors.

SS: That's true. A lot of choreographers choreograph because they can't dance anymore, or a job falls into their lap because they were the dance captain. It's not a vision for them. From when I was a very small child, I always wanted this.

BB: Were you aware as a kid that choreography was an actual job? Or did you have the urge to do it first and then figure out that it was a job?

SS: I always thought it could be a job. Because at my house, when a musical would come on TV, everything would stop. We'd bring out the TV dinners and the TV trays and we'd all sit in front of the set and watch Fred and Ginger movies. The idea of singing and dancing and doing it all in a story form, these movie musicals, were very much a part of my growing up, and I understood that they were how some people made their living.

BB: You grew up in Delaware. Did you come into New York to see Broadway shows as a kid?

SS: No. Sometimes Philadelphia but never New York. That was the big, mean city.

Crazy for You (book by Ken Ludwig, lyrics by George Gershwin, music by Ira Gershwin) tells the story of Bobby Child, who works at his mother's bank in New York during the Great Depression but dreams of being a performer. His mother sends him to Deadrock, Nevada, to foreclose on a theater, but instead, he falls for its owner, a young woman named Polly. To woo her, he pretends to be Broadway impresario Bela Zangler, creates a show, and brings the theater and town back to life. Susan Stroman choreographed the original Broadway production in 1992, which was directed by her soon-to-be husband Mike Okrent, with sets by Robin Wagner, costumes by William Ivey Long, lighting by Paul Gallo, and sound by Otts Munderloh. In 2017, Stro directed and choreographed a fully staged concert version of the show at Lincoln Center, which I designed.

BB: Speaking of traveling, you told me that when you started developing *Crazy for You*, you went out to Nevada and explored ghost towns? Can you tell me a little bit about how you went out West to research the feel of the story?

SS: I do a great deal of research on every show. You have to immerse yourself in the geographical area and in the decade to be inspired to make movement and develop the music. For that show, I went out to Nevada to a couple of mining towns—some were ghost towns and some were tourist towns. I drove all around to get the picture of what was in those towns—the feed stores, the general stores. To get a feeling for the clothes, for what the costumes could be. *Crazy for You* is an East-meets-West story, and the way that the people in the East dance is very different from the way people in the West dance. Many of the showgirls' positions in *Crazy for You* were inspired by art and architecture in New York City in the twenties. There are a lot of Art Deco women in interesting poses, so there were moments in the choreography where we hit those poses.

BB: Robin Wagner designed *Crazy for You*, and I think he's one of the very best. When I'm doing a new production of a show that Robin originally designed, I feel a big burden, a heavy awareness of the original set, because I saw some of his shows when I was young, and they had a huge influence on me. He moves scenery through space so beautifully, and that's what stage design is to me: the transformation of the physical world—the scenic

Crazy for You (clockwise): Robin Wagner's model for *Crazy for You*; Busby Berkeley tower made with pickaxes; "Up above the Stars" finale: chorus girls as string basses
Robin Wagner/Joan Marcus

world—over the course of a play. The way the scenery affects the structure and pacing of a show is more important to me than what the details are or what it looks like. I think it's crucial to figure out how the physical space can manipulate the viewers' perception of the story. Robin does that brilliantly.

SS: Robin is great with movement and choreography. His *Crazy for You* set manipulated the space brilliantly.

BB: Can you tell me about the car gag in the very beginning of the show? Bobby Child is on the street, his mother's limousine pulls up, and ten million chorus girls pour out of the car. How did that idea develop?

SS: Bobby lives in a fantasy world and always dreams about singing and dancing. We had a street set where a big black car drives up, and the mother tells Bobby

Robin Wagner was born in San Francisco in 1933. His first Broadway show was *The Condemned of Altoona*, at Lincoln Center Theater in 1966. His fifty-five Broadway designs include *Hair*; *Jesus Christ Superstar*; *A Chorus Line*; *On the Twentieth Century*; *Promises, Promises*; *42nd Street*; *Dreamgirls*; *Chess*; *City of Angels*; *Angels in America*; *The Producers*; and *Young Frankenstein*. His beautiful use of tracking/rotating units in the 1995 *Victor/Victoria* was a huge influence on me—to the despair of many assistants and technical directors, since they are tricky to engineer!

to get in the car and go back to the bank—she wants him to be a banker. While his mother and his fiancée are yapping in his ear, the lights change, and he starts to fantasize. The lyrics are wonderful: "Bad news, go away, come around someday, in March or May, I can't be bothered now." And Bobby starts to imagine what it would be like to sing and dance and be surrounded by beautiful showgirls. We'd discussed with Robin that we had to have a magic moment there, so he designed this magical car. As the women are talking to Bobby, he gets into the car and inside there's an elevator that rises up and he suddenly appears on top. So now he's dancing on top of the car, up among the stars, when he hears a knock. He jumps down to the hood, and *knock, knock, knock*. There's a girl hidden inside the hood of the car! She pops out and they start to dance together. Then all of a sudden, the car door opens. You think you're going to see Bobby's mother and fiancée, but instead, out pour ten chorus girls, one after another. Robin had figured out how to angle the car in such a way that he could put a tunnel from it to the set piece of the Shubert theater upstage so that the mother and fiancée could exit on their hands and knees through the tunnel and the girls could come through and keep coming and coming—like it was a clown car. It was a really magical thing because the audience couldn't see in—they didn't know where all these girls were coming from. After that came a big production number, and at the end it was even more magical because all the girls disappeared back into the car, and just as the last one went in, the mother and fiancée came out!

BB: I remember it vividly.

SS: Later we had a scene where the New York showgirls come into Deadrock. They appear upstage and I wanted them to just walk with their arms hooked up. So Robin gave me ten treadmills! Each girl was on the edge of a treadmill in open-second position and she'd start walking. [Music director] Paul Gemignani would conduct according to the tempo of the treadmill. When they stepped off, the town would come in. It was like they were coming up and over the horizon of the Nevada desert, getting closer and closer to the town. That's another image that sticks with me.

BB: It's simple in concept but not so simple to make it all happen!

SS: It was all about the movement of the girls and the slow movement of the saloon, the feed store, and the theater coming in. Robin doesn't just build a static set—he really thinks choreographically about how it will move. He figures out how it should come on and get off, and where it will be stored. He thinks like a choreographer.

BB: So the entire transition moves beautifully and fluidly.

SS: One day, we were sitting around talking about the finale, and I said, "We need something magical to happen when Bobby and Polly finally get together. It'd be great if they were actually dancing in the air." Robin picked his saucer up off the table where we were having tea and crumpets, raised it high in the air, and said, "What if they were dancing on top of this?" And I said, "Yes!" So, he designed this moment where the floor lifted up in the air and from under it came the showgirls. The idea was that Bobby and Polly's love would not only restore the theater but the entire town. Robin created this big Follies number at the end, with a glorious set. It took all of the departments to make it really magical—not only Robin but William Ivey Long and his glorious costumes, smoke from the special-effects department, Paul Gallo's lighting—everything. Everybody worked on that moment to make it magic.

BB: It was striking. You've seen a lot of locations and effects through the whole show, but I don't think there was any other point in the show where something came out of the floor—that was saved for the last ten seconds of the show. You almost never see that.

SS: It was that moment where everything came together. It wasn't just done for a fancy effect but in service of the story. I think that's Robin's genius. Whatever he did, it was all in service of the storytelling. Always.

BB: There were so many moments in *Crazy for You* that stick in my head visually. You talked about the tunnel, which was brilliant and ultimately so simple. Often the simplest idea is the best one. And the treadmills were a conceptually simple idea, too, though not technically simple.

SS: No.

BB: And ten of them are expensive. I don't know if any producer today would pay for something like that, just to be used for a single moment.

SS: It was a single moment but so iconic that everybody remembers it.

BB: Another perfect moment was in "Slap That Bass." It's really a lighting moment, not scenic. When we started working on the concert, I told you I remembered the entire number as the girls being the string basses. And you said, "Yeah, everybody remembers it that way."

SS: They were the basses for only about ten seconds, but people remember it. It's wonderful when you can create images that burn in everyone's memory. The downlight that Paul Gallo used just focused the image. It lasted for just four counts of eight, but people remember it as the entire number.

BB: It's the sheer transformative theatricality of it.

SS: That is truly the magic that choreography and lighting can create.

BB: It happens instantaneously. You're watching all the preparation for it and not realizing what you're watching until all of a sudden, the image is there: girls turned into bass fiddles in front of your eyes!

SS: It takes a careful collaboration to create that: that spool of rope over on stage left, how long the rope has to be, how much of it spools out for before Tess chops it off, Bobby flipping the axe, the girls running around into place. . . . I mean all of that had to time out perfectly with the props. We had to work it out with the dance arranger, the wonderful Peter Howard, to time that out musically and create that group moment.

BB: I'm assuming you must've had rehearsal props as you developed that number, to help figure all those timings? Bobby, with an axe, is chopping lengths of rope off a spool as it musically unrolls. Each girl dances past and grabs a length of rope that will become the "strings" as each girl becomes a bass. The moment the final girl has that rope, the light changes and they all suddenly become the bass fiddles! Timing all that out to the music must have been crazy.

SS: Yes, it was intense in rehearsals.

BB: The last number that I want to discuss from *Crazy for You* is "I've Got Rhythm." For the act 1 finale, the residents of Deadrock grab junk that's sitting around and begin to make music with it. The town is coming back to life, and even its discarded trash has a use again! When we began to put the number together for the concert version, I was terrified, because I thought every one of the props—the hubcaps and the bike pump and so on—were going to have to make a sound at a specific pitch. As I learned, it was all rhythmic; the pitch wasn't crucial. How did you figure it out originally?

SS: Robin had given me a general store onstage—a feed store—so we used all the things that you might find in a feed store. We imagined that since it was a dead mining town, the store owner would be trying to get rid of a lot of stuff like pickaxes and miners' pans. So they were out front with signs on them that they were on sale cheap! I had everything that a miner would need: a shovel, a hammer, helmets, mining pans, pickaxes, all that kind of stuff. We had already set up in "Slap That Bass" that Bobby and the girls had taught the unemployed miners how to have rhythm. By the end of act 1, Bobby has created a whole show, but he's forgotten about marketing it and getting an audience. They're about to do this big show, but nobody comes, and he gets very depressed. So the townspeople say, "So what if there isn't an audience? You've given us something more." And they show him how he's given them rhythm. They grab things they're comfortable with and create rhythm. As we developed the number, we wanted to give a nod to Follies girls. Eight showgirls stepped on top of pickaxes held in a horizontal position by men who raised them up, almost like a cake.

BB: A Busby Berkeley moment.

SS: Yes. We built the number so it would grow and grow and grow and peak, and ultimately it had the best button in the world because it was a cliffhanger. Bobby is pretending to be Bela Zangler, but the real Zangler comes to town on the button!

BB: As I watched you re-create the *Crazy for You* numbers, I realized one of the things that is so magical about them is how they all build and build and build. So often, I find that build missing in musical theater. Someone will do a good enough number, but the choreography is four stanzas that repeat themselves. Your *Crazy for You* numbers start big and keep getting bigger. By the end, you can't believe what you're watching, because it just keeps expanding. I try to do that kind of thing with scenery. I try not to do too much with a set right at the beginning of the show. I'd rather start quietly, show some tricks somewhere in the first act, and then let it build from there. I push directors to keep most of the bells and whistles hidden through the first few numbers. It's all about contrast. I think you need to build toward bigger and bigger effects; otherwise, it's anticlimactic.

SS: This is why I always want to be involved in arranging the music. I worked with Peter Howard on *Crazy for You*. He was a genius at making sure the numbers built properly. I have many music meetings before going into rehearsal—even before going into preproduction. I sit with the pianist, and we keep playing through the songs and talking about the storytelling. For example, in *Crazy for You*, in the song "Shall We Dance?" when I wanted Bobby and Polly to be coy and shy with each other, I'd have the music play in the tempo of a soft-shoe. When I wanted them to chase each other, we'd pick up the tempo to a fast two. When they were falling in love, we'd go into three-quarter time. The manipulation of the time signature helps propel the audience's emotions. The time signature of any song can help tell the story for you.

BB: I love watching you use the music to punctuate beats in the story, little percussive pings or slide whistles or drum hits. I did a show recently with a younger team, and there were a couple of scenic effects that were good but weren't landing, because the music wasn't supporting them. It didn't punctuate the physical action. The musical director and composer didn't have the experience to solve it. I'm too musically ignorant to know what to suggest, but I knew we needed musical support that we didn't have.

SS: It's something I recognized as a young girl watching those movie musicals. If Fred Astaire jumped in the air, the entire orchestra jumped in the air musically. If Fred hit the wall, the sounds would support that. All the departments supported one another to make the musical a success. The more you know as the director—about lighting, scenery, costumes—the better off your work is going to be. I can make the most beautiful dance step, but if it's done by somebody who's not in the right costume, it won't matter.

BB: And on the right floor!

SS: The right floor! That's the bane of our existence!

BB: Sondheim talks about not making his lyrics too complex because there's so much else happening onstage. If he makes the lyric too dense, he says, the audience will miss other things—because there is music and costumes and choreography and lighting all happening at the same time. All those parts need to be balanced so they can coexist without creating a jumble. Any one of them can take center stage for a moment, but they need to be in balance so the audience can take it all in.

SS: That's so important to storytelling.

BB: When we were developing *Be More Chill*, which is a musical with a science-fiction twist about teenagers battling issues of popularity and ostracization, there was a scene near the end where the characters are putting on the school play. We kept jumping from onstage to backstage. We'd figured out how to make the set flip back and forth so that sometimes you were seeing the action from the "audience's" point of view and sometimes you were seeing the "backstage" view. We realized in previews that there was just too much happening. The little scenic trick we were using, even though it was good, just confused things at a point when there was also a lot of plot development happening. We cut all the scenic effects and just kept it all "backstage."

SS: I think every department understands that balancing act. When I did *Contact*, I told William I needed a yellow dress for Deborah Yates. He made thirteen yellow dresses just to get it right. He decided it had to be a very specific color yellow, the color of a traffic light: *move with caution*. It had to be sexy but lay on her so it would never be lewd. It had to be made of a material that allowed the boys to lift her without slipping. He really went through the wringer with it. But he came up with the most beautiful yellow dress that for three and a half years was in advertisements on every bus in New York City!

BB: That costume became famous. I mean, the character is named after the dress!

SS: The whole idea for *Contact* came over me in a New York City club at Hudson Street and Hubert at one in the morning. Everybody was dressed in black, like every good New Yorker, and in walked a girl in a

Contact is a dance drama created by Susan Stroman (who directed and choreographed) and John Weidman. Without any words—only dance and music—it tells three one-act stories thematically connected by the characters' attempts to make contact. Act 1 is based on Fragonard's eighteenth-century painting, *The Swing*; act 2 features a gangster's wife in the 1950s; and act 3 is a modern New York scenario about a lonely advertising executive and a mysterious girl in a yellow dress. The set was by Thomas Lynch, costumes by William Ivey Long, lighting by Peter Kaczorowski, and sound by Scott Stauffer.

yellow dress. She stepped forward when she wanted to dance with a man, and then she'd retreat. I got obsessed watching her. Then she just disappeared, like a vision. I thought, *That girl's going to change someone's life tonight.* About two weeks later, I was talking to André Bishop at Lincoln Center and he said, "Do you have any ideas for a show? If you have an idea, we'll help you develop it." I said, "You know what? I do have an idea."

BB: That was the beginning of *Contact*—the girl in the yellow dress? Then you developed the other sequences?

SS: Yes, I called John Weidman, and we put together a scenario around that idea of the girl in the yellow dress. André and Bernie [Gersten, the managing director of LCT] gave us eighteen dancers and set us up in the basement of Lincoln Center. They didn't come down to check on us, they didn't see what we were doing for four weeks. Then they came down to see it, and they fell in love with it. They said, "Do you have any other short stories? We want to produce this, but it needs to be longer."

I have a lot of short stories in my head. So John and I put together two other short scenarios that had something to do with the word "contact." The first story was about three people who have no problem making contact. The second story was a woman in an abusive relationship; her husband could not make contact with her. The third story—with the girl in the yellow dress—was about this man who would die if he didn't make contact that night. Each story also had something to do with the word "swing." The first one was based on the Fragonard painting, *The Swing*. The entire short story took place on a swing going back and forth. It had a very hypnotic feel to it. The second one was set in the fifties, with "swingers." There was a very Rat Pack feel to the husband. The third one had swing dancing, but it was my version of swing dancing—about making contact.

BB: When you were developing the Fragonard story, I assume you had a swing in the rehearsal room to figure all that out?

SS: We did. I can't believe we didn't pull the ceiling down!

BB: The length of the ropes must be crucial to making it all work rhythmically. The swing would behave differently if the ropes were longer or shorter. Did you play with different lengths?

SS: We did. Ultimately, we had to figure out a swing that would work in the Mitzi Newhouse Theater. And as the show ran, the ropes got longer!

BB: They stretched?

SS: Yes. Our head carpenter would have to tighten the swing up.

BB: I have always loved that painting. I was introduced to Fragonard in a college art history class, but the teacher didn't point out how sexually explicit his work is. When you start looking, the paintings are full of sexual imagery: the guy lying on the ground is looking up her skirt, her dress looks like a vagina, the plants look like penises.

SS: I knew the painting because I used to live part-time in London with my husband, near the Wallace Museum, and *The Swing* was there. I thought it was beautiful. I thought that girl in the pink dress was beautiful. Then I noticed there was a cupid in the garden who had his finger to his lips like, *Don't tell.* I thought, *Clearly something else is going on that he would paint the cupid like that. The cupid sculpture was*

Scott Taylor, Sean Martin Higston, and Stephanie Michaels on Thomas Lynch's set for the original Broadway production of *Contact*
Photo © Paul Kolnik

watching them. So, when the swing sequence in *Contact* came to us, it was clear it wasn't just servant, master, and beautiful girl. It had to turn into something else.

BB: A theatrical ménage à trois on a swing! Speaking of two men and a beautiful girl, tell me how *The Producers* developed?

The Producers, by Mel Brooks and Thomas Meehan, based on Brooks's classic film, is about Max Bialystock, a Broadway impresario, and Leo Bloom, a meek accountant. They concoct a plan to raise $2 million to produce the worst play ever done on Broadway (a musical comedy about Adolf Hitler) and pocket the investment when the critics inevitably pan it and it closes. They hire a blond bombshell named Ulla as their secretary and convince legions of little old ladies to invest in the show which, against all odds, becomes a smash hit. Max and Leo go to jail for the fraud but are shown at the end happily working on another hit show behind bars. Susan Stroman directed and choreographed, the set was by Robin Wagner, costumes by William Ivey Long, lighting by Peter Kaczorowski, and sound by Steve Canyon Kennedy. The Broadway production won a record twelve Tony Awards in 2001.

SS: *The Producers* was a little different for me, because instead of immersing myself in the decade and the geographical area, I had to immerse myself into the cinematic world of Mel Brooks. First and foremost, I knew it had to be funny. Every moment had to be funny but not cartoonish. Robin [Wagner, the set designer] said, "It has to be a real set. Comedy plays best against a real set."

BB: A realistic approach, on a show with so many locations, means a whole lot of scenery.

SS: Within that real set, of course, we created lots of whimsical moments.

BB: My favorite moment was when the curtain opens on the second act and Ulla has painted their entire office white! She's just finishing painting the last tiny dreary square of the office!

SS: The last spot of white!

BB: Was that basically the same set and some flats got changed out?

SS: No, we had the entire white set hanging up in the air! There was so much scenery crammed into the Saint James Theater for that show that the first time we did the intermission shift in front of an audience, it took about fifty minutes. I went out and told everyone, "This is our first preview and we're having a little trouble so you should go out and have a drink, maybe a little dessert." Then I said, "You know what? You can probably have a whole dinner!" It took almost an hour. But then we figured it out. That complicated shift just had to be figured out.

BB: On big shows, it's always an issue. People who don't work backstage don't understand how tiny it is there and that hanging lots of big scenery overhead in the wings is one of the tricks that fits all that stuff into tiny backstages. The first time I do an intermission shift on a big show, it is going to take an hour as we sort out the puzzle of packing and repacking it.

SS: Yeah.

BB: But if the second time only takes forty-five minutes, then I know we're going to get there. We just have to do it a few more times. Often the producer comes to me in a panic about how long it's taking and I say, "Don't worry. It'll take half an hour the next time, then fifteen minutes the time after that." The crew has to rehearse like anybody else and figure it out. In tech, you're usually dealing with the show proper. You don't have time to really figure out the intermission shift.

SS: Yeah, that takes a while.

BB: In tech, we're often figuring out how each scene works on its own. When we start running it all in sequence, it goes so fast that inevitably we end up with a long scene change or costume change, or a lighting change that goes on for fifteen minutes.

SS: Absolutely.

BB: I want to talk a little more about *The Producers* and *Young Frankenstein*—both famous Mel Brooks movies that you turned into musicals, and both designed by Robin Wagner. In both cases, the musicals didn't just mimic the details of the movies. The way they looked was quite different from the originals.

SS: You have to throw the movie away and start again. A musical is a different animal. It's no longer a movie. You have to start with a whole new script for what you imagine onstage.

BB: I'm assuming there was never any discussion of doing *Young Frankenstein* in black-and-white, like the movie?

SS: No. That would have been too much. I don't think a musical comedy audience can stare at black-and-white for that long.

BB: There are so many movies that have been made into musicals. There are things that work in cinema with close-ups, things that are brilliant on film that don't work onstage. Often the hinge of a story, the turning point, can't be replicated well. I've fallen into that trap. [See my discussion of the car-door lock in *A Bronx Tale*, in chapter 10.] I've seen other shows fall into the trap. You try to re-create some iconic cinematic moment only to find that it has little impact onstage. I feel like you avoided that in both *Young Frankenstein* and *The Producers*.

SS: A musical is a completely different animal. We're never going to be in close-up. Film people sometimes don't understand that.

BB: Another thing in *The Producers*—tell me about the little old ladies' walkers: they are one of the more famous props in recent Broadway history.

SS: I love finding that image that's going to connect the audience to the show—that they'll take away with them. The walkers came from immersing myself in the world of Mel Brooks. What is funnier than a little old lady with a walker? There was a little old lady character who had a scene with Max, and I thought she could bring out a walker. Then I thought, *You know what would be funnier than that? Twenty-five little old ladies with walkers!* I didn't even know if you could dance with a walker, if it could hold a person's weight. So I got a real walker and went into a studio with it. I found out that not only could it hold me, I could tap dance with it and do acrobatic flips! So with my wonderful dance arranger, Glen Kelly, I worked on that idea. In the show, you see one walker, then two, three . . . and eventually there are twenty-five walkers on the stage! We had to have a big discussion with William [Ivey Long, the costume designer]. Is it a lot of different little old ladies? Or would everybody be dressed the same? We decided that it was funnier to dress them all the same. In rehearsal clothes, everybody looked different. With costumes, they were a kind of funny Broadway show chorus.

BB: Showgirls as little old ladies with walkers! It shouldn't exist, so when it does, it's funny.

SS: Exactly! And an image the audience takes away!

BB: I want to switch to a minimalist set that I designed for you: *The Scottsboro Boys*. When we started you said, "It's a minstrel circle of nine chairs." You wanted it to be modern and not feel like the nineteenth century. I think that's all you told me: "You've got nine chairs to work with. Figure out how to make all the locations we need."

SS: Sometimes a show happens because someone hands you a screenplay or a novel or just the vision of a girl in a yellow dress. *The Scottsboro Boys* happened because Tommy [book writer David Thompson] and I wanted to work with Kander and Ebb again. We sat down at Fred's kitchen table and someone said, "We are often in a fantastical world in the musical theater; what if we wrote about something true; something real?" We started researching famous trials in America and one of the most famous was of the Scottsboro boys. It had a profound impact on civil rights. It changed juries. It had a big part in changing a lot of laws in the country. We found out about some of the people involved—the lawyers and the judges—but the guys themselves, they were just called "the Scottsboro boys"—like they were a vocal group or vaudeville act. Kander and Ebb were interested in these nine young men wrongly accused of a horrific crime. They were attracted to it because it was about underdogs.

We all felt it was important to teach people the names of the guys—that they be presented as individuals. We learned that a lot of the reporters called the trial a "minstrel show." That idea set Kander and Ebb free. *Chicago* had been a vaudeville, and this would be some sort of minstrel show. That concept would allow me to put the actors in charge of telling the story. The characters could move the minstrel chairs around—they'd physically control the set—to become a train, a holding cell, whatever they needed to tell their story.

BB: Had you done a show with just chairs before?

SS: No. In *Crazy for You*, they all climb chairs like a barricade at one point, but I'd never used them for a whole show.

BB: I hadn't either. Now, everybody thinks I'm the chair man, I think it's part of why I was asked to design both *Little Miss Sunshine* and *Come from Away*! There's a real theatrical magic to it. Even with the biggest sets I design, my goal is to figure out the bare minimum I can put it onstage and still make the story clear. In *Scottsboro*, the audience very quickly understood how we were using the chairs.

SS: It also allowed these nine young men to walk away from the minstrel show at the end. They knock the chairs over and walk away from it. This really made them in charge of the story—being able to walk away from the form of it. Those chairs that you created were very *today*, very modern. They helped connect that injustice to current injustices so much better than if you'd done a cliché vaudeville bentwood chair.

BB: Let's move on . . . a less minimalist show that we did together was *Little Dancer*.

SS: Just as Robin did with his *Crazy for You* set, you made that final moment where everything comes together in service of the story. There's nothing in *Little Dancer* like the last ten seconds, where you transform that whole set with beautiful movement into a modern museum.

BB: We were talking before about visiting the real place where a show occurs, for research. It's hard, as a designer, to immerse yourself that way on every show. I have to do too many projects to be able to travel like that! But although theater is usually on a much faster timeline, in this case we had dates to present it at the Kennedy Center two and a half years ahead of time. I was doing a lot of international work in those years, so while I was traveling for work, I went to museums in Saint Petersburg, London, and Philadelphia, where there were a lot of Degas paintings. I went to Paris to wander around Montmartre and find where Marie's house would have been. It was inspiring to be there—in the real place—with the show in my mind. I could start to feel the world I was trying to re-create.

SS: Yes. And your idea to make walls out of painters' canvas was genius. Then the lighting department and projection department could soak your canvases with Impressionist color. You really immersed yourself in the art world, the Degas world, and it showed.

Little Dancer, at the Kennedy Center

Little Dancer, by Lynn Ahrens and Stephen Flaherty, tells the story of the Impressionist painter Edgar Degas and Marie Van Goethem, a young, impoverished dancer who served as the model for his famous sculpture *La Petite Danseuse de Quatorze Ans*. It contrasts the successful Degas, losing his sight late in his career, with the young Marie, sacrificing everything to pursue a life as a dancer. The bulk of the action takes place in Paris at the end of the nineteenth century, but the final moment unfolds in a modern art museum, where we see Marie transform into the sculpture. The show was originally mounted at the Kennedy Center in Washington, DC, in 2014. It was remounted at Seattle's 5th Avenue Theatre in 2019 under the title *Marie* in preparation for a Broadway production that is still in the works. Susan Stroman directed and choreographed, and I designed the set, with costumes by William Ivey Long, lighting by Ken Billington, projections by Ben Pearcy, and sound by Kai Harada.

BB: As I said, having time to learn about him and his painting techniques gave me the toolbox to build the show from. It wasn't a big leap that we'd want to re-create Degas's paintings, but it was a great challenge for me to replicate the ballet studio in those famous paintings, with that diagonal wall of arched windows. It's such a recognizable image.

SS: But the set also had to allow a clear floor for dance too.

BB: The whole set had to be able to open up, but we couldn't do automated scenery that would require deck tracks, because the dancers *en pointe* might catch their toes on them and trip. That's what led to the whole set being hung from above and able to rotate from giant trusses. The happy accident was that, because it floated, the set "danced" in a way that scenery usually can't. It literally floated just off the ground.

SS: There was something magic in that. Those walls spun. They did pirouettes. Whenever the set changed, the cast would be dancing downstage of it to help the transition take us to the new place, and the set was dancing along with the company.

BB: That set was extremely complex because it could smash into itself in multiple ways. It was time-consuming and difficult to program the automation in that show to avoid crashes. But once it was cued and working, the whole thing was uniquely beautiful.

SS: Absolutely.

BB: We've talked a little about the Broadway production of *Young Frankenstein* already. Now I want to bring up the reimagined version that you and I did in London two years ago. It came about because Mel [Brooks] wanted to rethink the show.

SS: Yes! Mel is a wonderful friend. I love him. But when a man in his nineties says, "OK, we're going to do *Young Frankenstein* in London," maybe you don't quite believe him. I said, "Yes, of course we will"—you know? He'd come to New York and we'd meet, but I was still thinking, *This is not going to happen.* Then, all of a sudden, there was an English producer and an English general manager sitting in my office and I thought, *Oh my God, this is really happening! I better pay attention.* Mel did that! He wanted to do a leaner, meaner version of it. It was a very big show originally.

BB: In the Hilton [now called the Lyric]—one of the biggest theaters on Broadway.

SS: Sadly, in a huge theater. That big theater was not good for us. I could see where Mel got the idea to scale it down, because he writes songs that are kind of like vaudeville songs. They fit a vaudeville aesthetic with hard-edged spotlights, footlights, and in-one song and dance. The idea made perfect sense. We went back at the show and cut it down. We cut about an hour off it, and it made the comedy stand out even more.

BB: I hadn't seen the show on Broadway, so I went to the Lincoln Center Library to watch what you guys had done originally. When I saw the Igor and Doctor Frankenstein number, "Together Again for the First Time," I thought, *It's such a vaudeville number. The entire thing can be very theatrical—all painted drops. We won't even care if they flap in the wind because the musical is so self-consciously theatrical.*

SS: The Garrick Theatre in London's West End was perfect for it. That backstage was very small, but the show really worked well there. People just loved it.

BB: I want to talk about a *Young Frankenstein* prop: the hay cart. In that particular case, I very nearly re-created what Robin had made for you in the original. It was the only place where I wanted to copy the original scenery—so I talked to Robin about it and got his blessing. The choreography and movement in that song are so tied to what that cart does and how it's built that it made sense to re-create it.

Young Frankenstein by Mel Brooks and Thomas Meehan, adapted from their 1974 film of the same name, is a spoof of the classic monster story. In this irreverent version, Dr. Frankenstein's grandson decides to reanimate his forebear's monster, and the hilarious mishaps that ensue include a musical seduction in a hay cart called "Roll in the Hay." The 2007 Broadway production had a set by Robin Wagner, costumes by William Ivey Long, lighting by Peter Kaczorowski, and sound by Jonathan Deans. The 2017 West End production had a set I designed, costumes again by William, lighting by Ben Cracknell, and sound by Gareth Owen. Susan Stroman directed and choreographed both productions.

SS: We had to fit that hay cart backstage, so the one in London had to be a little smaller. But we needed to be able to do those physical jokes with the cart and horses. We had to make sure Inga could do all her acrobatic feats to really support Mel's jokes.

BB: When you did it originally, I assume the first rehearsal version of the hay cart wasn't what it ended up being? You must've had a mock-up in order to develop the idea, yes?

SS: I went on at great length with Robin about what I needed from the hay cart—but yes, we rehearsed with something that ended up developing with the actors.

BB: No matter how much you feel you know about what you want from a prop like that, there's really no choice but to make a rehearsal piece and then alter it a hundred times.

SS: Yes, because of all the tricks. For one thing, we found we had a hay problem. We had to sew the hay to a hay blanket so it wouldn't spill everywhere.

BB: Then there was the rhythm of it rocking. It had to rock slowly at some points, then faster at others, depending on the action of the scene. Even though we had a relatively small budget in London, we built an automated rocker control into our cart to accommodate that!

SS: Yeah, that was quite an involved prop.

BB: I think I've come to my last question. Do you have a first memory of noticing stage design in a show?

SS: Yes, a couple of things hit me early. Right after I came to New York, I was performing in a show on Broadway called *Whoopee!* We were at the ANTA Theater, which is now the August Wilson Theatre. When we got out, I would walk over to the Uris Theatre and second-act *Sweeney Todd*. That set! I'd never seen anything quite like it—that look of Industrial-Age London. Eugene Lee's work was phenomenal and exquisitely supported by Ken Billington's lights. They had that giant set and that little barbershop—I thought it was the most incredible thing I'd ever seen.

I also have a vivid memory of seeing *Dreamgirls*—designed by Robin Wagner— and looking up in the air and seeing these men lowered from above on trapeze bars. Then in the same show, right when the lead character was going to hit a big note, she got sucked back upstage into the set. She was on a palette and as she held a long note the palette sucked her back. I thought to myself, *Oh my God, if only I could work with somebody like Robin Wagner someday.* I remember that image and thinking how musical it was.

When I was in college at the University of Delaware, one day I cut class and went to the playhouse and saw the tour of *Seesaw*. This girl came out covered in balloons, with this tall drink of water named Tommy Tune dancing on his toes in clogs. The set—Robin again—danced right along with them. I thought, *That is for me.* It was the greatest image—such a happy visual of this little girl *en pointe*, covered in balloons,

Robin Wagner's set for the original Broadway production of *Dreamgirls*
Robin Wagner

and the tallest thing in the world, dancing in clogs. These are design images that stick with you; you remember them forever.

BB: That's beautiful, like the great images you went on to create: showgirls turning into bass fiddles, an electric chair tap-dance nightmare, a Broadway chorus on walkers, or the girl in the yellow dress. I can't think of a better ending than *images you remember forever!*

FIVE

Windows

Designing *Much Ado about Nothing* for Kenny Leon

**Unless . . . to defend ourselves it be a sin
When violence assails us. —Othello, Act 2, Scene 3**

For twenty-five years, I thought that politics didn't make good theater.

I went to school at Vassar College with a lot of idealistic people who wanted to make a political or social point with plays. Sitting through one too many ill-conceived, political-axe-grinding productions taught me it wasn't a good idea. Beyond school, I've found that explicitly political theater easily gets preachy, and that preaching is frequently to the choir. Though I generally agree with the message, this doesn't tend to make for good storytelling. I found myself firmly against the whole idea of political theater until Kenny Leon showed me I was wrong.

In November 2018, Ruth Sternberg, the director of production at New York's Public Theater, emailed to check my availability to design for Shakespeare in the Park the following summer. There were a few jobs on my wish list at the time, and designing at the Delacorte Theater in Central Park was high among them. I'd known Ruth and the Public's artistic director, Oskar Eustis, for close to twenty years. I'd worked with them at Trinity Rep in Providence, and since they'd moved to the Public, I had bugged them to let me design a park show, to no avail. I'd pretty much given up on it ever happening, so the call was a nice surprise. Of course, that didn't mean it would pan out.

The two shows the Public was planning for the summer of 2019 were *Much Ado about Nothing* and *Coriolanus*. It was their rule to hire a single set designer for both productions in the hope that some elements could overlap to save money and—more important—time, because of the quick turnaround between the shows. Dan Sullivan, with whom I had never worked, was directing *Coriolanus*, and Kenny Leon, for whom I'd once designed a play called *Emergencee!*, was directing *Much Ado*.

Kenny is a tall man with a gleaming shaved head. He is classically square-jawed, handsome like a 1950s superhero, if 1950s superheroes had ever been Black. Among his many diverse credits are the Broadway premieres of the final plays in August Wilson's epic Century Cycle. I'd seen Kenny at the September opening of my production of Theresa Rebeck's *Bernhardt/Hamlet* on Broadway. "Great work, man," he'd said. "I'd love to get in a room with you again." After Ruth's query, I immediately emailed Kenny to say how much I'd love to do *Much Ado* with him. The theater is a hyperbolic, glad-handing world where people are often complimentary to your face and don't follow up. I didn't know Kenny well enough to guess if his kind words had been heartfelt or simply polite.

November turned into December without a word and then into January. I assumed they had found another designer. Then Ruth called again to say that, while Kenny really wanted me to design the show, Dan was worried I wasn't right for *Coriolanus*. Would I be willing to sit down with him and show him some of my work?

By that time, I'd amassed a stack of Broadway credits and a Tony Award. Some flourishing Broadway designers might balk at interviewing for an off-Broadway job, but I totally got where Dan was coming from. When I'd finished graduate school, my goal had been to design musicals and Shakespeare. I'd had the good luck to do quite a few musicals, and Dan was probably aware of this. I'd done some Shakespeare, too, regionally, but I hadn't done any high-profile Shakespeare in New York. I wasn't the least bit put off by the fact that he wanted more information before hiring me. I trundled up to his Upper West Side apartment, my portfolio stocked with Shakespeare designs. An hour later, I was hired to design the two shows. Both were a treat to do, but I want to focus here on just one of them.

Much Ado was scheduled to tech in May. After quickly rereading the play, I arranged a call with Kenny to start discussing the production. Kenny lives in Atlanta when he's not working in New York or Los Angeles, so much of our design process would happen by phone and email. I would soon learn that Kenny can be a man of few words; his side of the correspondence often consisted of either "yes," "no," or "I don't think so." But he was always clear, and when something needed more explanation, he'd provide it or say he wanted some time to think it over.

In that initial call, he told me he was planning an all-Black production set in modern-day, middle-class Atlanta. In fact, he wanted to set it slightly in the future and to have a *Stacey Abrams 2020* poster on the set. Abrams, a Democrat, had recently lost a nationally covered governor's race in Georgia, where serious voter-suppression issues had contributed to her Republican opponent's victory. Kenny knew Abrams personally, and there was talk that she might run for senate or even president in 2020. He thought the poster would be a succinct way to establish time and place while offering a nod to current politics.

I love designing Shakespeare plays, but I hate the trend of picking a "period" to place them in. The plays are great enough to survive it, but I've gotten a bit tired of seeing them set in random historical contexts for no particular reason. That said, I love setting them "now." The Elizabethan language can be jarring at first, but audiences are so attuned to the nuances of the clothes, surroundings, and behavior of our own time that I think it deepens the storytelling. Most of the plays work brilliantly in the present and can easily withstand the occasional anachronistic sword or dagger. I was very happy that Kenny had decided to place the play in contemporary America.

He tossed out a few other images. He wanted to include a place for a live DJ on the set. He wanted an American flag and an old car up on blocks. "Most of the play is a comedy," he pointed out. "It's about love and deception and marriage. It deals with people—in this case, Black people—going about their everyday lives. But of course at the beginning, they're coming back from the war."

"So they're American military?" I asked. "Coming back from Iraq or Afghanistan?"

"No," he said. "I'm talking about the war that's going on in America right now."

I paused for what felt like five minutes to digest what he'd said. I'm a middle-class, middle-aged white guy working in a fairly liberal industry, living in a fairly liberal city. I try to be "woke." I've gone to more protest marches, mailed more letters to representatives, and written more postcards to likely voters than I can count. But my personal experience is massively different from that of a Black man, and I knew it. This was eighteen months before the murder of George Floyd and the international explosion of the Black Lives Matter movement, but I was aware of the awful statistics: the massive numbers of Black people incarcerated and killed. I would have described those as terrible civil rights violations, but Kenny had used the word "war," and that had set my mind reeling. It reframed my perspective in an instant. *If I were a Black man*, I thought, *watching my people being imprisoned and killed, facing the reality that it might well happen to me, how could I describe it as anything but a war?*

In that moment that felt like an eternity, I was grasping an idea that was new to me. A window cracked open, and I saw a slice of the world through new eyes. Could we build a production that would open that window for others? It's what art is always supposed to do but seldom does.

I think I just said, "OK, got it." We chatted a bit more. I told Kenny I'd send him some ideas soon.

Like one that draws the model of a house beyond his power to build it. —Henry IV, Part II, Act 1, Scene 3

The next day I went up to the Delacorte. I'd seen many shows there but had never seen it empty and wanted to get a sense of the size and feel of it. It's a big stage—seventy-five feet wide, which is almost twice the width of the average Broadway proscenium. It's a thrust stage with some masking right and left that slightly frames it. Upstage, it is wide open to a lake (the turtle pond), Belvedere Castle, the trees of Central Park, the skyscrapers of Midtown, and the sky. The house holds 1,800. Much has already been written about how Joe Papp battled Robert Moses for permission to build it in the early 1960s, so we'll skip to the happy ending: The Public has been producing free shows there to packed houses ever since. I was ecstatic at the opportunity to work there.

The Delacorte Theater

I was meeting Hugh Morris, the Public's shaggy-haired head scenic artist whom I'd known for years, and Nick Moodey, their burly, round-faced technical director, whom I did not know well. I had designed outdoor shows before but wanted their recommendations on how best to proceed with the design. The differences from indoor scenery surprised me. First of all, there was less weatherproofing than I'd expected. These sets are outside but only for about eight weeks, between tech and the run of the show. Most indoor scenic materials can survive that, and Hugh has a lot of experience selecting paints and sealers that can help. Wind was the bigger concern. Anything tall had to be sturdy enough not to be blown over. "Don't make anything taller than twenty-four feet," Nick warned. Indoors, twenty-four feet can seem massive. But when you are outside and competing with a seventy-five-foot-tall tree just off stage right, it doesn't seem so tall. (For reference, the little black masking panels in the picture above are eighteen feet tall.) Hugh outlined the various ways they tried to make the flooring less slippery for actors, since the stage was often damp, and he pointed out that smooth, shiny surfaces are harder to keep safe than broken-patterned ones. Finally, he warned, "We don't use any real plants or trees." I was shocked. We were in a park, for heaven's sake! It turned out that the city was deeply worried about invasive species. Technically, we could use live plants if they were native, but the red tape involved in getting permission was onerous.

I asked the two men when they'd need finished designs. It was late January, and we didn't tech until mid-May, so I wasn't feeling rushed—that is, until Nick replied. "I know you got hired late," he said, "so maybe we can push the design due date until late February?"

I must have turned white as a sheet. I had an unusually busy February ahead of me, juggling the techs for three off-Broadway productions (Tom Kitt and John Logan's musical *Superhero*; Lin-Manuel Miranda, Tommy Kail, and Anthony Veneziale's *Freestyle Love Supreme*; and Joel Grey's all-Yiddish *Fiddler on the Roof*) plus the West End opening of *Come from Away* and the Broadway production of *Be More Chill*. I'd been counting on having March to finish the Delacorte designs, but Nick laid out the schedule: If they weren't able to start building by early March, the scenery might not be ready by May. It was the kind of timeline I'd expect on a big Broadway show, but I hadn't been thinking about it that way. I hadn't factored in the physical size of the Delacorte, which made the construction more time-consuming than for a typical off-Broadway set. "Well," I said as I ran for the exit, "I'd better get to work!"

The other thing I did before I started to design was email the set designer John Lee Beatty. A well-timed piece of advice from John Lee had helped me solve some problems on *Act One* at the Vivian Beaumont, and I knew he'd designed many sets in Central Park. Who better to ask for advice?

A few mornings later, in a conference room at Manhattan Theater Club, John Lee gave me a crash course in designing for the Delacorte. "Don't fill the whole stage," he began. "The front of the stage is a big semicircle. You can pull your playing space back a full eight feet and it will hardly be noticed. I know that sounds like a lot, but it'll shrink the playing space, make the actors feel bigger on that giant stage, and save money on materials. And watch out for sightlines, especially stage left."

The Delacorte's thrust stage is surrounded by a curved amphitheater. The house-left audience has a clear view past the stage-left masking, into a backstage office area—and at 1,800 seats, if even 10 percent of the audience is looking into the wings, it's a lot of people. John Lee told me a lot that morning, but the piece of advice that really stuck with me was his suggestion that I use artificial foliage for masking, which could easily blend in and soften the visual transition from stage to park. I'm not sure I would have figured that out on my own—in fact, I'd probably have avoided the fake stuff altogether, figuring it wouldn't look good next to the real thing. It turned out to be a useful insight.

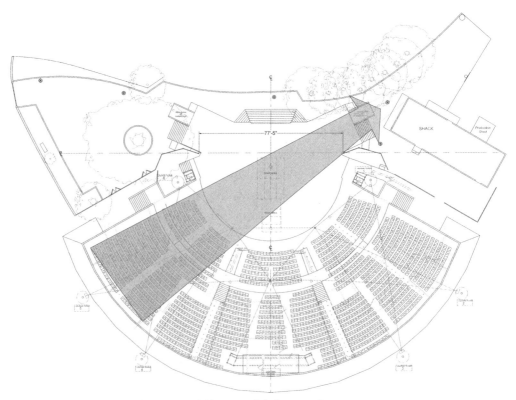

Plan of the Delacorte showing stage width, open sightlines, and trees

Having finally gotten my wish to work in this beautiful place, I was gripped with fear that I'd screw it up. I wanted my first Delacorte set to be perfect, but the desire for perfection can be paralyzing. The fear of making a wrong decision can keep you from making any decision at all. I flailed around for a specific style.

Scenic style is secondary to, and reliant on, scenic concept. If I have a solid concept or theme, it illuminates what the visual style must be. For example, *Act One* was the story of youthful artistic exuberance growing into a more measured artistic maturity. I saw *The Scottsboro Boys* as a historical event retold and physically controlled by the very people who were its victims. I don't always define my set concept in a sentence, but doing so can be helpful in guiding my style choices: what the production will look like. *Act One* was a massive, old-fashioned-looking structure that the actors moved through, ultimately leaving a dirty, squalid area behind to exist in a cleaner, more expansive realm. The *Scottsboro* set was dominated by simple, modern chairs controlled and manipulated by the performers within a disconcerting, menacing surround.

It was clear that in *Much Ado*, Kenny wanted to express the spirit of Black Lives Matter without literally stating the phrase. Because I was rushing, and the outdoor theater was an intimidating new venue for me, I didn't fully think through how best to support that idea before I started asking myself style questions: *Should the set be realistic? Poetic? Completely abstract?*

Most of my work is designed for traditional indoor theaters. When the house lights go down, the stage is all the audience can see—so I'm free to define the style of the visuals. At the Delacorte, Central Park is always part of the image. The sun does not go down until well into the performance, so real trees and a lake are part of the set whether wanted or not. The presence of the surroundings is a big part of what makes the experience unique. The set needs to work in harmony or in some sort of intentional disjunction with those surroundings.

Shakespeare wrote most of his plays to be performed with essentially no scenery, at the Globe or another Elizabethan playhouse. I believe that because his audience was familiar with the architecture of those places, they ignored it; it became a blank canvas. Most Shakespeare plays unfold across multiple, ever-shifting locations, much like modern screenplays. The playwright took care to have his characters tell us where we were at any given moment—for example, "This castle hath a pleasant seat; the air/Nimbly and sweetly recommends itself unto our gentle senses." With that, we are situated. Because this is true, I have always tended to make my sets for Shakespeare plays poetic rather than realistic. That doesn't mean my set may not have realistic elements; it just means that the overall feel of the set is poetic enough that the words can transport viewers wherever they need to go. Which begged the question of how to deal with Central Park's very real trees and lakes. Modern audiences, unlike Shakespeare's contemporaries, see the physical set as part of the storytelling and see meaning in it. That isn't to say they will ascribe significance to the reality of Central Park in relation to the play, but they will be aware of it, and that reality will affect their perception of the set I place in that park.

Thinking about it further, I realized that, atypically for Shakespeare, *Much Ado* doesn't change location often. With the exception of a few comic scenes and one at a family grave site, almost all of it takes place in and around Leonato's home. Perhaps in this case, the set *could* be relatively realistic without being at odds with the language. In any case, a certain level of realism would be important in communicating contemporary Atlanta for Kenny. My goal became to find a way to balance that realism with the essentially poetic nature of Shakespeare's work.

I decided to focus on the characters, hoping that might lead me to what set they should inhabit. Kenny had mentioned a middle-class Atlanta world, so I found pictures of people picnicking and having a block party. I suggested that perhaps we could set it at an Atlanta barbecue joint, maybe called "Leonato's." There is a crucial aborted wedding in the middle of the play and a completed ceremony at the end, so I looked for wedding images. And he had mentioned an old car on blocks and the idea of soldiers returning from the war. I compiled all of the images I found, sent them to Kenny, and arranged a phone call to discuss my ideas.

Kenny was nice but firm. "I don't think any of this is right," he began. "I don't want to do some sort of 'cool' production. Middle-class Black folks in Atlanta have a lot of money. They have some really nice houses. At the beginning of the play, an army of like thirty people shows up to stay with Leonato for the weekend, and it's not a problem. He has to have a house that can handle that!"

Kenny's tone was neither condescending nor mean, but I felt like a jerk. Apparently, I was the stereotypical white guy who assumed a "Black" production had to be urban and rough. "I guess maybe I thought the car on blocks implied the place wasn't fancy," I ventured.

Kenny thought for a moment and said, "You're right. Forget about that car. Give Leonato a really nice house! I like that last painting in your research; that feels right."

He was referring to the painting on the following page, with the park and the horse and the barbecue oven—a refined and manicured location I'd come close to omitting. I tamped down my embarrassment and went back to work.

Research collage

Leonato's house was an important symbol of his wealth. I realized that an attractive upper-middle-class home conveys stability. Once established, that stability could be in jeopardy as a result of the war the characters were returning from. By making the characters' lives concrete in this way, perhaps it would help make a war in defense of those lives more poignant to an audience that might initially recoil from the idea of an internal American war. We hadn't yet defined whether our "war" was a Black Lives Matter protest or a second American Civil War or something in between. But we were certainly presenting a war more consequential than the bloodless, cheerful adventure Shakespeare seems to have had in mind.

Putting a house on a stage surrounded by trees tilts the style away from abstraction. I had to decide what kind of home would make sense in the midst of the surrounding parkland. Maybe a lake house was better than an urban home? Kenny was fine with that, as long as I could make it clear that it was near Atlanta, so I researched lake houses in North Georgia.

There were a few practical considerations:

Much Ado has several very funny scenes in which hidden characters overhear others talking about them. The set needed to provide plausible hiding places in view of the audience, so viewers could see their reactions. The Globe Theatre had an upper

Research collage

gallery onstage that served as Juliet's balcony and the battlements prowled by Hamlet's father's ghost. *Much Ado* doesn't necessarily require this kind of gallery, but a raised central space could be useful for the eavesdropping scenes.

The script mentions an "orchard," an "arbor," and a "honeysuckle bower." On an abstract set, the language would have to establish those locations, but this set was realistic. I'd have to provide these specifics, or their absence would be felt.

When working on a thrust stage such as the Delacorte, it's good to think of the set as a big M with its middle point thrusting down toward center stage. A lake house with a raised deck area could do that. It would also partially hide Belvedere Castle, which is prominently visible behind the theater. (For many Shakespeare productions, this Victorian structure provides a charming addition to the landscape, but for a production set in Atlanta in 2020, it seemed like something to obscure rather than emphasize.)

The color and brightness of the house would be important. As I've mentioned elsewhere, when the shade of a piece of scenery is brighter than that of the performer's face in front of it, it is difficult for the lighting designer to make the performer pop out. If a spotlight aimed at a dark face is also hitting a light wall upstage of that face, the wall, not the actor will be the brightest thing onstage, so when I work on a show

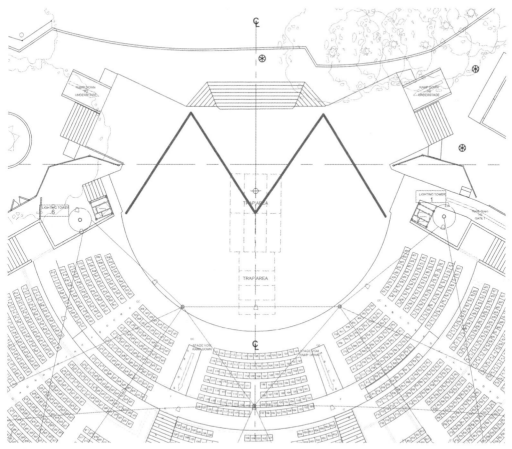

An M superimposed on the Delacorte stage

with Black actors, I try to push the set darker to make sure they are properly visible. At the Delacorte, there are no overhead lighting positions, as in an indoor theater; all the lighting comes from towers behind and around the audience. There's backlight and sidelight but no ability to use light from directly above to isolate actors from what is immediately upstage of them. This was another consideration in making the performers stand out.

As I wrestled with all these matters, I was juggling the five other productions I was committed to. Much of my design work on *Much Ado* was being done at tech tables. I started a Photoshop sketch of the set but very quickly realized I'd need to build a physical model.

In a proscenium theater, everyone in the audience sees the stage from essentially the same angle, so a sketch can be made to represent the basic ideas. In a thrust theater, the set is seen from multiple angles. I'd have to create my set in three dimensions—as sculpture.

Early, unsatisfactory Photoshop sketch of the set

Some designers hire assistants to build their models, but I've always used model-building as a tool for discovering what the set is. For *Much Ado,* that model-building had to happen on occasional free mornings and my one day off each week. As I refined the models, I did create parts of them digitally at my tech table and had those parts 3D-printed or laser-cut to speed up the assembly process.

I started with a very rough model, attempting to figure out how a house might sit in the space without compromising the theater's wide sightlines and still create some good acting areas. I have boxes of old model parts around, so my rough models often are patched together with those. The Victorian balcony and stairs in this model were remnants from another show. I placed the house stage left to partially mask Belvedere Castle. Not wanting the actors to be dwarfed by the huge Delacorte, I included a patio that I hoped would frame them and focus the scenes. I then created some sitting areas around the patio's edges to augment the chairs and chaise longues.

I never showed this rough model to Kenny. I'd made it for myself, so I could figure out space and proportion. It was the stepping-stone to the second model. In this more finished version, I placed a photo of the actual park view at the back to get a sense of the scale of the background in relation to the scenery. (Some designers create an unpainted "white model" as part of their process, but I find color too important an element to ignore at any stage.) In this model, the grass and trees were appropriately green. I intended to make the house darker, but before I did, I was seduced by the elegance of a white house in the midst of a verdant park.

The first rough model

I sent Kenny a photo of the model, and he replied that he liked it and looked forward to seeing it finished. Still attached to the idea of an all-white house, I sent the photo to our lighting designer, Peter Kaczorowski, and set up a call to discuss it.

Tall, angular, and with an almost permanently pugnacious expression on his face, Peter is both immensely talented and not known for sugar-coating his opinions. A colleague once said to me, "I think Peter actually derives energy from fighting with people." I've always had a lovely relationship with him and have appreciated the way he lights my scenery, but I wasn't surprised when he blurted out his judgment that the set was "utterly un-lightable!" He mentioned the difficulty of showcasing dark-skinned actors against white walls and noted that the big glass windows of my lake house would reflect the low-angled light back at the audience, blinding them. The windows couldn't be glass, and the set couldn't be white!

I went back and found images of darker houses and then started a new model that would meet all the diverse needs of the show. (See research collage 2, above.)

When I sent Kenny new pictures, he called me right away. "I don't know, it feels kind of small," he said, "Doesn't it? I want Leonato to seem wealthy. But maybe I need to see the model in person. Can we wait until I'm in New York in a couple weeks?"

I knew I didn't have a couple weeks to finish the set; Nick needed a design to start building. And Kenny was right that the house felt small. When I made it dark instead of white, it lost the elegance of the rough model and started to look like the cheap college housing I lived in my senior year at Vassar!

The second model

The third model

Atlanta mansions, including Tyler Perry's home (bottom left) and the brick-and-stone many-windowed house (bottom right)

He went on, "I know you sent me images of lake houses, but it just doesn't feel like Atlanta to me. Let me send you a few pictures of what feels right, OK?"

I was grateful for the offer of visual guidance and encouraged him to send whatever he could find.

"And don't forget," he added, "I want an American flag. These people are patriotic!"

Within hours, he emailed me a picture of Tyler Perry's mansion outside Atlanta, saying, "This is probably too much, but it's the right direction." Then he sent me another picture that really helped me, of a mixed, stone-and-brick home. I realized I could use masonry to make a very elegant home with a dark surface. Why hadn't I thought of brick on my own? Perhaps more important, the house had lots of windows. Peter was worried about Plexiglas reflections, but I could use black window screen instead—an effective stage substitute when glass is problematic. Windows imply people and life beyond them; they suggest a populated world. By inviting us to imagine what's going on inside, they nudge the audience to participate in the storytelling.

I made a quick new model from cardstock. To avoid the white-model trap I'd fallen into with the lake house, I Photoshopped color onto it. I balanced the stage by putting the patio on stage right, disconnected from the house. That created another focused acting space, in addition to the balconies of the house. A low wall upstage of the patio would provide additional places to sit and something to hide behind in the eavesdropping scenes. Per Kenny's request, I added a big Stacey Abrams banner and an American flag. I also returned to his early idea of a car, but instead of a junker

The fourth model

on blocks, I put in a clean, suburban SUV. In case anyone missed the "2020" on the banner, the car would signal that this was no old-fashioned production!

"That's more like it," Kenny emailed. He liked the balcony as a hiding place but worried about how he would get actors up to it and back down quickly.

"Fair point," I replied. "I'll add some stairs." He reminded me that he was thinking about having a live DJ, and we'd need a spot for her. I said I'd make some space and prepared to go to work on these final refinements—but before I did, I sent some photos to Nick at the Public. I wanted to make sure I wasn't designing more scenery than they could reasonably build within the time and budget available. I was relieved by his quick response, "Looks great, we can do that!"

I added stairs to the balcony and a dormer window above it with its own balcony for the DJ. To balance the dormer, I added a cupola with a lightning rod on the house's stage left wing. In realistic set design, more adornment is generally good.

The fifth and final model

Inspired by Kenny's research picture, and to create some visual variety, I made part of the house stone and part brick. The orchard referred to in the script would be a Georgia peach orchard, of course.

Kenny arrived in New York in early March to audition actors, and we were finally able to meet in person. He stared at the model for a few very long minutes and then said, "I love it. It looks like Atlanta."

Build there, carpenter; the air is sweet. —Troilus and Cressida, Act 3, Scene 2

We were down to the wire and needed to get the set under construction. After a quick meeting with Ruth Sternberg and Oskar Eustis to get their blessing on the design, I handed the model over to Alexis with a plea that she draft the technical drawings as fast as she could. "I need it last week!" I insisted.

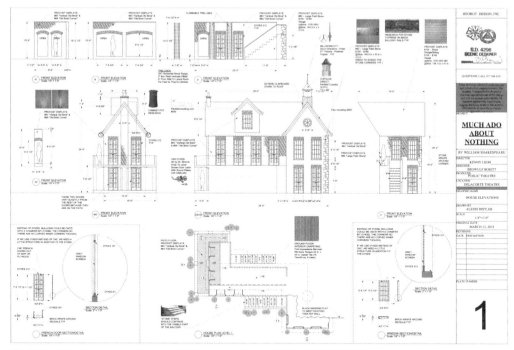

Drafting of the house

Correct architecture is crucial in realistic design. When something is off, the audience can't necessarily pinpoint what it is—but they know that what they are looking at seems false and stagey. Working quickly, Alexis cleaned up and clarified the architecture as she drafted. Among other things, she detailed the many wooden windows set into the brick-and-stone walls. We made sure to specify screen in the windows, not Plexiglas. Miraculously, by mid-March, Alexis had completed the drawings and the shop could start building the set.

With the set under way, it was time to think about the props. The Public had hired a props supervisor I didn't know but would learn to love: Sydney Schatz. There's a quip that all you need to stage Elizabethan plays is a "Shakespeare bench." Face it toward the audience and you're in the royal court, turn it ninety degrees and you're in a tavern, flip it on its side and you're on the battlefield. This is an oversimplification, of course, but it's true that working out what the actors will sit on is enormously helpful in staging Shakespeare. In our case, the "Shakespeare benches" would be lawn furniture, and I wanted it chosen quickly so Kenny could try it out in rehearsal.

As for the DJ, Kenny had changed his mind about having her be a constant presence. I decided to keep the dormer window anyway, as it made the third floor feel populated, and the whole house seem bigger and more full of life. To simplify construction, though, I got rid of its practical balcony. The DJ would instead appear occasionally on the lawn, so I suggested a mobile DJ cart that could be wheeled out from the house—our version of the strolling lute or guitar player who graces many Shakespeare productions.

I mentioned earlier that one of the only scenes set in an alternate location is the graveyard scene, where Claudio and the Prince pay homage to Hero, whom they think is dead. Light is often used to focus and define individual scenes by making the rest of the set disappear. I've seen this attempted in the park, but I was skeptical that we could make my enormous brick house disappear. Carrying a prop grave onstage and pretending there wasn't a house looming behind it would feel silly.

To solve the problem, I suggested we set up a memorial portrait of Hero on the patio. Many people create informal shrines around a dead relative's portrait in their homes. After September 11, makeshift memorials sprang up all over New York and other cities, and you can see versions of them at the sides of highways, memorializing fatal car accidents. I sent Kenny some research, and he liked the approach.

It was a lower priority, but we would also need to dress the interior of the house with furniture and pictures. Key to making all those windows feel real was the indications of life which could be seen through them. I hoped we could pull much of this

A makeshift memorial

dressing from the Public's prop stock and not spend a lot of money on it. It wouldn't be the focus of anyone's attention, but I wanted it to feel modern and upscale so it wouldn't detract from the gentility of Leonato's mansion. I sent Sydney some pictures of the general style without asking for specific items.

For any walls that might be visible, I suggested paintings by Romare Bearden, an artist of the Harlem Renaissance. Years before, I'd worked for and become friends with the Black actor/director Billie Allen. She had several original Beardens in the Manhattan duplex she shared with her husband Luther Henderson (who had been one of Duke Ellington's arrangers). Beyond the TV living room of the *Cosby Show*'s Huxtable family, that was pretty much the extent of my personal exposure to the artistic taste of a wealthy, urbane Black family. I thought Leonato might have some of these paintings. My only other specific request was for a copy of Shepard Fairey's Barack Obama "Hope" print.

Style of decor for the house interior

The show began rehearsal in mid-April. The cast was filled with classically trained actors who were off-Broadway Shakespeare regulars. Among them was my friend Chuck Cooper as Leonato, who I knew would be brilliant. (Chuck graces the stage in the chapters about *Act One* and *Prince of Broadway* as well.) I had assumed that Danielle Brooks, who was playing Beatrice but had come to prominence playing Taystee on the Netflix series *Orange Is the New Black*, might be less well-versed in classical theater. I was wrong. Even in the first rehearsal she was charming, funny, and she knew her way through the script better than most of the rest of the cast. Thirty minutes of read-through banished any worry that our star wasn't a trained classical actor. Thirty seconds on Google told me she'd trained at Juilliard. Kenny later told me that there is a rampant notion that Black actors can't do Shakespeare, but I think my personal prejudice had more to do with whether "just a TV star" could handle it.

We were still figuring out how "military" our army was going to be at the beginning of the show. I wondered if they ought to arrive in something other than an SUV. I found some photos of pickup trucks converted to battle wagons called "technicals" in African and Middle Eastern guerrilla wars. I suggested that a vehicle like these would really drive home the image of a war, especially in contrast to the calm, suburban home center stage.

Military "technical"
Magharebia

"Might work," Kenny responded. "We have to have a balance of banners and mega-phones. We are fighting and protecting our communities. We are not the aggressor. Maybe one big gun like that would allow us to carry fewer personal guns. Hmmm."

Kenny loved bouncing around these kind of ideas as he developed the show, and so did I. After a few days, though, he decided the quasi-military truck wasn't the way to go—that it would tip the balance of the play in too aggressive a direction. "I don't want the 'army' to feel too violent, or the white audience may shut down and won't hear what we're trying to say," he explained.

When I saw the first run-through of the show, the army marched on in the opening scene with military precision. We hadn't decided yet whether they would be carrying guns, but their entrance signaled an established military unit, not a band of disparate protestors gathered for the day. Most of the play then spooled out as a very good if fairly traditional telling of *Much Ado*. As Kenny had said, "There are times when we fight, but between those times we're just living our lives, we're joking around, we're getting married."

In the middle of the show, for a dance at the aborted wedding ceremony, the composer Jason Michael Webb and the choreographer Camille A. Brown had cre-ated a celebratory dance that was distinctly Black. It was wonderful and appropri-ate to the production, but it didn't strike me as making a political statement. At the end of the show, when the weddings were finally carried through, the dance was reprised—but this time, the long, slow wail of a police siren shattered the joy of the celebration and cut it short. Members of the army stopped in their tracks, formed ranks, and marched offstage. Even in the rehearsal room, my blood ran cold. In one simple but powerful theatrical moment, Kenny had turned a celebration of life into a march back to war.

Our costume designer was the zen and cheerful Emilio Sosa of *Project Runway* fame. (Professionally, he goes by ESosa.) When I asked him how he planned to dress our army, he told me the uniforms would be based on those worn at military acade-mies—meaning they'd have a somewhat nineteenth-century feel, as modern military dress uniforms do. Perhaps a Black audience would understand that our soldiers were civil rights warriors, but I worried that a white audience might not.

I emailed Kenny that evening to ask whether he thought some protest signs might help establish our soldiers more specifically. My concern was that without this con-crete addition, the stakes at the beginning wouldn't be clear—and that might sap the power of the ending. He replied quickly, "You might have a point. In my mind, these people decided to organize, and that included designing uniforms based on the contributions Blacks have made historically in the military. Maybe one big banner? Or two or three signs? *Our Lives Matter, Remember the 14th Amendment, We Can Kneel* and *Serve, Equal Education for All: 1865–2020, Let Us Be Free.*" I was game to try any or all of them, but after a few more days of discussion, Kenny nixed protest signs altogether, and I trusted him on the point. At least for the moment.

As the show rehearsed downtown at the Public, the set was beginning to take shape at the Delacorte. The Public has a small scene shop, but most of the set for *Much Ado* was built in place. In March it still snowed from time to time, and the carpenters actually had to shovel before they could work. By the end of the build in May, temperatures had risen to ninety-nine degrees and the sun beat down on the stage.

As the house rose under the watchful eyes of Nick and Hugh, it began to look for all the world like a real house that had been in Central Park for ages. And like a real house, it was framed by two-by-four stud walls so that it could withstand the wind. The brick, stone, and shingles were Vacuform stapled to plywood—exactly what we'd use in an indoor production.

I wanted to use real turf for the lawn, but because of the "invasive species" rules, we had to use a roll of what amounted to high-end Astroturf. Hugh and his right-hand painter, Tacy Flaherty, assured me that they had developed ways of clipping and layering it to appear less uniform and thus more real.

As the set progressed, I made plans with Sydney to "landscape" the yard. Although I come from a family of gardeners—my grandmother's gardens outside Boston won national prizes and are recorded at the Smithsonian—I did not inherit that green thumb. In fact, I've killed almost every plant I've ever owned. Perhaps Leonato's gardens, albeit artificial, would be my chance to redeem myself!

I researched the flora of Georgia and made Sydney a map of the foliage I liked. I wanted some honeysuckle because it's mentioned in the script, along with other plants that could conceivably be found there. Most audience members wouldn't know the difference or care, but that sort of accuracy is nice for those who do recognize it—as long as it doesn't draw attention away from the story. As much as I try to be accurate, it's worth mentioning that I hate it when a clumsy or confusing bit of staging or scenery is explained away because, "It's what they would have done . . . what they really had . . . what it really was." If being accurate (historically, biologically, zoologically, whatever) confuses matters, it's best to take some license. I'm an artist, not an anthropologist. But luckily, on *Much Ado*, botanical accuracy met our needs just fine!

The set under construction

MUCH ADO FOLIAGE

This could be honeysuckle if we find an affordable honeysuckle. Otherwise it could be ivy.

English ivy

Aezaleas around patio or some leafy shrub people can hide and peek through.

White Honeysuckle on trellises

6'-8' pine tree in corner

I think this is a rose bush, could be some other shrubby plany with reddish flowers.

Foliage map

The wind and the rain. —*Twelfth Night*, Act 5, Scene 1

In mid-May, as we approached tech, I met with the props team to dress the interior of the house. I'd discovered that the Public had a policy of not using reproductions of artwork without clearing and paying for the rights. I couldn't argue with that; it's a noble, if slightly novel, policy for a theater. But I didn't want to spend money on licensing Romare Beardens and an Obama poster that would only be glimpsed through the windows. It seemed wiser to spend what budget we had on the exterior and pull random, innocuous art from the theater's prop stock.

On the day we dressed the set, it was pouring, and I learned firsthand that the roof of our structure wasn't very watertight. It's the first time I've ever dressed a set while juggling an umbrella!

The next day, our stage manager, Kamra Jacobs, led us into tech. We rehearsed with the actors for five hours in the afternoon and five hours in the evening, just as we would on Broadway, but in the park, the setting sun became a factor in our schedule. Peter and the lighting team had only a few hours of darkness each evening while the actors were present. After rehearsal, they'd stay to write cues late into the night. Each afternoon, Kenny would work on staging; each night, we would start a run of the show at eight so Peter could run cues in real time as the sun set.

The fact that we had a single set and fairly continuous realistic action should have made our lives easier—and would have, if nature had cooperated! The first day of tech, it was fifty-five degrees and pouring. The simple folding sunshades over our tech tables soon gave way to ramshackle hovels made of plastic tarps in a semisuccessful attempt to keep us dry, and we found ourselves watching the stage through a tiny window at the front of our leaky little hut. The poor actors wore rain ponchos and carried umbrellas but were soon soaked. At least they could go warm up in their indoor dressing rooms between scenes—no such luck for us. After dinner, Nick brought us a little electric heater to try to warm up the inside of the tent. It helped a little. Despite all the cold and damp, I was having a ball. I'd always wanted to design at the Delacorte, and I wasn't going to let the rain dampen my spirits!

After that first day, both Alexis and I came equipped with rain boots, long under-wear, and several layers of coats. Thankfully, the weather got better, and we ended up worrying more about sunburn than hypothermia. The evenings were perfect—comfortably cool without being cold. Because the set was static—different from most of those discussed in this book—it didn't transform physically. The transformations relied on changes in lighting—and of course, we had the most magnificent light source of them all. Over the course of act 1, the sun set behind the audience and the sky behind the actors morphed from a pale cerulean to a deep rich sapphire to the peculiar slate gray of the Manhattan-lit night. I spend so much of my life trying to "create" sky on an indoor stage that having the real sky as my cyclorama filled me with awe. As the stage darkened, the lighting began to shape and mold the space, some-times focusing tightly on a few actors, sometimes encompassing the entire stage. For another sort of transformation, we had covered almost every shrub and tree on the set with white Christmas lights. They glowed to life instantly for the wedding scenes, realistically reframing the house and yard as a place for celebration.

In the end, the power of the set came from its lack of transformation—its appar-ent solidity within its surroundings. It felt like a real house on a real lawn in a real parkland, although only one of those things was true. I think that helped make the characters seem real and grounded as well—recognizable and of-the-moment. In the end, it contributed to the idea that these lives were real. They mattered.

The weather improved, but nature never entirely left us alone. I don't know how many raccoons live in Central Park, but there's a sizable colony of them in and around the Delacorte. I'd been warned they'd visit us sooner or later and to keep my distance. Still, it was a shock the first time I watched one brazenly march through the seating risers toward a garbage can, climb it, push open the lid, root around inside, reopen the lid from inside, jump down, and happily stroll away. Where I grew up, fearless raccoons meant rabies—but I'd read that New York City had a good raccoon rabies-vaccination program, so these visitors were unlikely to be sick. They were used to being around people, pretty adorable, and very entertaining. At one point, they

With Kenny on the first day of tech

With Alexis, huddled in the scenery tech-tent

Delacorte raccoons and their handiwork in their "natural" habitat

climbed our artificial Georgia peach trees to sample the Styrofoam fruit. Apparently, they didn't care for the taste. I came to love their visits, even when one marched across a tech table during a preview of *Coriolanus* and sat down to watch the show!

Wild Kingdom aside, tech flowed smoothly into previews. When the Prince drove onstage in an SUV, the audience laughed and applauded at its concrete, contemporary reality. For the most part, the set worked well, but Kenny was having some difficulty with the pivotal wedding scene in the middle of the play, where Claudio accuses Hero of being unfaithful. He'd set the conflict at center stage, which made sense, but the set was so asymmetrical that the moment was not focusing properly. I suggested we add some wedding scenery to help. Actors could place big wedding bouquets on the stage right patio, as if the characters were creating an altar for the wedding. Kenny embraced the idea, we quickly gathered the props, and the scene proceeded well.

Later in the play, when Claudio comes to atone for the actions he believes had led to his erstwhile bride's death, we redressed the patio with funeral flowers and a portrait of Hero. This worked well until we had our first audience. When Hero's portrait was revealed, it got a big laugh—not at all the reaction we were going for! "Let's give

Margarette Odette, Tyrone Mitchell Henderson, Jeremie Harris, and company in the wedding scene

it another night," Kenny insisted. "I think maybe that laugh was the audience recognizing that Leonato is pulling out all the stops in order to fool Claudio."

The second night, the same thing happened. It shattered the sadness of the scene. Kenny and I looked at the portrait together. "Maybe it needs to be smaller," I suggested. "I wanted the back row to be able to see it well, but maybe it's comically big?"

"Maybe we need a different picture of her," Kenny mused, "something less casual?"

The next day, Sydney printed and swapped in a new portrait, slightly smaller, and the audience didn't laugh! Although the second portrait wasn't that different from the first, it was perceived differently. It never got a laugh again. That's the strange alchemy of theater.

In previews, I discovered an unexpected pitfall of our realistic set. There's a point at which the villains of the story are sneaking around, and they hear a noise. One of them—Conrade, played by Khiry Walker—passes it off as "the vane on the house." Khiry had asked me if we had a weather vane, and I'd pointed out the lightning rod on the cupola, so he made a little gesture toward it when he said the line. But that led one of the theater's artistic staff to ask me why it wasn't a proper weather vane. I argued that a lightning rod was good enough, but it got under my skin, and within twenty-four hours, I had decided I needed to make it into a real weather vane. It was a throwaway line written for an Elizabethan playhouse, but because the set was so

The 'funny' portrait of Margarette Odette and the replacement portrait

realistic, I felt it needed to refer to something real. I didn't want any of the audience members to wonder why a lightning rod was called a weather vane when they should have been watching the action!

The problem was the cupola was at the very peak of the roof, and the roof was made of theater flats covered with Vacuform shingles. It wouldn't support the weight of a carpenter climbing up to place the weather vane. Even I knew it was a bit extreme to re-erect scaffolding to add this tiny detail. To my delight, Nick figured out a crazy way to lay a ladder across the roof safely enough for a nimble carpenter to slip my crossbar in place!

The army appeared at the beginning of the show and left at the end, in the uniforms ESosa had created. Kenny had decided they should not carry weapons; he wanted them to be peaceful warriors. But I continued to worry that the audience might not understand we meant them to be warriors nonetheless, battling for civil rights. Nervously, I decided to bring up the idea of protest signs one more time. I didn't want to question Kenny's authority or presume that I knew better how to define a protest, but the army was so important to the message of the production!

Kenny must have been having similar concerns because this time, he welcomed the idea—though he was quick to add that he wanted the signs to carry only positive messages, nothing angry, and sent me a photo as an example. With ESosa's maroon soldiers' uniforms in mind, I created several examples in fonts ranging from casual to more clearly military.

We tried several options over the next few nights. Sometimes only the Prince carried a sign, and sometimes several other characters had them as well. Sometimes a single slogan appeared on a number of signs, and sometimes there were a variety of slogans. Ultimately, we chose the military stencil font and a variety of slogans. To me, this made the intent of the army crystal clear.

In 2019, the phrase "Black Lives Matter" was in use but had not yet been embraced by the general public; even in liberal New York, it wasn't in the mainstream. Kenny wanted to avoid it, but we intentionally came close in several recognizable slogans and also evoked well-known historical rallying cries of the civil rights movement. (By 2021, when I designed *Merry Wives* in the Park, the world had evolved, and I placed a large Black Lives Matter mural prominently on the set.)

With the various adjustments we made during previews, the show was settling nicely, its message resonating with audiences. The heart of *Much Ado* is the romance of Beatrice and Benedick, and Danielle Brooks and Grantham Coleman played their brilliant scenes to perfection. That in itself would make for an entertaining evening, but the social and political brackets we'd placed around the play made their story all the more poignant. When Benedick marched away with the army at the end, leaving Beatrice alone onstage, it was heartbreaking. It added the tension of a life-and-death struggle to a comedy where the stakes are less dire. It gave a classic story added depth.

Kenny had also managed to make sense of a part of the play that tends to be problematic. As Shakespeare wrote it, Hero is falsely accused of infidelity by Claudio, but as soon as he repents, she forgives and marries him. It's difficult for a modern audience to swallow that, and because Hero has so few lines, it's hard to convey her motivation. Many productions sidestep the problem by focusing heavily on Beatrice

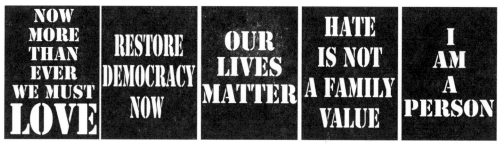

Protest signs

Chuck Cooper, Danielle Brooks, Margaret Odette, Grantham Coleman, Jeremie Harris, and company

and Benedick, a more modern, equally matched couple. Kenny's idea was to open the show with Hero stepping onto an empty stage and then work her into every scene possible, placing her in the thick of the action so she could react physically, if not verbally.

Margarette Odette is an actress with a great deal of charisma, and her Hero felt as important and present as anyone else in the play. When Claudio finally asked for her forgiveness and her hand in marriage, she offered her response with ferocity: "One Hero died defiled, but I do live." The hand she offered him was a punch in his mouth. As he staggered back in shock, she continued defiantly, "And surely as I live, I am a maid." Then she kissed him and it drew applause every night. It placed Hero in control of the moment, so the reconciliation of the couple felt joyous.

Just before we opened, I added one final prop. For budget reasons, I had given up on the specific interior artwork I'd wanted, but as we started previews, Sydney told me we had enough money to buy an original Shepard Fairey Obama "Hope" print. *Yes, please!*

The print was procured and put into a watertight frame, and together we placed it over the mantelpiece in Leonato's living room. It was a detail, but a surprisingly large percentage of the audience could see it, and a number of people mentioned it to me. It was the perfect punctuation mark for the set.

The show was well received and, to my delight, Stacey Abrams flew north to see the production that forecast her next political move (incorrectly, as it turned out, though she would go on to create massive political waves in 2020 nonetheless).

The view through one of the doors to Leonato's living room

Most theater is ephemeral, but we were fortunate that PBS decided to film our *Much Ado* for its *Great Performances* series. Mind you, a televised version of a live play isn't the same as the original—and of course I am always concerned that scenic imperfections will be visible in close-ups. Film is able to present grand wide shots and detailed close-ups in a way theater never can, but the experience of viewing theater involves looking at a full picture and simultaneously making decisions about what to focus on. I tend to miss that extraordinary feeling of participation when I see my productions on film. All of that said, it was thrilling that a show I loved that had such a brief run would be memorialized this way.

With the opening came the reviews and, unlike some theater people, I tend to read them. If they praise me, I'm happy about it, but positive or negative, I try not to give them too much weight. In this case, I was startled at how consistently the critics seemed to get Kenny's message; the ideas he'd shared with me so many months earlier had come through loud and clear. Most of the reviews were positive, but even the mixed ones seemed to understand that the "war" was in defense of the lives of those who populated the play. In *New York* magazine, Sara Holdren wrote, "In this *Much Ado*'s version of next year, America is in fact at war with itself, with civilian militias holding the line against what are presumably the Trumpian forces of evil." In *Newsday*, Barbara Schuler wrote, "This war, it seems, is of the moment, but the community values worth fighting for take a more personal turn in the love stories at the heart of the play." Jesse Green, in the *New York Times*, said, "That's what's so successful about this fresh version of one of Shakespeare's most popular plays: Its politics, though unmistakable, cloud neither the romance nor the comedy." I don't think I've ever seen a group of reviews so clearly mirror the director's intent as those did.

I loved that our "war" was a more serious frame to the play than the seemingly bloodless conflict usually implied. I have always preferred Shakespeare's more serious comedies, *Twelfth Night* and *As You Like It*, because their life-or-death situations raise the stakes. Kenny's superimposition of an existential struggle onto the brilliant fun of *Much Ado* gave it poignancy and made the story deeper.

I knew that our references to Black Lives Matter, however oblique, would be regarded as a political statement. What shocked me was that the reviewers seemed to think that simply casting Black performers in the roles was political in itself. *Much Ado about Nothing* was written by an Elizabethan Englishman about characters in Sicily. I hadn't thought setting it in an affluent Black suburb was any more radical than setting it in nineteenth-century Europe or any of a hundred other choices a director could make. That shows my naïveté, I guess. Because every review mentioned the all-Black cast—often in the headline—as if that were a bold choice.

And so, I guess it was. The production hinted at the Black Lives Matter movement, it's true; but mainly, it presented a group of Black lives being lived. I guess Kenny and the cast understood all along that the casting itself was political. I learned by working on the show with them. In addition to everything else it accomplished, the show cracked open a window and let me look through.

SIX

Backyard

A Conversation with Kenny Leon

Setting: *Kenny Leon's backyard in Atlanta, Georgia. Kenny lives in a quiet, tree-lined, Atlanta neighborhood full of elegant brick town houses built in classic Southern style right down to their black shutters and white Doric columns. He lounges comfortably in a white rocking chair. Only a tall glass of sweet tea is missing to complete the picture.*

KENNY LEON: I hope sitting outside works?

BEOWULF BORITT: It's great. We'll talk about *Much Ado*, as well as some of the other shows you have directed and your approach to working with designers in general. But my first question is, how did you become a director?

KL: I grew up poor. I was raised first by my grandmother; then I moved in with my mother and stepfather. Together, they made maybe $10,000 a year. I was a member of a program called Upward Bound, which really helped me find my way to college. Angela Bassett was in that same program. We grew up in the same town. She ended up going to Yale. I went to Clark College, a historically Black college here in Atlanta, where I ran into people like Samuel L. Jackson.

BB: That's very cool.

KL: It was great. I met Sam and his wife LaTanya Richardson and the great late Bill Nunn. Spike Lee was studying film at Morehouse. We had our own little Harlem Renaissance. I liked hanging around these cats. I was a political science major, but I spent all my time around these theater folks and started doing plays. I'd grown up in the church, acting in plays and stuff, so I thought, "This is fun." Pretty soon all my electives were in theater, and I spent all my summers doing shows at the Atlanta Street Theater, where I got paid to act in plays for kids.

BB: So you were getting work as an actor even while you were in college?

KL: Yes, I was. After college, I went to law school, until there was an emergency at home and I had to withdraw for a year. While I was waiting to go back to law school, I didn't want to stay in Florida, so I came back to Atlanta to get a job. The Academy of Music and Theater had auditions, and they were specifically looking for a Black person to be in their company. I got that job. We used improvisation techniques to build shows for high schools and elementary schools. I also ended up working with prisoners, teaching them to act and tell their stories, and with the homeless population. At night we would do traditional plays like *Hamlet* or *Richard III*. Other folks in the company would direct the plays for the main stage. I would direct my prison and homeless and high school students but never directed for the main stage.

Finally, I got to direct a play called *The Wishing Place*. It was a surreal play with snow in the living room and leaves blowing through the interior of the house. I had a great time. I had never experienced that before. Acting in a play felt like being a slice of the pie, but when I was directing, even that first time, I felt like, *I have to choose which pan to use, I have to know how the sweet potatoes go in, the whole recipe*. I loved it, and I was really pretty good at it. But the artistic director said, "Well, Kenny, we don't think you have the skills to direct. We think you could be the next really famous Black American actor." I said, "OK, but I really like directing, and everybody else gets to be a director here." He said, "We want to have you in our company as an actor but not as a director." And I was like, *Wow, OK. It's time for me to leave*. And I left.

BB: Just like that, you walked away from a secure acting job?

KL: I did. During that time, this great woman, Timothy Near, was the new associate artistic director at the Alliance Theater in Atlanta. She saw my production of *People Are the Bricks* at the Academy of Music and Theater. She saw me act in a play called *Split Second*. She saw me do community work. She told me, "The National Endowment for the Arts and Theater Communications Group have a directing fellowship program. I think we should apply for it, for you to come to the Alliance and be in residence for a year and work on issues of multiculturalism."

I got the grant but with one stipulation: they said, "We do not want you to stay in Atlanta." I was like, "Wait a minute, I'm trying to get through the doors at the Alliance Theater. They don't have any Black folks working there." But they said, "Take it or leave it."

BB: What did you do?

KL: I was newly married, and my wife said, "You've got to do it."

BB: Good for her!

KL: I said, "OK, well, where do I go?" Growing up poor in the South, I hadn't ever been anywhere. Going to college was the first time I'd been out of Florida. I looked at a map. I was afraid to go to New York because it was too big, just too much, too intense. I saw Washington, DC, and thought, *I don't want to go there. That's the government, that's too busy.* Then I saw a place called Baltimore, Maryland, right in between. Baltimore had a theater called Center Stage. I met the artistic director, Stan Wojewodski. He was a great director, very different from me, very into classical theater. He was a great person, a great leader. He said, "We don't want to just have you come here and be an assistant director. That's not a good use of the fellowship. You can assist me on this show, but you should also sit in on the board meetings, learn how a theater runs." So I did that and hung out with different staff members. I was so curious.

BB: It was sort of like your graduate school.

KL: Yeah. Then I took a group of community people and board leaders to New York on a bus trip to see a Broadway play by this new, young playwright, August Wilson—*Fences*. James Earl Jones and Mary Alice were in it. This was 1988, and there I was, at my first Broadway play. I was like, *Wow.* I heard and saw things that I'd never experienced on a stage before. I was like, *I know what it smells like when my mother puts the hot comb on the stove to heat it up to press my sister's hair. I know that smell. I know what it's like to see someone sit on the porch and eat a watermelon, like I used to sit on the porch with my grandmother. I know what it's like when poor men come home on Friday from a job they hate and sit around in the backyard and talk.* Seeing that onstage made me realize, *Whoa, this is what I want to do with the rest of my life.*

Then I met August. He said, "Hey man, you're that Black cat in the NEA program." We talked about his

Fences, August Wilson's 1985 play, won the 1987 Pulitzer Prize for Drama and the Tony Award for Best Play. Written in Wilson's signature poetic style, it takes place in the 1950s Pittsburgh backyard of Troy Maxson, a talented baseball player who never broke the color barrier and now supports his family as a garbage man. Troy's brain-damaged brother Gabriel drifts in and out of the house which Troy purchased using a government settlement for Gabriel's brain injury. The original Broadway production was directed by Lloyd Richards with a set by James D. Sandefur, costumes by Candice Donnelly, and lighting by Danianne Mizzy. Kenny Leon's 2010 revival had a set by Santo Loquasto, costumes by Constanza Romero, lighting by Brian MacDevitt, and sound by Acme Sound Partners.

plays for a while, and he said, "If you ever get a chance and you want to do one of my plays, you can do any of them. Whenever. You don't have to wait till it gets to Broadway." So we formed a partnership.

BB: What an amazing moment.

KL: At the end of that year, I was offered two or three jobs and one of them was back in Atlanta, at the Alliance Theater. Timothy Near had left to run San Jose Rep, and the Alliance hired me as associate artistic director. I contacted August and he sent me this play that hadn't been published yet called *Joe Turner's Come and Gone*. That was the first play I directed at the Alliance and it was a huge hit. The community loved it.

Two years later, I was named artistic director, and that season I did *Fences*. Every other year after that for the next ten, I did one of August's plays. He would come down during tech and previews to give me notes, and I got to know him really well. So that's how I found my way to becoming a director.

BB: So let's talk about how you, as a director, work with designers.

KL: OK, well, here's an important lesson I learned. I was doing *Fences* at the Huntington in Boston, and Marjorie Kellogg was designing the set. I told her, "I think everything in this play is bigger than life. The house is bigger, the tree is bigger—you know?" I came into the theater the day before the set was finished; before they were ready for me. The set wasn't done. It just had work lights on it. I was like, "Oh my God, what *is* that, Marge? It's horrible. That big tree. Oh my God, the house is *too* big. Oh my God!" I went off on her: "This is not what we talked about!" But the next day, when she had finished her work and it was lit properly, it looked great. And she said, "You have to promise me now to always ask a designer if they are ready for you to see the set." To this day, I always say, "OK, are you ready for my notes?"

BB: You're really good about that.

Marjorie Bradley Kellogg was born in Cambridge, Massachusetts, in 1946. Her first Broadway design was for the musical *Where's Charley?* at Circle in the Square in 1974. Her twenty-five Broadway designs include the original productions of *Requiem for a Heavyweight*, *Steaming*, *The Best Little Whorehouse in Texas*, *A Month of Sundays*, and revivals of *American Buffalo*, *Arsenic and Old Lace*, *Present Laughter*, *The Seagull*, and *Death of a Salesman*. She went to college at Vassar, as I did, and was one of the first professionals I looked up upon my arrival in New York. Marjorie gave me some invaluable advice, including the admonition that to pursue a career in the theater and stand out among its hyperbolic personalities, one needs to be extrapushy. I listened and learned and found her to be absolutely right.

KL: Well, now you know why. I learned not to respond before people are ready.

BB: The people who are making something, building something, rehearsing, writing, whatever . . . don't want notes until the right moment. We want to feel our work is complete enough to express what we we're trying to say. Then give me your notes!

KL: Right.

BB: Let's talk about some of the plays that you've directed—starting with Charles Fuller's *A Soldier's Play* at the Roundabout. I saw a touring production of the play when I was in high school.

KL: Probably half of what I've done on Broadway has been new work and the other half revivals—but I always treat revivals like they're new work. I'm always looking at who's in the audience right then, what's happening in the country. *How does this play relate to our world now?* I'm always trying to make the piece feel current, even if it's twenty or thirty years old. For *A Soldier's Play*, which is set in 1944, that's exactly what we did. We're going through a lot of dissension in the country in terms of race. I wanted the viewers to know visually that these people in the play love their country. It's a myth that they don't love that country.

BB: They're patriots.

KL: You and I worked on *Much Ado* right before *A Soldier's Play*. I think that my productions talk to each other, and you could draw a line from *Much Ado* to *A Soldier's Play*. Those two productions had things in common visually, whether I purposely tried to do that or discovered it along the way. They both had prominent American flags. They had contemporary music that helped make my point. And in both cases, I needed viewers to know that the characters loved their country. In *A Soldier's Play*, I knew I wanted a big American flag. I didn't know where it would be, but I said to my set designer, Derek McLane, "Give me a way to have a big American flag."

A Soldier's Play is Charles Fuller's 1982 Pulitzer Prize–winning murder mystery set in the segregated US Army of 1944. The murder of a Black sergeant named Vernon Waters is investigated by a Black officer, Richard Davenport. After looking into the local Ku Klux Klan and racist white soldiers, Davenport discovers the surprising truth. Originally produced off Broadway in 1981 and directed by Douglas Turner Ward, the cast included Denzel Washington and Samuel L. Jackson. The set was by Felix E. Cochren, costumes by Judy Dearing, lighting by Allen Lee Hughes, and sound by Regge Life. Kenny Leon directed the Tony Award–winning Broadway premier in 2020 with a set by Derek McLane, costumes by Dede Ayite, lighting again by Allen Lee Hughes, and sound by Dan Moses Schreier.

BB: So you gave him that image from the beginning? You told me the same thing when we started *Much Ado*.

KL: Yeah. I love sitting in a room with a designer, playing around with the model. Derek had a little cloth American flag and he happened to put it on one of the beds in the model. I said, "Oh, wait a minute. If you put an American flag on a bed, it looks like a casket. These Black soldiers have sacrificed their lives for this country. Once we put those flags on the beds, I knew we had to make them look like caskets and have the big flag for the last statement.

BB: That moment with the flags on the beds was beautiful. We'd been watching those beds define the barracks all evening, and then suddenly you transformed them into coffins. When an object is one thing and suddenly transforms into something else, that's theater magic.

KL: That's what theater is, right?

Blair Underwood, Jerry O'Connell, and the company
Monique Carboni

KL: I ended the show with a Nipsey Hussle tune. Nipsey Hussle was a community activist who was killed in LA in 2019. If you were sitting in the audience and you didn't know hip-hop music, you probably thought, *Wait a minute, man. That's not 1944.* But I was trying to make a statement in that last scene by playing that particular hip-hop tune as the lights went down on two Black men saluting the flag—you know? I was mixing the origins of hip-hop and blues, looking at American and Black history, and putting all that together. Because it was a murder mystery, we were able to get the audience involved in the mystery and keep them from focusing on race. But with that last image, I wanted them to focus on race—so they'd go home thinking about it.

BB: Switching to a show that's more explicitly about race, let's talk about the Christopher Demos-Brown play, *American Son*—which you directed on Broadway in 2019. It took place in one very realistic location. How did you and Derek McLane approach that one?

KL: The play unfolds in one room in a police station. But most important was the storm outside. I felt like it was the fifth character in the play. I needed to have the rain and lightning because that kept the play threatening. Derek came up with a set that had a window upstage center, so there was this three-dimensional world through the glass.

> Derek McLane was born in London in 1958. His first Broadway design was for *What's Wrong with This Picture?* in 1994. His forty-three Broadway designs include the original productions of *I Am My Own Wife, 33 Variations, Million Dollar Quartet, Bengal Tiger at the Baghdad Zoo, Beautiful, China Doll, American Son, A Soldier's Play,* and *Moulin Rouge!* He has designed Broadway revivals of *Anything Goes, The Pajama Game, The Threepenny Opera, Follies,* and *The Heiress.*

BB: We saw it rain through that window for the entire show. Technically that must have been a pain in the butt.

KL: Yeah, we had our problems with it. There was a leak into the trap room of the theater.

BB: If there's a tiny pinhole, water will find its way through that hole.

KL: At least I didn't have to fix the leak! I think designers appreciate a director who admits what he doesn't know how to do. But what I did have to go through the play and figure out was when it should sprinkle and when it should pour and so on. That determined how much water we needed.

BB: The rain was great. It made the characters seem even more trapped in that police station.

KL: One of the things I always do when approaching a play is read it five or six times before I form any judgment about what it's about. Then I write down two or three words that come to mind when I think about it. Is it beautiful? Fluid? Patriotic? Heavy? The next thing I do is determine the rhythm I think the play moves in. By the time I talk to a designer, I know how fast it moves. Does it call for scenic changes that move fast? Do the people speak faster? With *American Son*, I understood the intensity and tempo of the whole piece going in.

BB: You used the water, the rain, to help establish that. One of the things this book is about is how the physical production can help create the tempo of a show. A designer has to be sensitive to the show's rhythm and figure out how to help establish and enhance it. We've all seen shows where the production steps on the rhythm of the language and wrecks the show. The trick is to take something that's written down and figure out how it's physically going to transform over time in front of an audience. Once you figure out the rhythm of the show and what it is really about, you'll know what it should look like.

KL: I agree. The most important thing is the rhythm. How does it move?

BB: You mentioned our *Much Ado About Nothing* earlier, I want to return to it now. I was constantly aware that we were telling the story of a wealthy Black family through Shakespeare's play, and that's not a world I know intimately. I understood that if I were going to work on this particular version of *Much Ado*, I'd need you to guide me more than if we were doing an Elizabethan version. That's one of the things I love about the work I do: Every show presents me with a new world to explore.

We set our production in Leonato's backyard. At one point I suggested changing our suburban SUV into a truck with a big machine gun mounted on it. I thought we needed a stark image showing how these folks had literally gone to war to defend themselves. You decided that was too aggressive—that it would turn off the audience.

Rendering of *Much Ado About Nothing*

Danielle Brooks, Margarette Odette, Chuck Cooper, and company under a changing sky.

Danielle Brooks, Chuck Cooper, Grantham Coleman, and company under a changing sky.

Tayler Harris, Denzel DeAngelo Fields, and company during the final wedding scene under a changing sky.

Great Performances opening aerial shot
Great Performances

Rendering of *Prince of Broadway*

Emily Skinner, Schuler Hensley, Tony Yazbeck and Nancy Opel in *Follies*

Brandon Uranowitz in *Cabaret*

Chuck Cooper in *Fiddler on the Roof*

Michael Xavier and company in *Company*

Janet Dacal and company in *Evita*

Karen Ziemba and Chuck Cooper in *Sweeney Todd*

Janet Dacal and Michael Xavier in *It's a Bird . . . It's a Plane . . . It's Superman*

Michael Xavier, Tony Yazbeck, Brandon Uranowitz, and Chuck Cooper in *Damn Yankees*

Brandon Uranowitz in *She Loves Me*

And, once we had an audience, I could see that even without something as literal as that machine gun, they understood the struggle we were presenting—really got it. I thought, *How does Kenny thread the needle so that people get the point without hitting them so hard that they stop paying attention?*

KL: Here's something I learned early in my career. When I got the job running the theater in Atlanta, we had twenty thousand subscribers—and here I come, trying to diversify these white folks' theater experience. I wanted to bring something new to them but maybe wasn't mindful enough about what I was taking away—or what they might think I was taking away. I don't regret anything I did, but if I had to do it over again, I would be more careful about that. I did eleven plays in a season—including for example, one by Lorraine Hansberry, an August Wilson play, a new play by Pearl Cleage—and people would say, "Oh, you're turning this into a Black theater?"

BB: Because three of the eleven plays were by Black authors?

KL: Yeah. How was that a Black theater? But it didn't matter. It was their perception. When I did *Joe Turner's Come and Gone*, I piped the music into the parking deck. When people got out of their cars they heard drums, guitars . . . all this beautiful African music. The Black folks were like, *This is hip!* But the white people were like, *What the fuck is that?*

BB: Uh-huh.

KL: Look, I'm not one of those directors who does a show that's difficult to watch and thirty percent of the audience walks out, and the cat is like, *That's OK, that's my point.* In fact, that's my greatest fear as a director—maybe because of my political science degree. I'm trying to talk to the audience. I'm like, *OK, you didn't, like, like that idea? I've got 999 more.* I'd rather try something else than hold onto one idea that isn't working. So when I noticed the reaction to the *Joe Turner* music, I thought, *Oh, white people, as a rule, they don't understand two-four time.* That's cultural. That's specific to what we listen to; it's R&B. When I took the drums and bass way down, the whole energy of the white patrons changed.

BB: That's amazing.

KL: I didn't get any more complaints. I could still have my music but I had to learn to give a little, so people could come in and enjoy the play.

When we started *Much Ado* I thought, *What's in the mix in 2019?* What was in the mix was the notion that Black people didn't love their country because they were taking a knee at football games. On top of that, I was aware of the skepticism around a whole twenty-four-member Black cast delivering Shakespeare—a perception we're not classically trained. *It won't be funny; it's going to be hitting us over the head.* I had to keep in mind that at least sixty or seventy percent of the audience would be white, and I wanted to keep them in their seats all the way to that last scene. My goal is always that last scene.

In *Much Ado*, we led up to that big, magnificent song, the Black National Anthem ["Lift Every Voice and Sing"] integrated with "America the Beautiful." If I had just used the Black National Anthem by itself, Black audiences would have understood, but white audiences would have said, "What the hell is that?" I didn't want that. I'm not just doing this work for a Black audience. So we marinated and mixed it up and people were like, *Wow, that was good. Let's think about that.* Directorially, I'm always trying to get to that last moment.

BB: That last moment was powerful. The police siren blared, the couples were separated, and the soldiers marched off. It hit me in the stomach really hard. *This is so beautiful and sad*, I thought.

KL: It was a little ahead of its time, man. That production would be so perfect to do right now, you know? All our protest signs—*I Am a Person*; *Our Lives Matter*—it's all happening right now, in the summer of 2020.

BB: When I talk about what we did, I keep calling it a Black Lives Matter protest, although we were never specific. But our army was making a political statement, and we wanted people to perceive it that way. The thing that shocked me—although maybe you expected it—was that reviewers and audiences in 2019, in New York City, considered just the fact of a bunch of Black people doing Shakespeare "revolutionary." Maybe I was naïve, or maybe "white privilege" allowed me to be, but—

KL: When it comes to critics from the dominant press, I've never had one from my own culture write about the work I do. I don't know what that feels like, to have someone from my culture write about my work. This wasn't the first fully Black Shakespeare production, but I knew that people would comment on it. If you remember, even in rehearsal, people at the Public were saying, "Be careful." When I first talked to Oskar Eustis about it, I said, "I want to do *Much Ado* all Black." He was like, "Do you really?" But we talked and decided it needed to be all Black to make a statement.

BB: Right.

KL: And then there was our Stacey Abrams banner. Oskar pushed back on that because he was worried it was too specific for Shakespeare. But you made that banner happen. You said, "Let's try it out and if it feels wrong, we can always take it down." I'm so proud of that decision. Stacey came to the show and she loved it!

BB: You had a sense of those currents—the torrent of frustration underlying BLM, the rising tide of Democratic voters in the Atlanta suburbs—before a lot of white people had a clue what was coming, and you put it out there in the production.

KL: It was a-fucking-head of its time.

BB: Let's talk a little about *A Raisin in the Sun*. You've directed it on Broadway twice. Can you talk about the differences in your approach to the set each time?

KL: That was my first Broadway show, in 2004. The reason I got to direct it was that the Hansberry estate demanded a Black director. They tried one director who didn't work out, and then they came to me.

Like I said earlier, whether I'm doing a new play or one that's five hundred years old, I approach it like it's new. I look at it in light of the time we're in. Who's in the audience? How will they receive it? What does it mean to us today? I'm not interested in people watching museum pieces or looking at parts of history. It needs to be a living, breathing organism right now.

I had directed a lot of regional theater and directed the play before then. I knew the play well. But it was the hardest thing I've ever done. The second time around, in 2014, I won a Tony for it—but it was that first time that I earned it. My lead actor, Sean Combs, had never acted before and there he was, playing opposite Audra McDonald, who had won four Tony Awards; Phylicia Rashad, who had played Claire Huxtable on *The Cosby Show*; Bill Nunn, who had played Radio Raheem and a bunch of other roles in Spike Lee movies; and the amazing Sanaa Lathan! I've got all those people in one room, and

A Raisin in the Sun, Lorraine Hansberry's 1959 play, tells the story of a Black Chicago family headed by the impetuous, frustrated Walter Younger; his wife, Ruth; and his mother, Lena. An insurance settlement from the death of Lena's husband, Walter's father, will allow them to purchase a home in a white suburb and move out of their Chicago tenement. Walter rashly loses a portion of the money on a business speculation, and a white representative from the suburb arrives to try to scare them out of their intended move. By the end of the play, the Younger family has triumphantly pulled together and is ready to move on. The original 1959 Broadway production was directed by Lloyd Richards, with a set and lighting by Ralph Alswang, costumes by Virginia Volland, and sound by Masque Sound Engineering Company. Kenny Leon's 2004 revival had a set by Thomas Lynch, costumes by Paul Tazewell, lighting by Brian MacDevitt, and sound by T. Richard Fitzgerald. His 2014 revival had a set by Mark Thompson, costumes by Ann Roth, lighting by Brian MacDevitt, and sound by Scott Lehrer.

I've got to massage them into the same story with the same tone. One thing I did was have Sean Combs stay still while the women moved around him a lot.

BB: So you needed the furniture arranged to allow that kind of staging.

KL: It was different in 2014. Now I'm doing it with Denzel Washington, the most famous Black actor in the world. I'm doing it at a time when we have the first Black president. So that's a different feeling. As I work on it, I really don't think about the production from ten years earlier—not at all. I just think about the words that come to mind in 2014. I wanted to tell an intimate version of a big story.

This time around, I was working with a designer from the UK, Mark Thompson. I said to him, "People think *A Raisin in the Sun* is the big Black classic. How can we make it intimate?" And he said, "What if, as soon as the lights come up, we move the set down close to the audience?" So, as the show started, I had Sophie Okonedo—who was playing Ruth—scrambling eggs. People were visually glued to her when suddenly the set started moving downstage—about to land in their lap!

In 2004 I'd tried to keep Sean Combs very still, but in 2014 I had Denzel, who's a big, physical actor. The actors I cast dictate to me how I tell the story and what the rhythm will be.

BB: His big presence allowed you a big scenic gesture—like the set moving so dramatically.

KL: Yes.

When I work with the costume designer I always say, "Let's not be a slave to the period. Let's have the characters wear clothes they might have worn in 1940 but also in 2020, because fashion repeats often."

BB: I'd go even further and say that it's important not to be trapped by historical accuracy if it muddies your storytelling. I do the research, so I know what's correct. I make a set accurate if I can. But if some inaccuracies help tell the story more clearly, I don't hesitate.

KL: That's reinforced for me by August's work, because he always fudged in his storytelling. In one of his plays—I think it's *Seven Guitars*—a character says, "In Romans 3:2, God said, 'blah, blah, blah, blah.'" When the line came up in rehearsal, one of my actors was like, "August, that's not Romans 3:2." And August said, "No, no, I know that. I made that up. That's the address of my first house in Pittsburgh."

BB: And that's how people talk too. They spout stuff and get the details wrong all the time!

KL: *Joe Turner's Come and Gone* is set in 1904. The steel mills weren't even there then, but August, he's like, "People know Pittsburgh from the steel mills. So I'm gonna make this all about the steel mills." Not once have people questioned the presence of a steel mill in 1904 Pittsburgh—even though it's historically incorrect. August would say, "I'm not telling history. I'm telling a general idea about these ten years."

BB: You've directed three August Wilson plays on Broadway: *Fences*, *Gem of the Ocean*, and *Radio Golf*, which you directed in 2007. I read an interview where you speak about the production and said, "August always wrote about community. He was saying, here at the ending of the twentieth century, let's find our collective voice and not break apart."

KL: *Radio Golf* takes place in an old neighborhood the characters are trying to save. For the set, we talked about what was happening in that neighborhood, and it was all about gentrification—white folks coming in and taking over neighborhoods.

Radio Golf, the final installment of August Wilson's ten-play Century Cycle, tells the story of two real estate development partners: Harmond Wilks, a rising politician, and his friend Roosevelt Hicks, a bank executive. A conflict arises between them when they realize that the land they intend to raze in order to build a large development includes a house once owned by Aunt Ester, a mystical figure in many of Wilson's plays. The house stands as a symbol of the spiritual heart of the local Black community. Roosevelt and a white financier backing him insist that it be demolished, causing Harmond to break ranks and fight to protect the house. Kenny Leon directed the Broadway production with a set by David Gallo, costumes by Susan Hilferty, lighting by Don Holder, and sound by Dan Moses Schreier.

BB: So Dave Gallo's set is literally showing the community disintegrating?

KL: We wanted to communicate what that neighborhood was and what it was becoming.

BB: One of the main conflicts in *Radio Golf* is about whether to tear down Aunt Ester's house. I read an NPR interview where you describe her as "the mother of all of us. Symbolically, [her 366-year-old age] represents the length of time that Africans have been in America." You went on to say, "When you lose the spirituality from our neighborhoods, when you lose the morality, you lose the guiding post in our community. So Aunt Ester represents all of that." In *Radio Golf*, the destruction of her home is the symbol of that, and though we hear about it, we don't see it. But the set we see is helping show the loss you're describing. We do see Aunt Ester's home in *Gem of the Ocean*, which you directed in 2004.

KL: As an actor, I created the role of Citizen Barlow in *Gem of the Ocean* at the Goodman in Chicago. The great Marion McClinton was directing. A year and a half later, August called me from Boston and said, "Hey, Marion got sick, I want you to come

David Gallo's set for *Radio Golf*
David Gallo

in and take over the show. I want you to take *Gem of the Ocean* to Broadway." I was like, "Oh my God." That was my second Broadway show.

BB: David Gallo designed the set. Did you end up changing it, or was it basically what he'd designed for Marion?

KL: We changed some minor stuff, made the playing space smaller, but that was done mainly with furniture and things like that.

BB: You made it more intimate, but you couldn't completely put your stamp on it since the physical set already existed.

KL: Yeah.

BB: You said *Fences* was the first play you saw on Broadway. You ended up directing it, with Denzel Washington, a few years ago. That must've been an amazing experience.

KL: That was one of the joys of my life.

BB: The backyard where it takes place certainly isn't as nice as this one! I read a Broadwayworld.com interview where you talked about wanting to see the family's life inside the house, not just in the yard. Santo Loquasto's set had three large windows into the kitchen that frame that interior action. That set also has Troy's house pushed to stage left, with the yard spilling toward stage right, was there a reason for that?

David Gallo, born in 1966 in Dover, Delaware, designed his first Broadway show, *Hughie*, at Circle in the Square in 1996. His thirty Broadway designs include *The Drowsy Chaperone*, *Memphis*, *Dance of the Vampires*, *Xanadu*, and *Thoroughly Modern Millie*. He designed the Broadway productions of August Wilson's *Jitney*, *King Hedley II*, *Gem of the Ocean*, *Radio Golf*, and a revival of *Ma Rainey's Black Bottom*. He designed Kenny Leon's productions of *Stick Fly*, *The Mountaintop*, and *Holler If You Hear Me*.

KL: August always said, "When you do my plays, you have to figure out who the witness is." Not the audience, but who is the witness among the *characters*. In *Fences*, my image of the witness is always Gabe, with that piece of watermelon, looking through the screen door as Troy and Rose fight.

BB: Oh! So the house pushed to stage left lands that screen door right at center stage.

Santo Loquasto's set for the 2010 Broadway revival of *Fences*
Joan Marcus

Santo Loquasto was born in 1944 in Wilkes-Barre, Pennsylvania. David Rabe's *Sticks and Bones*, in 1972, was the first of his seventy-nine Broadway shows, which include the scenery for the original production of David Mamet's *American Buffalo*, *Bent*, *Fosse*, *Lost in Yonkers*, *Shuffle Along*, *Bullets over Broadway*, Jerry Zaks's revival of *Hello, Dolly!*, and Kenny Leon's *Fences*. He has designed numerous productions in a long collaboration with choreographer Twyla Tharpe as well as the costumes for *Grand Hotel* and *Ragtime* on Broadway. His long list of film designs includes *Big*, *Mighty Aphrodite*, and *Desperately Seeking Susan*.

KL: I wanted to create stage pictures where the audience could see who was witnessing. I wanted them to see through Gabe's eyes. I had a screen door to frame him—that was important—but I had to have the windows in the kitchen through which we could see him as well. Everything about that set was built around the image of Gabe at the screen door, eating a piece of watermelon, watching his brother.

BB: Beautiful. What a great way into the play. The settlement money from Gabe's brain injury paid for the house, and it's creating a frame around him.

BB: My last question for you will take you back much further. Do you have a first memory of theater design? Your first awareness of it?

KL: I can't say the first time I noticed it as an audience member. But I remember really realizing the power of design on my first big directing job outside of Atlanta. It was 1988, and I was directing Lanford Wilson's *Talley's Folly* at the Milwaukee Repertory Theater. It's the story of two people in love, and it's still one of my favorite plays. The guy—Matt—comes out at the beginning and says, "I'm gonna fall in love with this girl, Sally Talley, and it's going to happen in ninety minutes." He's at a gazebo and he gets into a boat with her. The two of them sit there with the moon going down. I remember thinking, this can't be a set. It can't be fake. There has to be real water. We have to believe it's a real lake and they are in a real boat. This is the ultimate love story and everyone in the audience—excuse me for saying this—has to be *moist*, like, *Oh my God!*

The set designer, Art Johnson, put a few inches of real water on the stage and the day he put light on it, I believed it was a lake. When Matt sat in that boat after saying that line about falling in love, Sally ran her fingers through the water. That was the money shot, you know? Just that simple, romantic gesture said it all.

BB: It's a great through-line in your work. Whether its moonlight on the water for a romance or Gabe framed in the screen door of the house his injury paid for or American flags to display the patriotism of Black Americans, you find these key images to convey the ideas, the words, you want to drive home with your productions.

Art Johnson's John Lee Beatty-influenced set for Milwaukee Repertory Theater 1988 production of *Tally's Folly.*
Mark Avery

SEVEN

Chasing Complicity

Designing *Prince of Broadway* for Harold Prince

Sprint

Harold Prince was directing a musical compilation of his long career, a revue called *Prince of Broadway*. The *Playbill* press release said that Susan Stroman was codirecting and choreographing it, Tommy Thompson was writing the book, Jason Robert Brown was the music director, William Ivey Long was designing the costumes, and Howell Binkley was designing the lights. But I wasn't designing the set. I was green with envy and more than a little hurt.

The project had been suggested by the Canadian producer Aubrey Dan and Canadian set designer Jerry Sirlin, who had designed *Kiss of the Spiderwoman* for Hal. Jerry was going to design the show.

It was 2011. I had met Hal many years earlier, when I had just graduated from NYU. In those days, all the design schools held a collective bazaar for their graduating classes at Lincoln Center. "Ming's Clam Bake"—as it had come to be called in tribute to its organizer, Yale design guru Ming Cho Lee—was a chance for the New York theater community to meet the new kids coming to town. It was there that I had the good fortune to meet and speak to Hal Prince.

Hal isn't a large person physically, but his overwhelming, bombastic charisma makes him seem like a giant. I had known him for several years before I realized that, not only was he not larger than I but he was significantly smaller! His neatly trimmed white beard and those signature glasses perched atop his bald head complete a look he had maintained since about the time I was born.

Harold Prince   •   **10 ROCKEFELLER PLAZA**   •   **SUITE 1009**
NEW YORK, N. Y. 10020

Telephone
(212) 399-0960
Facsimile
(212) 974-8426

June 4, 1996

Beowulf Boritt
111 4th Avenue
Apartment 3-A
New York, NY 10003

Dear Beowulf Boritt:

I returned to the office Monday after my sessions at the Performing
Arts Library so exhilarated by what I'd seen.

I thought your work was first-rate and I have your resume near of
hand.

I'm off for the Summer but hope that sometime next season we can
sit down and talk. Meanwhile, have a fine Summer yourself.

Best always,

Harold Prince

Hal's letter

A few days after the Clam Bake, Hal sent me a nice letter wishing me well. I eventually learned that he'd sent a similar letter to anyone there whose work he'd enjoyed, but I took it as an invitation to stay in touch with him.

Over the ensuing years, I sent him a postcard for every show I designed, no matter how small and insignificant. About twice a year I sent him an updated résumé with a letter reiterating my desire to design for him. It was patently absurd of me to think that this legend would hire a kid with just a handful of off-Broadway credits, but he did occasionally write back, always politely—and once invited me to his office to have a look at my portfolio.

In 2000, he recommended me to his daughter, Daisy, a talented director in her own right, for a musical she was developing with Jason Robert Brown called *The Last Five Years*. I designed that show in Chicago and then in a splashy, off-Broadway production. It didn't run long but was well received, and it introduced my work to a new stratum of the New York theater community.

When I interviewed with James Lapine to design *The 25th Annual Putnam County Spelling Bee* off Broadway, James asked how I'd come to work on *The Last Five Years*. "Hal Prince recommended me," I said, and I saw his eyebrows raise. Hal's stamp of approval clearly meant something. I don't know if it influenced James, but I did land that *Spelling Bee* job.

Spelling Bee was a huge success and transferred to Broadway, giving me my first Broadway show. Before it even opened, I got a call from Hal asking me to design a Broadway-bound musical he was developing called *LoveMusik*. That's how, after some good luck and ten years of persistent letters and postcards, I ended up designing a Broadway show for Hal Prince.

Hal's résumé hardly needs recounting, but the high points begin with *Pajama Game*, which he produced when he was twenty-four, followed by *West Side Story* and *Fiddler on the Roof*. He soon moved into directing, beginning with Kander and Ebb's *Cabaret*, followed by six groundbreaking Stephen Sondheim musicals in a row: *Company*, *Follies*, *A Little Night Music*, *Pacific Overtures*, *Sweeney Todd*, and *Merrily We Roll Along*. Along the way, he also directed *Evita* and *Phantom of the Opera* for Andrew Lloyd Webber. And these are just the highest of high points.

LoveMusik, about the composer Kurt Weill and his wife Lotte Lenya, got a mixed reception, but I was immensely proud of my work on it and loved working with Hal. Next, I designed a musical for him called *Paradise Found* that was intended for Broadway but never made it. We ended up doing it at the Menier Chocolate Factory, a tiny but fashionable theater in London. It was terribly produced and perhaps not a good show. Afterward, Hal said his memory of the tech was me standing onstage screaming, "Fuck this fucking, fucked, fuckheaded theater." Suffice it to say that the experience was difficult and somewhat traumatic for all involved. All of which is to say that, having done a few shows for Hal, I felt I had earned my stripes. I was terribly jealous that I wasn't tapped for *Prince of Broadway*.

A year later, in early 2012, Hal's right hand, Dan Kutner, called me and surreptitiously inquired about my availability. Dan looks like a guy who stepped out of a Woody Allen movie and got dressed in the dark. He is also a dear friend, so I quickly forced out of him what was going on. Hal was unhappy with Jerry Sirlin's design for *Prince of Broadway*. It relied almost wholly on video, which isn't something Hal used much, with the exceptions of *Evita* and *Kiss of the Spiderwoman*. An attempt to re-create his cannon with projections seemed ill-conceived at best. Dan told me that Hal was considering replacing Jerry, but they already had dates set to do the show the following autumn on Broadway and needed to know if I could step in fast. The answer was obviously *yes*. The answer is always *yes*. Dan promised they'd decide within the week.

A week passed. Then two. Then three. Initially I had been ecstatic, but now I was hurt and jealous again. I assumed that either they had decided to stick with Jerry or had opted for someone other than me. Then one morning, I was going to a meeting in the West Side building I've already written about, where Stro lives and both she and James Lapine have offices. Broadway folk Lynn Ahrens, Billie Allen, and Charles Strauss lived there, too, among others. I'm in and out so often that the doormen know me on sight. That day, I bumped into Stro in the lobby and we exchanged a few pleasantries. I desperately wanted to ask her what had happened with *Prince of Broadway*, but it felt rude to bring it up so I just made tortured small talk.

The fear that I'd been making inexplicable faces as we chatted led me to email Stro that evening to apologize for my weirdness—and to ask her directly about the show. And that, I guess, helped move things along. The next day, Stro called Hal and said they needed to decide what to do about the set. Hal fired Jerry and offered me the job. I'm ever thankful that I happened to cross paths with Stro in her lobby that day! Luck.

The next morning, I read the script and was in Hal's office at noon to discuss it. He said he wanted each excerpt from one of his shows to feel as if it were lifted right out of the original production. I was free to redesign, but he wanted me to try to capture the feel of the original, not reinvent it.

A day later I was in Stro's office to talk it through with her and Tommy Thompson. Like Hal, they wanted a set that was tangible—forget about projections—something that felt handmade and in keeping with the texture and spirit of Hal's famous productions.

The revue would be narrated by a projected, animated Hirschfeld drawing of Hal that would recount anecdotes from his life as a frame for the numbers. Sometimes a single song would represent a show. Sometimes three or four songs from a show would be connected by bits of dialogue to form a musical synopsis that conveyed the whole story. Dan sent me a compilation, and I played the songs over and over as I worked—from *Pajama Game* (1954) through *Parade* (1998) and all the hits in between. In a brilliant overture, Jason Robert Brown had managed to tie together the themes of about twenty scores into a coherent and thrilling piece of music.

Holding it all together would be the idea that even a stellar theater career like Hal's depends on luck. Talent and hard work are crucial but even if you have those, you need a lot of good luck. Either I had come to the same conclusion on my own, or my years as Hal's protégé had instilled it in me—or maybe it's just a fact. Whatever the case, I believe it wholeheartedly. I loved that it was the spine of the show.

As usual, I began by charting out the structure of the overall show, including the number of pages each sequence took up in the script. That structure would determine the pace at which the space needed to transform. I began to muse about what sort of space it should be. I did some rough digital renderings that included a proscenium, a red curtain, a brick wall, and show logos . . . but somehow it kept feeling like a collage instead of coalescing into a single idea. I really dislike collaged scenery; I was looking for a set, not a collection of research images onstage.

When you're stuck, it's a good idea to go back and reread the script. The opening sequence was a Kander and Ebb song called "One Good Break," from *Flora the Red Menace*. Hal had told me he wanted to present it on a bare stage with actors picked out of the darkness. That was it! Picking the important details out of the darkness should be the crux of the design. Hal often talks about theater as a black box where you provide just enough information to make the audience imagine more. As he explains, "That makes the audience complicit in creating the production. By filling in the blanks with their imagination, they become active participants in what's happening on stage."

Hal by Hirschfeld
Al Hirschfeld © The Al Hirschfeld Foundation.
www.AlHirschfeldFoundation.org

That describes my own experience of walking into an empty theater: it's a blank canvas, an empty volume of space, and I imagine filling that blank space with a world. The set for *Prince of Broadway* would be a classic dark, empty theater. Within it, I could introduce a single, small, scenic gesture, and it would instantly dominate the space, fill it visually, the way a small sketch can fill a blank piece of paper.

Of course, I could fill the entire space on occasion, for sheer spectacle. But full sets for every sequence would be overwhelming for the audience in a show encompassing twenty-six distinct musicals. The idea would be to keep most of the scenes simple and essential.

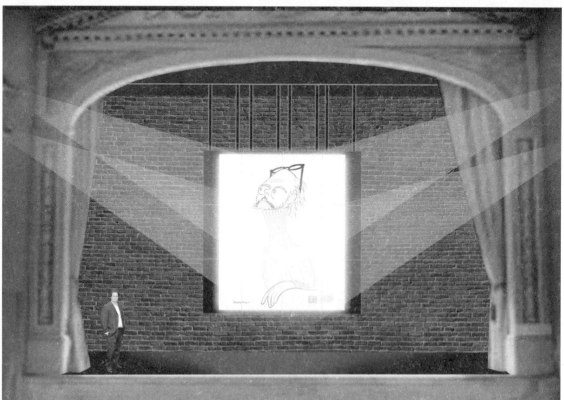

First sketches for *Prince of Broadway*

In this sketch by Eugene Delacroix, a small detail commands the entire page. The distant house seems of utmost importance, though it is tiny in comparison to the space it inhabits.

This wasn't a revolutionary idea. In fact, the bare backstage set pops up frequently—perhaps too frequently. But it was the perfect surrounding for a story about a life in the theater. What's more, the bare industrial feel of the brick, water pipes, and ropes of a traditional backstage area would be in keeping with the feel of nearly half of Hal's oeuvre, from the factory world of *Sweeney Todd* to the dank prisons of *Parade* and *Kiss of the Spiderwoman*, to the tatty underground club of *Cabaret*.

It was mid-March. I had six weeks to design and draft the entire show if I was going to meet the schedule for a fall Broadway opening. I wanted to get some ideas out quickly and see if they appealed to Hal, Stro, and Tommy, so I scheduled a meeting with them in five days' time and got to work. Instead of starting with a model, which is my preference, I decided to make a quick series of Photoshop renderings. As it turned out, drawing up enough scenes to explain my idea would take the whole five days. I would be going in without a backup idea, so if they hated my approach, I might face Jerry Sirlin's fate.

I began with a digital rendering of the theater and put my backstage set within that. Then I made a sketch of the opening number, followed by individual scenes to show how the bare backstage would be a springboard for all the other locations.

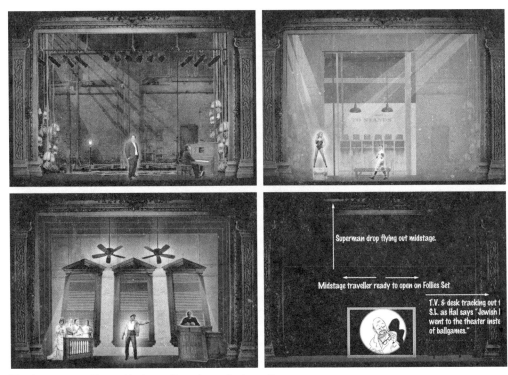

The bare stage, *Damn Yankees*, *Parade*, and a transition sequence

With my heart in my throat, I marched into the meeting. When Hal asked how I was getting on with the design, I was too nervous to make small talk. Without any preamble, I spewed out the basic idea and spread my renderings across his desk for all to see.

Hal got it. And he loved it. "That's it!" he said. "When can I see the whole thing?"

That's when the sprint began. Ideally, I'd have a year to work out the designs for a show on this scale—not that the design itself would take a full year, but that would give me time to research, kick around bad ideas and jettison them, and let thoughts percolate in my subconscious. Instead, I had ten days to create renderings of the whole show before I'd have to make a model and get everything drafted.

Under that kind of time pressure, any research would have to be quick. I owned lavishly illustrated books about Boris Aronson and William and Jean Eckert. Between them, they'd designed more than half the musicals referenced in *Prince of Broadway*. I paid a visit to the theater archives at the Lincoln Center library to find additional visual material, and found a lot. Puzzling were several Art Nouveau–styled, original Boris Aronson model pieces in a folder labeled *Follies*. The *Follies* "Loveland" set had famously looked like an array of big pink valentines. I didn't remember any Art Nouveau scenes, and when I asked him, neither did Hal.

Beyond research, I needed assistants to take my sketches and models and turn them into technical drawings for the shop that would build the show. For smaller productions, I sometimes do the drafting myself, but big shows are a lot of work, so I employ an associate designer for the purpose.

Alexis had joined me on *The Scottsboro Boys* in 2010, but I hadn't yet used her as my associate on a big Broadway musical. Because this one was going to be fast and furious, I felt I'd better hire a veteran associate. I spoke to several great people before asking Eddie Pierce to join me. For years, Eddie had overseen Eugene Lee's sets for *Wicked*; he knew his way around big shows better than I did. We immediately hit it off.

Now I faced my most important decision since committing to the empty-theater framing device. In any revival I work on, I try hard to avoid copying the original designs of the show. I don't even look at pictures of previous productions for fear they'll get stuck in my subconscious. Of course, this can be difficult on classic shows where the original scenery is well known—but I try to do my own thing, always. This show was different. In *P.O.B.*, I was tasked with honoring the work of a singular director, and one of the things that makes Hal *Hal* is the way he collaborates with designers in the creation of a show. In an interview with Tommy Thompson he said, "If you know what your set is, you can understand how your show will flow, how the scenes will move, how you get from moment to moment. It becomes the motor of the show."

I needed to represent those original sets, so I decided to treat the original designs as I would any piece of architectural research. If I were designing a scene that included the Eiffel Tower, I wouldn't feel I had to reinvent the Tower; I'd use its particulars without concern that I was ripping off Gustave Eiffel. I decided to approach the original sets of Hal's musicals in the same way.

For the next ten days I felt like a graduate student at NYU again, with way too much work for the available time. In fact, one of the most valuable things NYU taught me was to think coherently about design when I was so exhausted that I couldn't speak without drooling. Emergency room residencies and military basic training involve exhausting the participants in the hope that they will learn to do their jobs competently even when bone-tired. So did my design school and to this day, I'm grateful for it, though admittedly design is a less life-and-death endeavor. I'm normally not an early riser, but for those ten days my dog, Hermione, got a predawn walk, and I saw the sun creep over the buildings across First Avenue from my studio. Something magical happens when your mind slips into semicoherence: you become more open to your own subconscious, and that's a big help when you need to work fast.

When I roused myself from the fever-dream I had, the entire show storyboarded in a visual plot of the transformation of space over the full time of the show. Every scene and—perhaps more important—every transition were rendered, from opening to finale. I got my first full night's sleep in a week and a half and woke prepared to present it to Hal, Stro, and Tommy.

I added a twist to my initial, empty-theater idea. In addition to specific scenery appearing, the theater set itself would transform to support the locations of the scenes. For *West Side Story*, I added some fire escapes and a fence but then transformed the "theater." The top of the back wall lifted away to reveal a starry sky with a silhouetted New York water tower. Hidden lightboxes in the remaining brick wall set it aglow. Seventy-five percent of what had been there to start with stayed the same, but a few added details changed the context of the brick theater wall into the *West Side Story* set.

For *Kiss of the Spider Woman*, a jail cell sat small and lonely against the tall bleakness of the black brick wall with a spiderweb projected on it. When that little cell spun around, voilà: Mrs. Lovett's *Sweeney Todd* pie shop. A back-wall panel moved to reveal the giant, filthy, factory window that completed the transformation. Hal's metaphor for the show had been society as a machine grinding its unfortunates into fuel. For the original set, Eugene Lee had reassembled an actual New England factory inside the Uris Theater, including giant, grime-encrusted skylights. My window recalled the gritty realism of that set.

Some moments needed to break out of the skeletal mold for visual variety but also, and more importantly, to reflect the breadth of Hal's career. His most famous shows were intellectual, conceptual projects, but he's done his share of lighter fare as well. For *It's a Bird . . . It's a Plane . . . It's Superman* (Yes! Hal Prince directed a *Superman* musical in the sixties!), I created a giant comic-book page with "Ben-Day"* dots. It filled the proscenium end to end with a colorful image unlike anything else in the show. The transition into it was based on a fun idea Stro had, that Superman could leap onto the bare stage as a rope fell from above for him to "pull" to reveal it.

At the end of the *Superman* sequence, the drop flew out to reveal my rendition of Boris Aronson's valentine set for the *Follies* "Loveland" scene, which in turn flowed into the decrepit backstage that defines most of that show.

---

*"An inexpensive mechanical printing method developed in the late nineteenth century and named after its inventor, illustrator and printer Benjamin Henry Day Jr. The method [—seen most obviously in newspaper comic strips and adopted by the pop artist Roy Lichtenstein as a signature technique—] relies upon small colored dots (typically cyan, magenta, yellow, and black) that are variously spaced and combined to create shading and colors in images." https://www.moma.org/collection/terms/145.

Within this image: "SPIDERWOMAN CELL REVOLVES TO REVEAL SWEENEY PIE SHOP. BLACKS IRIS OPEN TO REVEAL SWEENY WINDOW."

West Side Story, Kiss of the Spiderwoman, transition from *Kiss of the Spiderwoman* to *Sweeney Todd*, and *Sweeney Todd*

It's a Bird . . . It's a Plane . . . It's Superman transition and scene, the beginning of the *Follies* sequence, and the second part of *Follies*

"All I Need Is One Good Break," our opening sequence, *Grind*, *Fiorello*, and *On the Twentieth Century*

I'd rendered all of the transitional narration as well, and roughed in the projected Hirschfeld animation. From the moment I'd completed the renderings, through all of the ups and downs that followed, the design remained essentially the same; I don't think more than 15 percent of it changed from my presentation of it to our opening night on Broadway five and a half years later.

But I'm getting ahead of my story. The opening dash of the sprint was past, and it was time to start the second. Eddie and his team of draftsmen started to draw what they could, based on my two-dimensional renderings, while I built a model to detail the sculptural elements. As I've mentioned, I seldom hire assistants for model building; I discover a lot by building the model myself. It forces me to think about the details of the show and solidify my design decisions. Besides, I love model making. I love the process of figuring everything out in miniature. After the race to render this complex show, the weeks I spent refining my design by building the model felt almost relaxing.

During breaks from working on the model, I contacted the designers (or their heirs) who had worked on each of Hal's shows. My work was an interpretation of theirs, so I wanted to get their blessing and any comments they might have.

Boris Aronson with his model for *A Little Night Music*
Martha Swope, ©Billy Rose Theatre Division, The New York Public Library for the Performing Arts

Boris Aronson had died in 1980, and the person I was most eager to speak to was his widow, Lisa. I had met her several times at Hal's Christmas parties, and had once driven up to Nyack, New York, to visit her in the house she and Boris had owned. Nonetheless, I was nervous to speak with her. Boris was responsible for the original sets for *Cabaret, Fiddler on the Roof, Company, Follies, A Little Night Music,* and *Pacific Overtures.* I was reinterpreting more of his work than anyone else's—and copying his designs more exactly than the others—both because his sets were so visually unique and because they had so deeply influenced Hal's own aesthetic. I've felt Boris's presence in the room for every design discussion I've ever had with Hal.

When Lisa invited me to share a lovely lunch at her home overlooking the Hudson, she was ninety-some years old, sharp as a tack, and looking like a mystical European elf. She had been Boris's design associate when her husband worked with Hal, so she knew the details of the shows intimately. Among other enlightening things, she finally explained the strange Art Nouveau model pieces from the *Follies* set. Apparently, Boris's original design for "Loveland" had been an Art Nouveau extravaganza. Makes sense, since *Follies* was written as a nostalgic look back from the 1970s to earlier days, when the Follies were a fashionable form of entertainment. But the day before the first rehearsal, Hal had sudden misgivings. He told Boris that Art Nouveau was all wrong, that the number should look like a frilly valentine full of silly cherubs. With no time to really think it through, Boris had gone home and found a box of old valentines and a bundle of paper doilies used to display pastries. Working through the night, he chopped them up and assembled them into a model of the "Loveland" set. Mystery solved! Before I built the model for the *Follies* sequence, I went to the grocery store and bought two packages of doilies for the purpose.

After lunch, with some nervousness, I began to show Lisa my renderings from start to finish. She listened politely to my explanations, asked very few questions, and was extremely supportive. I had worried that she would feel I was appropriating too much of Boris's work but, on the contrary, she seemed to love how closely I'd stuck to the originals. In fact, her only note was that she wished I could add a big upstage mirror to the set for *Cabaret*.

Cabaret was the first set Boris designed for Hal, and the mirror had come as a delightful surprise to the director. The message of *Cabaret* is that the threat of fascism lies just below the surface of society—that we should never think of Nazism as simply something from a faraway place and time. Boris's huge mirror reflected the audience back at themselves as they walked into the theater, reinforcing that idea of self-examination.

Ultimately the mirror didn't make it into *Prince of Broadway*; it just didn't lend itself to the specific songs that had been chosen. But I did use a shiny mylar rain curtain in the sequence, as a spiritual nod to the great designer. Lisa died a few years later, before *P.O.B.* made it to the stage, but I'm grateful to have had her blessing on the project.

The minute I finished the model, I took it to Hal. I wasn't sure he'd totally understood from the renderings the jigsaw-puzzle aspect of the set's back wall, how it was designed to transform and reveal various surprises. He may not have fully understood how it worked even with the model, but he was excited by what he saw, acting like a kid on Christmas morning each time the wall reconfigured itself.

When I mentioned the surprise mirror in *Cabaret*, Hal told me that Boris would surprise him with some element in each set. I've surprised him myself (usually pleasantly, thank God) a few times over the years, though the "revelations" were always things I'd shown him in the model. It makes me wonder . . . maybe it wasn't that Boris had planned to surprise him but that Hal hadn't been fully attentive to what he'd approved.

Hal and I stepped through the entire show, Hal describing the action while I moved the model pieces around. Over the next few weeks, we'd replay that performance for

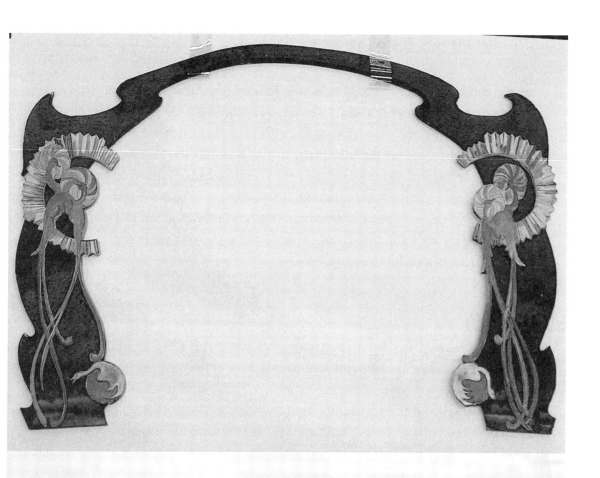

The Art Nouveau Loveland and its Valentine replacement

larger and larger groups of collaborators. I'd learned in working with him on *Love-Musik* that this was key to Hal's development of the show. He was literally directing it as we stepped through it. The model, with its scale figures of the actors, allowed him to play the story out and edit it as we went along. By the time we got to the first rehearsal, we were well rehearsed, and the narrative had solidified in the director's mind. Our presentation had become an entertainment in its own right.

Inevitably, things change in rehearsal, tech, and previews. But Hal would always start rehearsal with a thorough blueprint of the show, and those successive model presentations helped him form and develop it.

Stumble

Aubrey Dan and Peter Lamb, our producers, scheduled a big, old-school backers' audition/cocktail party. Aubrey was providing most of the financing for the show, but he wanted to attract some additional investment. In a grand room overlooking Times Square, we laid out the entire storyboard of the set, along with William's costume sketches. Jason played his brilliant overture as Stro sang out the titles of Hal's thirty-two Broadway musicals, which we would ultimately project onto the show curtain.

Our cast of Broadway stars, including Linda Lavin, La Chanze, Shuler Hensley, Emily Skinner, Sierra Boggess, and Sebastian Arcelus, mingled with the potential investors. As we all chatted and sipped cocktails, Dan Kutner introduced me

Hal checking his notes before the backers' presentation

to Hiroko Murata, a Japanese producer he'd worked with in Tokyo who planned to invest in *Prince of Broadway*. Hiroko asked me if I would come to Tokyo to design Dan's next project there. *Of course I would!*

The room was packed with high-powered producers, from the then-mighty Bob Weinstein to *Wicked* producer David Stone, and all of them seemed fascinated by our project. It felt like a dream to me, enhanced by the glitter of Times Square shining in through the picture windows. At the appropriate moment, Hal, signature glasses in place atop his bald head, walked toward the stage to describe the show, tripped going up the steps, and nearly fell on his face. Standing next to me, Dan winced and muttered, "I told him to wear his glasses!"

Rattled at first, Hal soon recovered and picked up steam as he spoke. When he'd finished and accepted polite applause, he descended the stairs and tripped again— and recovered again, thank God. In the moment, it was a bit scary. Soon it would seem like an omen.

Over the following days, Peter Lamb assured me things were full-steam-ahead and we ought to bid out the set drawings. We hoped the backers' audition might yield a specific theater for the fall, but even if it didn't, everyone was confident we'd get one. It's frustrating but not unusual for me to find myself designing a set without knowing what theater I'm designing for. (As I mentioned earlier, *Act One* at the Beaumont was an exception and a godsend.) Commercial shows come and go quickly, so it makes sense that we might not know in May what theater would be available in October. There's lots of jockeying for the "good" theaters, lots of politics and personal relationships involved in the process—none of which I can control. Luckily, most Broadway theaters are similar enough in size that I can design for a general space and adjust to the reality later.

Eddie sent our drawings to the main Broadway scene shops and after a few weeks of back-and-forth, we had our quotes. They reflected the sheer volume of scenery we needed; most of the bids were well over our budget. But my old friend Warren Katz at Global Scenic really wanted to build the show. At around my age, Warren was the youngest of the big shop owners (he has since tragically passed away), and Global was the newest of the big union scene shops. His price for *P.O.B.* was close to our budget and he reassured me that with some tweaks, we could get most of what I'd designed for the money. On first impression, Warren could come across like one of the Jewish gangsters from the *Sopranos*, but he had a genius for figuring out how to produce quality scenery cheaply, and I trusted him.

The day Warren and I shook hands on the deal, our general manager called me. "Submit all your outstanding expense receipts right now," he said gravely. "The show's in trouble." It seemed that Aubrey Dan did not want to foot the bulk of the $12-million budget after all and, despite a few other investors joining the project, we were dramatically short of money. Aubrey was pulling the plug. I never learned whether he had initially intended to finance the whole thing and gotten cold feet or if he'd assumed others would line up to pay for it. Whatever the case, the entire creative team was in shock. Our show had fallen flat on its face.

Marathon

Once he sinks his teeth into a project, Hal Prince never lets go. While the rest of us were recovering from this blow, Hal was looking for new producers. By the middle of summer, he invited us to meet our new bosses: a group of men who'd had some gigantic hits in the early 2000s, including *The Producers*, with Stro, and *Hairspray*. But the theater is fickle, and they had recently fallen on hard times. They warned us that they personally would not be able to finance the project but said they were excited to raise the money to produce it. We all hoped that their impressive resumes would be more attractive to investors than that of the relatively inexperienced Aubrey Dan. We planned another backers' audition for investors; among them was Hiroko Murata, who was still excited by the project.

I'm not good at gauging audiences, but even I could tell we weren't making the sale. The performances had been organized quickly. There was a lot of talent on display but very little evidence of the through-line that Tommy Thompson's book was designed to provide. As we watched one energetic performance after another, the whole thing felt more like a benefit concert or "Broadway night" on a cruise ship than the next Broadway blockbuster. We didn't raise any money.

By the following spring—2013—our replacement producers had lost hope of getting the show to Broadway. They stepped away, and the show collapsed for a second time.

But, as I said, Hal never gives up. Later that spring, Dan called me and said, "Hiroko Murata still loves the show. She wants to produce it herself. In Tokyo."

I was skeptical—especially since the show that Hiroko had asked me to design in Tokyo had disappeared when she decided it was too expensive to fly me over and hired someone local. *She likes to make flamboyant offers and then disappear*, I thought.

Much to my surprise, *Prince of Broadway* in Tokyo didn't disappear. The Japanese have greater reverence for age and experience than flash-in-the-pan Broadway. There were very few living artists with Hal's experience, and even if Broadway backers didn't see dollar signs in that, Hiroko saw something more valuable. She was the artistic producer for a Japanese railroad conglomerate called Umeda, which also presented cultural events. *Prince of Broadway* would be a prestigious feather in their cap. The production was planned for October 2014. Hal insisted that this was just our stepping-stone back to Broadway. Doesn't everyone do their Broadway tryout in Tokyo?

To save on airfare, the producers wanted to use Japanese lighting, video, and sound designers. I suspect they also wanted to emphasize that they had great artists in Japan, too, and that not everyone had to be imported. Hal told us we'd be working with the lighting designer Sonoyo Nishikawa but avowed that Howell Binkley would return for Broadway.

At that point, we had a year-and-a-half to mount the show, and I naïvely assumed the designs were finished. But Hal kept thinking and tinkering. Every few months, I'd find myself back in his office with Stro and Tommy, with the model or my sketches, and we'd talk through some change in the song order or minor change to a scene. And this process improved the show.

As we tweaked things, Hal decided he wanted me to change my show proscenium. I'd always thought it should be simple and just suggest "Broadway theater" without

The Arno proscenium, representing, from left to right: producers, managers, sound designer, lighting designer, costume designer, set designer, orchestrator, musical director, choreographer, director, librettist, composer, lyricist, actors, singer, dancer, and theater critics (burning in hell).

any other agenda. But he decided we should make it a collage of all the people who collaborate to make a show—and that it ought to be in the style of Peter Arno, a *New Yorker* cartoonist from the 1950s. My attempt lasted one meeting before we returned to the more traditional proscenium.

Hal had a complicated relationship with *Phantom of the Opera*, his record-breaking megahit. Because the physical production is such a spectacle—and a currently running one that anyone could buy a ticket to see—the act of replicating a piece of it satisfyingly was troubling him. I must have redesigned the sequence twenty times in those eighteen months.

I made versions that were somewhat original and versions that slavishly copied Maria Björnson's brilliant set. I made a (quickly rejected) pitch that we *had* to have the famous chandelier. Finally, after my umpteenth iteration, Hal announced, "What's great about *Phantom* is candles and a lot of smoke. Let's do that on a black stage." Smart. Easy. Sold. Done.

Hal also decided that he didn't like the idea of himself as a Hirschfeld-cartoon narrator. It now felt childish to him. Hiroko hired a famous Japanese commercial video

Phantom of the Opera copying Maria Bjornson's candelabra, *Phantom of the Opera* as if seen from backstage looking toward the audience, with the famous chandelier in the distance, and the final *Phantom of the Opera* sequence

designer, Atsunori Toshi, to show Hal and Stro a video hologram of Hal as the narrator, but it was underwhelming. We finally settled on a simple voice-over. For a man with ego to spare, Hal was bizarrely shy about putting "himself" onstage in this show where *he* was the connective tissue of all the disparate parts. I remained a fan of the Hirschfeld cartoon because it was big and theatrical, but the idea was cut—to the detriment of the show.

Our next hurdle was financial. Because labor and materials costs vary from place to place, I always try to understand what a dollar (or yen) will buy in the place I'm working. Often I ask for pictures of a set built with a budget similar to mine, in order to get a sense of it. But *Prince of Broadway* was already designed. I wouldn't be conceiving it to fit the budget, so I had to hope the budget would buy what I'd conceived!

The set would be built by Yuichiro Kanai, a svelte, dapper man who flew to New York to discuss it with me. In addition to modern productions, Kanai's family has been building the scenery for traditional Kabuki theater for generations. He understood the ideas perfectly, and I immediately felt at ease with him. I asked him about scenery costs in Japan relative to New York, and he told me that prices were comparable. But when I asked if our set budget was the equivalent of the $1.1 million we'd planned for in New York, he said that Hiroko and Umeda had budgeted just the equivalent of $500,000. We were in trouble.

Kanai suggested that we get rid of the show's automation and have stagehands push the scenery on and off. That would save us the cost of the machinery for the automation as well as the significant cost of an entire raised show deck to house the automated tracks.

I was horrified. Stagehands pushing scenery? Were we doing summer stock? I talked it through with Hal, and Dan came to the rescue. He'd directed several shows in Tokyo and said that not only did Japanese stagehands wear head-to-toe black like ninjas but they moved so stealthily that you could barely see them. More convincingly, he also explained that Japanese audiences were very used to the convention and wouldn't see it as cheap. What choice did I have? I had to save money somewhere.

Somehow that one alteration solved our budget problem completely. I never understood how cutting the deck, which might have saved $250,000 on the high end, got us from $1.1 million to $500,000, but it did. I suspect Kanai swallowed the excess costs and built the set at a loss. I've always been grateful to him for that, though he never confirmed my hunch. Another hurdle cleared!

The show rehearsed in New York. Because they were Tokyo-based, Hiroko and Umeda had hired an elegant independent producer named Kumiko Yoshi to be their New York representative while we developed the show. She was a quiet presence, always in the background. Down the road she would become a key player.

Follies drop under construction in Tokyo. The giant doilies were hand-cut from industrial felt
Jen Price Fick

Relatively late in the rehearsal process, Stro added an unplanned dance sequence. In developing the song "Right Girl" from *Follies*, Stro worked for the first time with Tony Yazbeck, who was playing Buddy. She and Tony were made for each other. What might have been a brief soft-shoe turned into a stunningly violent tap sequence in which Tony's feet drummed the stage with machine-gun ferocity. It was brilliant. And I knew the thin plywood deck surface we were using to save money would last about two performances. I emailed Kanai to warn him. He said we had no more money, the deck was already built, and we'd have to hope for the best.

Nervous about that floor and everything else, I boarded the plane for Japan with the cast. It happened to be my birthday and, because we were crossing the international dateline and jumping ahead twelve hours, I missed most of it. I've joked ever since that I have been aging backward from that day.

After everything that had happened leading up to it, the tech for *Prince of Broadway* was one of the smoothest I've ever experienced. Hal yelled a lot in tech, but I'd learned during *LoveMusik* not to take it personally. Sonoyo, our lighting designer, had spent time with us in New York and knew the show well, but I could tell that first day that she didn't know what hit her. She scrambled to get her footing as Hal screamed about this or that and then screamed again when she didn't correct it fast enough.

Hal and Stro kept wanting to adjust the cueing and timing around the buttons of various numbers. Sonoyo's experience had mainly been in opera, and she was completely confused. Finally, she came running to me in a panic and begged, "What the hell is button?"

By day 2, Sonoyo had gotten into the swing of Hal and Stro's rhythm, and the lighting was starting to look good. The video was another story. It had been clear even in New York that Toshi wasn't really understanding the aesthetic the show demanded. He did a good job with some of the projections, but I had to step in and help out with others, as I had a better idea what Hal was looking for.

Hal watches Schuler Hensley and Nancy Opel in tech in Tokyo

Video images for a sequence where Times Square evolved from the 1950s to the 2010s, paralleling Hal's career
Chris Ash/Beowulf Boritt

I'd hired an associate projection designer—the bookish, bearded Chris Ash—who made some video sequences for me. Those went into the show smoothly. But as tech wore on, I started stepping in and rebuilding more and more of Toshi's images to better match the show's aesthetic. I was never sure whether Toshi was offended or relieved by my intervention.

The first time we assembled the *Follies* set for Hal, he felt that I had hung one of the drops too far upstage; that the overall image was too spread out to be effective. He was right, but the fix wasn't simple. Every pipe was being used, so there was no obvious place to move the misplaced drop.

A large-scale musical involves a complicated integration of pieces, and the domino effect of moving one bit of scenery can disrupt six other scenes. But, after poring over our ground plan for a while, Jen Price Fick (who had drafted the show with Eddie and was with me in Japan) found a smart solution. By relocating two drops and two pieces of hard scenery to different pipes, we could achieve the look Hal was asking for. On Broadway, a scenery swap like that might involve a day of arguing with the production manager, a day of arguing with the crew, a day to plan the moves, and a day or two to execute.

With some trepidation I went to Kanai and explained what we wanted to do. After discussing it briefly with the crew chief, he came back to me and said, "It will be done in twenty minutes."

My jaw dropped to the floor as four pipes of scenery flew to the deck, about a hundred black-clad stagehands swarmed the stage, and the scenery was rearranged into its new positions. Japanese efficiency is a marvel!

As I'd feared, the deck surface became an issue for Tony's *Follies* tap dance: It was getting chewed to pieces, and a shower of splintered wood chips would erupt around him each time he performed the number. When it was clear that the situation was becoming dangerous for the dancer, the producers finally agreed to pay for a new, harder surface on the downstage portion of the stage deck. It was painted and installed.

One minor (literal) earthquake later, we were approaching the *Phantom* sequence at the end of act 1. As Hal had requested, it involved candles and a lot of smoke. It looked great. "Wulfie, where's the giant cross that says Daaé?" thundered Hal into his God mic. I reminded him of his decision to keep it simple and flipped through all my rejected *Phantom* sketches. To no avail. He wanted a big cross. Finally, I got him to agree to a projected one for Japan, with the promise that I'd give him a real one for Broadway.

The show was on its feet. Ever since our failed second backers' audition, my great fear had been that it would feel like a benefit performance on steroids, a collection of songs sung well by talented performers rather than a coherent show. But it cohered. And the set helped tell that story.

Ramin Karimloo and Kaley Ann Vorhees in the *Phantom* sequence

The empty theater as a frame for the show worked well and felt appropriate. At times it felt present as a real thing, and at others it receded so that the sequence-specific scenery could dominate visually. The back wall transformed effectively and almost indiscernibly into a tenement skyline, a factory wall, a prison courtyard—and back into the wall of a theater. Its chameleon nature sat in contrast to the more traditional scenery that joined it. Small pieces, such as the *Damn Yankees* lockers and the *Parade* jail cell, coexisted comfortably with it, and their rotations to reveal the *West Side Story* fence or the *Sweeney Todd* pie shop had an exciting theatrical flair.

I was particularly happy with *West Side Story*. My set referenced a little wooden fence with a boxing poster from Oliver Smith's lyrical original set. But as the light came up on that fence and Ramin Karimloo, playing Tony, launched into "Something's Coming," the top of the theater back wall lifted away to reveal a tiny patch of unreachable sky and twinkling stars. Window light boxes transformed the wall into a tenement slum. The extreme forced perspective provided a twist on the conventional fire escapes and helped make the hopeful sky even more remote.

The main empty-stage set could disappear when more involved sequences demanded more fully realized scenery. *Superman* wiped away the blackness with bright comic-book color and then just as quickly flew away to reveal my favorite sequence in the show. To the thunderous introductory chords of Sondheim's "Beautiful Girls," my homage to Boris Aronson's lace-and-pink "Loveland" set was revealed. Reon Yuzuki, in a massive Follies-girl costume, elegantly descended the pink center-stage stair, and as suddenly as it had appeared, the "Loveland" vision evaporated to reveal a rusty iron backstage stair and piles of broken detritus. Most strikingly, the upstage drop collapsed into an angled, messy pile on the floor, melting away before the audience's eyes. In seconds we played out visually *Follies*' theme: the excitement of youth dissolving into memory and regret in the blink of an eye.

In the *Company* sequence, which encompassed several songs, the multilevel, constructivist towers created a complete world of vertical acting space—then that, too, slipped away, leaving Evita on her balcony, isolated in a tight spotlight. The longer sequences in the show—*Cabaret*, *Company*, *Evita*, and *Follies*—felt like condensed versions of entire shows, while the briefer segments—*Parade*, *Phantom*, and *Forum*—left audiences wanting more. Interspersing these sequences of various lengths created a dramatic rhythm I'd worked hard to mimic visually.

In the end, we'd managed to create a lovely evening of theater, and the Japanese audiences were eating it up. Hal seemed visibly shaken by watching his career play out in front of him as a musical. You'd think he'd have been prepared after so many

In Tokyo with Hal Prince
Dan Kutner

years of development, but I think he'd gotten lost among the trees and hadn't taken in the forest until we were up and running in front of an audience. After three and a half years, we'd finally crossed the finish line!

Then Hal reminded me: Tokyo was our stepping-stone back to Broadway. And Hal Prince never lets go of a project once he sinks his teeth in.

In Tokyo with Susan Stroman, and Jason Robert Brown
Mimi Bilinski

Final Hurdle

It was December 2015 and Jeffrey Seller, the producer of *Hamilton*, was flying to Tokyo to see our show. *Hamilton* had opened on Broadway a few months earlier, and although it hadn't swept the Tony Awards yet, it was already the musical of the decade. Such is Hal Prince's legacy that when he called Jeffrey and asked him to bring *Prince of Broadway* back to New York, Jeffrey jumped on a plane.

A month later, Jeffrey had Lynne Meadow, the artistic director of Manhattan Theater Club, on board to produce the show the following autumn. Kumiko Yoshi was on board as well. She had the entire Japanese set packed into shipping containers, sent halfway around the world by boat, and loaded into MTC's storage facility. If we could find a few million dollars of commercial enhancement, we would finally be on Broadway.

Between the box-office grosses for *Hamilton* and those for *Phantom of the Opera*, I'd have thought Jeffrey and Hal would consider this additional funding pocket change—but neither of them had gotten where they were by throwing their own money around. In fact, I learned later that Hal had stopped investing in his own shows after losing a good bit of his personal fortune on *Pacific Overtures* in the 1970s. I believe Jeffrey did ultimately put in a sizable amount, but it was hard to attract additional investors who felt, *If it's so good, why doesn't Hal finance it himself?* Getting the show on slowed to a crawl; I wondered anew if it would ever happen at all.

Our proposed opening moved from autumn of 2016 to May 2017 and then to August 2017—which put it on a collision course with the London production of *Young Frankenstein* I was designing and Stro was directing. Like *Prince of Broadway,* it had been on-again, off-again for several years. Wouldn't you know that it finally had a theater—for August 2017.

I'm shocked at how frequently in my career major projects have collided. It doesn't make it easier to do good work. Stro tried in vain to get one or the other production shifted by a couple of weeks, but West End theater availabilities were as tough as those in New York. We'd just have to be in two places at once. Stro would head to London at the end of *P.O.B.* rehearsals and miss the tech. I'd stay in New York for tech and a few previews but would then have to leave an associate in charge and head to London. I called Eddie Pierce. He was available to continue with the project but was used to being paid considerably more than what MTC—a nonprofit Broadway producer—generally budgeted for a design assistant. I called MTC and haggled and managed to get both Eddie and Jen Price Fick hired to help me reconstruct the show. They built me a beautiful model box of the Samuel J. Friedman Theatre, which is a

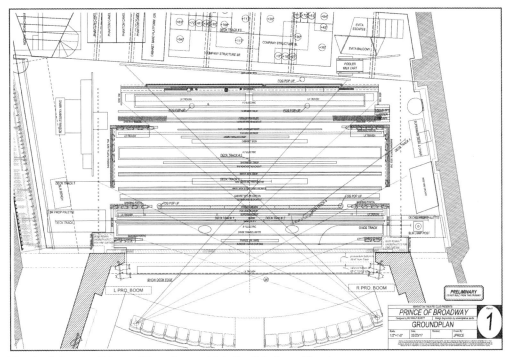

Plan for fitting the *Prince of Broadway* set into the Friedman Theatre

third the size of our venue in Tokyo, and I adapted my original set model to fill it. As it turned out, the small units for each segment looked good in the smaller space. I just had to figure out how to fit them all backstage. I laid out a basic ground plan and determined that if we trimmed down the edges of the flown scenery and hung it very tightly, it just might fit.

Techniques for fitting massive amounts of scenery into typically tiny Broadway theaters include such methods as kicking sheaves, splitting pipes, and using flown storage. The processes aren't artistic, they're technical, but they're worth a moment of explanation.

In most traditional theaters there are a series of flying linesets (pipes) hung one after another from just behind the proscenium to the stage back wall. Their spacing varies from one theater to another, but the pipes are typically two inches in diameter and hung every eight to twelve inches. So, for a twenty-eight-foot-deep stage, that would mean about thirty to forty pipes. In many theaters that's what you have available to hang scenery, lights, and masking. You can't add more pipes; they won't fit.

But on Broadway, I typically have the time and money to reconstruct much of the stage machinery to suit my set. First, we can "kick" sheaves. Sheaves are pulleys that guide the steel cables that lift the pipes. We can often move them around (kick them) on the grid and pack them more tightly together than the typical eight to twelve inches. Of course, the pipes can't get closer together than the thickness of the scenery, so if it has dimension, that's that. Simple painted drops, though, are thinner than the two-inch-thick pipes from which they are suspended—meaning that the pipes can be hung every four inches: two inches for the pipe itself and two inches of clearance. That configuration allows for a lot more scenery.

Splitting pipes is the second space creator. We can rerig the grid, so we don't have to rely on full stage pipes that span the distance from stage left to stage right. In *Prince of Broadway*, I had masking legs that looked like brick theater walls, draped with ropes and sandbags. They were thick upstage-downstage—about nine inches—but sat at the edges of the stage. Between them when they were hung, center stage, was a hole nine inches deep and the width of the space between the two masking legs. My thicker scenery would fit into there.

The *Cabaret* sign was covered with light bulbs, so it was thick and fragile. It fit nicely into a space between the masking. We "split" the pipe that would have gone all the way across the stage into three parts, and each masking leg was on a short pipe. Between them was the *Cabaret* sign, on its own separate pipe so it could fly in and out.

The third method for creating extra space is flying scenery into the wings. Broadway theaters tend to have very shallow wings but, just as there is fly space over the stage, there is airspace over the wings. We typically hang motorized winches there that can lift props and scenery pieces into the air so they can be stored above everyone's heads backstage. The show crew fly them down to the deck just before they are needed and replace them with pieces coming offstage.

On big shows, wing storage might be packed two or three items tall, with act 2 scenery hung up high during act 1 and then brought down and swapped with the first-act scenery at intermission. It's like a giant, three-dimensional Tetris game.

This may sound like a lot of technical jargon, but if you want to design a show with any complexity (and you aren't working at Radio City Music Hall), you're going to end up splitting pipes, kicking sheaves, and/or utilizing vertical backstage storage. I used all three methods in fitting the *P.O.B.* set—designed to go into the eight-thousand-square-foot Orb backstage area—into the two-thousand-square-foot Friedman backstage.

After all the stops and starts, I still didn't quite believe the show would happen. But on a February afternoon in early 2017, I found myself in a freezing warehouse with Josh Hellman, MTC's curly haired, affable, worry-wart of a production manager, as a crew unpacked my Japanese set. It had survived reasonably well, considering it had traveled halfway around the world and then sat in storage for a year and a half.

Out came the pink valentine drops of the *Follies* set, the silver steel superstructure of *Company*, a special packing crate protecting the *Cabaret* sign, and acres and acres of gray "backstage" brick. The set wasn't about to reconstruct itself, but it was here!

I talked Hal and Stro through the show for the umpteenth time. They liked how the set looked within the proportions of the Friedman. They must have asked me fifty times if all that scenery would really fit, but I was confident it would.

We were reconceiving a few scenes. Hal decided to cut the song "Lovely" from *A Funny Thing Happened on the Way to the Forum* and replace it with "Everybody Ought to Have a Maid." I quailed internally at the choice, though the change didn't affect the set. The new song is sung by four dirty old men extolling the pleasures of ogling (or worse) their pretty servants. In the context of *Forum*, maybe the song makes a point. As a stand-alone number it felt gross. Sondheim's lyrics are clever. The song captures a truth about the way men look at pretty women, but it also makes a salacious joke of that. I was uncomfortable, but I was just the set designer, so I kept quiet.

In Japan we had done the song "Now You Know" from *Merrily We Roll Along* on a bare stage, as an emotional accompaniment to some narration about Hal's eight Broadway flops in a row in the 1980s. I decided that I wanted to add to the effect by

Forum for Broadway

Merrily for Broadway

opening the back wall to reveal the *West Side Story* skyline again, with the addition of an illuminated theater marquee spelling out *Merrily We Roll Along*.

And of course we had to discuss *Phantom of the Opera* again. The sequence was moving from the end of act 1 to become the penultimate sequence in act 2. That made sense. It's Hal's biggest popular hit, but it's different from most of his work. The new placement would give it importance without clustering it among the more conceptual shows that are his trademark. Luckily, this didn't create scenery challenges, because we hadn't made physical *Phantom* scenery in Japan. I'd promised Hal that for Broadway I'd replace the projected Daaé grave with a real one. He loved the surprises revealed by the theater back wall, so I proposed we add a *Phantom* surprise. I repurposed a part of the brick wall to reveal a giant Gothic arch with an iron gate. Upstage of the gate would be the Daaé cross. We were still trying to avoid too literal a re-creation of the real *Phantom*, but I hoped mine captured its dark, melodramatic spirit. Downstage, I placed four giant palettes of candles, and the use of dry ice would evoke *Phantom*'s mysterious underworld. Hal was happy. We were ready to go.

Although Sonoyo, our Japanese lighting designer, had done a great job, she was replaced by Howell Binkley, as planned. I had essentially taken over the projection design in Japan, so I became the official projection designer. Designing both scenery and projections can be artistically rewarding, but if things don't go smoothly, it can spread a designer thin. My technical knowledge of projectors, lenses, and the programs that manage everything is woefully limited, so I can only tackle projections

Phantom for Broadway

with the help of a strong, knowledgeable associate designer. Chris Ash, who had built some content for me for Japan, agreed to join me.

Jen Price Fick began the meticulous process of redrawing the scenery so a shop could precisely trim it to fit the Friedman. Almost all the drops and full-stage scenery would have to be reduced by a few feet. The deck scenery fit unaltered except for my *Follies* stair. A tall staircase is dramatic onstage, but the higher it goes the more space it inhabits, and my backstage wasn't big. I could retain the full height of the staircase by making each step taller and having fewer of them—but that would cause trouble for the actors, who had to descend gracefully in heels and elegant costumes. The steps had to stay shallow, so I ended up reducing the size of the staircase and hoped it would look grand enough.

Reon Yuzuki on the *Follies* stair in Tokyo

Janet Dacal on the *Follies* stair on Broadway

Our budget wouldn't allow for as many stagehands as we'd had in Japan, so I'd need to automate the deck scenery—not an insignificant expense in its own right. It would require raising all two thousand square feet of the stage by nine inches so that under it, we could run the cables and guides for moving the scenery.

Having learned my lesson in Japan, I knew the deck surface would have to be strong enough to withstand Tony Yazbeck's tap sequence. We chose a very hard material called EPS (also known as Arboron), made from compressed paper but extremely durable. It can bear the weight of heavy scenery and I was pretty sure it could survive Tony. We'd paint and texture it to look like dark, wooden planks.

Almost exactly five years from the day we sent the original *Prince of Broadway* set out for pricing, Jen and Eddie had the whole show redrawn and ready to send to shops. As I flipped through the fifty-one pages of technical drawings, I realized just how big a show it was and how little money we had to reconstitute the set.

Then Eddie hit me with a bombshell. He'd underestimated the time for redrawing the show and had burned through much more of our assistant fee than expected. We'd have just enough money left to pay the two of them to load the show in—but they wouldn't be able to tech it with me. Shocked, I was not terribly diplomatic. I said they had better do the full job for the agreed-upon fee and that was that. Though polite, Eddie was unwilling to budge. Ultimately, we decided that Eddie and Jen would withdraw from the project, and I would take whatever funds were left and find an associate to finish the show with me. I'd have to call in a favor.

I had two associates I'd trust with anything: Jared Rutherford and Alexis Distler. Jared was going to England with *Young Frankenstein*, but maybe Alexis was available. (As you'll recall, in 2012, when I started work on *Prince of Broadway*, I wasn't sure Alexis had the experience to handle it. But by 2017, she and I had done multiple big shows together.) There are many advantages to establishing long-term working relationships with associate designers, but one of them is that you can occasionally beg them to work on a project for less than they're worth. I called Alexis and explained the situation, and, to my great relief, she joined me.

I waited nervously for the pricing to come back and when it did, I found that my luck had held! *Prince of Broadway* could easily have cost twice my available budget, but May is a very quiet time for Broadway scene shops, and that helped. Most commercial sets are built and in their theaters by April. After the Tony Awards in June, some shows close, and the shops get busy again, building new sets for the shows that will take their place. But, in April, May, and early June, the shops are quiet, hungry for work, and ready to cut a deal.

Neil Mazzella, the president of Hudson Scenic Studio, called me and said, "I want to do the show, and I can do it all for the budget you have." Neil is a small guy with waist-length hair who is usually dressed in biker leather. He looks like he could beat up someone twice his size. But he has a heart of gold and has worked on Broadway for longer than I've been alive, making him a savvy liaison between the artistic staff, technical staff, and financial managers. Knowing that Neil and his shop would be reconstructing the set for Broadway was a huge weight off my shoulders.

Around that time, I met the house carpenter responsible for the Friedman stage: Fran Rapp. He was quiet and guarded until he got to know me, but I soon discovered that he had vast experience with musicals and the tricky task of making big shows fit into little spaces. He would prove vital to making the show work—more good luck.

With the set under way, I turned my attention to the projections. Most of them were simple, but a few sequences were more involved. We had to re-create the overture sequence, during which the titles of all thirty-three musicals Hal had directed or produced would be projected onto the show curtain. Toshi had built the montage in Tokyo, but to avoid having to pay for the rights to the logos, he'd made fake versions, different enough from the originals to avoid copyright issues. I hated the fakes and felt that for Broadway audiences, we'd need the real logos. Hal agreed, but the legal department did not. They simply didn't have the time or resources to secure the rights to the logos. Hal asked me to make "plausible" fakes and, though

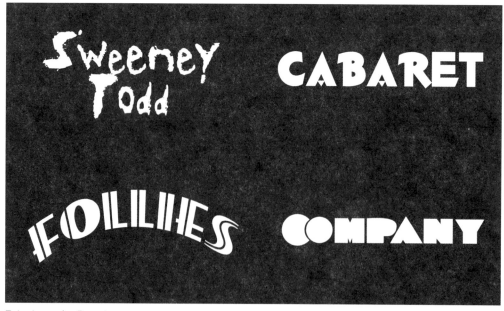

Fake logos for Broadway

I'd have preferred to just show the titles in some classy font, I had no choice but to try. It was a long, tedious, project but in the end, I didn't hate what I'd come up with. Or maybe I *wanted* to think they were good. There is a constant danger when you work hard that you begin to believe it's good simply because you're happy to have conquered the challenge.

As rehearsals approached, we held a flurry of final meetings. One day, chatting with Stro, I mentioned that I was uncomfortable with "Everybody Ought to Have a Maid." Stro has the most amazing poker face I've ever seen. In the ten years I've worked with her, through some pretty difficult situations, I've only seen her composure slip a couple times. In this moment, I saw the slightest shadow cross her face. "You ought to mention that to Hal," she said quietly.

I'd kept my mouth shut up to that point, but the #MeToo movement was gaining steam, and I'd heard man after man in the industry admit that he'd seen women mistreated and hadn't spoken up. Perhaps a jokey, slightly off-color song wasn't comparable, but words matter. That evening, I sent Hal a long, carefully worded email outlining my concern that the song, when removed from the context of the show it was written for, was offensive. I took a deep breath and hit *send*.

I soon got a polite but firm response from Hal saying that I was being too politically correct. "The song is funny and harmless," he insisted. But, to ensure that people got the joke, he said that he'd costume the men as extra-disgusting perverts. I wasn't sure how that was going to help, but maybe I *was* too sensitive.

The first day of rehearsal arrived. We were actually doing *Prince of Broadway* on Broadway—I presented the model as Hal narrated the action for the cast. It was a routine we'd been practicing for five years; no surprise it was polished and entertaining.

When we'd finished the *Company* section at the top of act 2, I revealed the *Forum* scenery. Hal paused. He turned to the cast with a wink and said, "Wulfie thinks 'Everybody Ought to Have a Maid' is too anti-feminist. But we don't care, do we? We think it's funny . . . right?"

I was mortified that my attempt to stand up for something was being publicly mocked—until several of the younger women in the cast audibly gasped. Kaley Ann Voorhees, who was playing the young ingénue in the piece, actually put her hands over her mouth in shock.

The next day Dan Kutner called me. Hal had cut the song, and thus the *Forum* sequence, from the show. He said that my email had gotten under Hal's skin, and when he'd seen the reaction of some of the cast, he realized I might be right. In fairness to Hal, what is offensive can change radically from generation to generation. It

Tommy Thompson, Hal Prince, Susan Stroman, William Ivey Long, and Alexis Distler in a design meeting

was typical of Hal that, having surrounded himself with younger people, he decided (in this case, anyway) to take their views seriously.

As noted, fitting all that scenery into the Friedman was a nail-biter. It worked on paper—just—but what if a pipe had a small bend in it, suddenly taking up three or four inches of depth instead of two? Those inches could add up, and suddenly the set wouldn't fit.

Josh Hellman, our Eeyore of a production manager, hadn't done a lot of big musicals. He was terrified of the volume of scenery I was trying to cram in and kept asking me what I would cut when it inevitably didn't fit. He was so obviously concerned that Jason Robert Brown said, "You can tell Josh knows we're all going to die. We've made a show so big it's going to kill us all, and he's resigned to the fact that we're hurtling into the abyss and there's nothing he can do about it."

I wasn't worried. It's true that I had designed everything with only inches to spare—but theater is a collaborative art, and I had great collaborators. Neil's shop had re-created the pieces to perfection and the carpenters—under Fran Rapp's expert supervision—had installed them meticulously over three painstaking weeks. In the end, everyone's care and professionalism paid off. With just a couple of tweaks, the sets fit and flew in and out without a hitch.

We were ready to tech the show. Stro was about to leave us for *Young Frankenstein* and had left her associate, James Gray, in charge of the choreography. James is a British dancer with the most irrepressible good spirits I've ever encountered. Before Stro left, we visited the theater with Tony Yazbeck to test the floor for his *Follies* tap dance. I'd used a similar floor on another project with Tony, and he'd liked it. This time it was clear that he hated it. The sound wasn't good and it was too slippery. "Couldn't we have a sprung hardwood floor, like the one in my home studio?" he pleaded.

After twenty-four frazzled hours, we decided to rip out the downstage eight feet of our deck, replace it with oak sprung floor, and stain it black to match the rest. Tony was happy, and the dance was exquisite. It was worth the extra effort.

The cart we'd used for Tevye in *Fiddler on the Roof* in Japan hadn't arrived with the rest of the set, so we'd had to build a new one. Despite my props team beating it up, it looked too pristine. Shops can be hesitant to "go too far" with this kind of prop abuse. When I want scenery to look old, I build it from real materials that I can continue to distress in a real way. Nothing looks more like broken, splintered wood than real broken, splintered wood!

Early in tech, armed with a hammer, chisel, and wooden club, I stripped to my T-shirt and hauled the *Fiddler* cart out to the alley beside the theater. Two minutes later, Greg Livoti, our stage manager, appeared and said I was making too much noise—they could hear me onstage. I ended up on the sidewalk of Forty-Seventh Street pounding and chopping away at the wood and splashing it with dirty paint washes and amber shellac.

Scenery on the sidewalk of the theater district isn't all that unusual, but my vigorous activity managed to draw a small crowd. Soon, like Tom Sawyer with his whitewash, I had some new friends lending a hand. One retired scenic painter and two trans women who'd been sharing a joint added their personal touches. To finish off the job, I pulled a scrap of paper from my pocket that said Аронсон—*Aronson* in Cyrillic. I planned to hide the names of the original designer in each of the sets, and a Russian friend had transliterated it for me. Carefully, I chiseled the letters into the side of the cart.

In Japan, *A Little Night Music* had been represented by Emily Skinner singing "Send in the Clowns" on a bare, black stage. The song is so well known and has been sung by so many people that the simplest possible staging felt perfect. In New York, Hal added another song from the show to precede it, "You Must Meet My Wife,"

The *Fiddler* cart on Forty-Seventh Street

performed by Michael Xavier. We added a settee so Emily could sit and listen as he sang it. Unexpectedly, the addition of that piece of furniture made the stage feel lazily empty instead of magically empty—as if we'd bought a sofa but forgot the rest of the set. That's the strange alchemy of the theater.

Hal turned to Howell Binkley and asked for gobos—lighting stencils—to create a forest of birch trees against the black curtain upstage. The original Aronson set had featured just such a forest, but Howell hadn't prepared any such thing. Luckily, I'd had a similar idea and had worked up a projection. It would take Chris Ash just minutes

Michael Xavier and Emily Skinner in *A Little Night Music*

to set it up. I hate it when projections are used to replace physical scenery—except when I don't. The subtlety of those white birch trees, barely visible on the black velour drop, was ethereal enough to feel like a well-considered choice. It also allowed me to inscribe *Aronson* up the trunk of one of the trees and get the master's name onto another of the sets he'd originally designed.

We continued to tech and Hal continued to yell, impatiently driving us forward. Despite his typical bombast, I could tell he was having a good time. The show was looking good. The little vignettes staged within the empty theater set felt more present in the intimate Friedman. The only sequence that disappointed me was *Follies*. The grandeur of the music and scenery had been exhilarating in the giant Orb. They came across fine at the Friedman, but the smaller staircase felt a bit puny, and the moment when the pink "Loveland" backdrop melted into the stage was less monumental. But Hal was happy.

Until we got to *Phantom of the Opera*.

Since we'd moved *Phantom* close to the end of the show, we were nearly through tech before we hit it. When we finally did, dry ice clouds filled the stage, palettes of candles rolled out, the upstage wall moved to reveal the massive Gothic gate and beyond it a very real, very large cross with light-up letters that spelled *Daaé*.

"Wulfie, what the hell is that?" Hal bellowed. "That's not what you promised me! It looks like a church! That's not *Phantom*!"

I didn't even try to ascertain what Hal thought I'd promised. I yelled for Dan to bring the storyboards and showed them to him yelling, "This is what you approved! There are candles, there's a gate, there's a cross! It's all in this rendering! I'll change anything you want if you don't like it now, but don't accuse me of not delivering what we agreed on."

"Wulfie, what's gotten into you?" murmured Dan. "You're screaming at the boss!" The look on my face must have revealed my chagrin because he quickly added, "Don't worry! He loves it!"

For all of his yelling in tech, Hal could take it as well as dish it out. He had to admit that what was onstage looked like the picture. In twenty minutes, he cut half the candles and put the rest in a different spot. The Daaé cross went out to the dumpster and Howell took most of the light off the gate so it came across as just some dim and distant architecture. Finally, Hal was happy and we could finish teching.

I have a slight aversion to the first time an audience arrives. After weeks of having the show and the theater to ourselves, its jarring to invite the public in—which is odd, since that's the point of the whole exercise. I love creating a show, but once the audience shows up, my part in the creation is all but done. That always makes me a little sad.

Of course, there are things to love about previews—especially the backstage energy as everyone works to find their sea legs. I love to stand in the darkness of the wings and listen to the hubbub as the audience files in. By that point, I've spent so much time worrying about what the stage looks like from the front that the view from the wings feels exotic and new.

Hal's career, and thus *Prince of Broadway*, covered such a wide swath of theatrical history that a lot of theater legends—as well as longtime theatergoers—wanted to come see how we'd handled it all. One night, I sat in the last row of the orchestra a few seats from Joel Grey. When the *Cabaret* sequence began, with Brandon Uranowitz as the Emcee, I couldn't help glancing over at Joel, who had, of course, created the part. I was rewarded with a smile bright enough to light Broadway and a fountain of tears rolling down his cheeks.

Not everyone loved all of it. A few days later, I was standing in the lobby during the second act, chatting with James Gray. Suddenly, the door to the theater burst open, and a very unhappy-looking Stephen Sondheim marched past us and out of

Mimi Bilinski, associate choreographer James Gray, Joel Grey, and Hal Prince backstage

the theater. Steve was amply represented in the show, very favorably, I thought, so I couldn't fathom what he'd reacted to. I learned later that it was the point in the show when Hal said, "I had eight flops in a row," followed by "Now You Know" from *Merrily We Roll Along*. Steve is justifiably proud of the score for *Merrily*, and I guess he took issue with it being referred to as a flop (though it's hard to argue with the financial realities). The next day, Hal cut the *Merrily* marquee from the set and delayed the song's opening bars so they didn't overlap with the narration.

Working closely with Hal, and more peripherally with Steve, has been an honor for me; they're among my greatest professional heroes. The two remained very close friends—and friendly rivals—until Hal's death in July 2019. Steve's displeasure at *Prince of Broadway* mirrored a moment in 2010 when Hal had stormed out of *Sondheim on Sondheim*. On that occasion, Steve had asked that we remove the thing that had offended him. Hal was returning the favor.

Prince of Broadway settled into its final form, and just like that, my five-year odyssey was over.

I flew to the UK to tech *Young Frankenstein* as planned and—very sadly—missed opening night. As I've expressed elsewhere, I have mixed feelings about opening nights, but they do serve an important purpose in the peripatetic life of a theater artist. Like graduations or marriage ceremonies, they mark the end of one chapter and the beginning of the next. Consequently, I always want to be present even if I don't always enjoy myself. I'd tried to arrange a quick trip back to New York for the occasion but couldn't find a combination of flights that would work—the *Young Frankenstein* tech was not going smoothly (but that's another story).

The reviews were mixed, and maybe we shouldn't have been surprised. We were, after all, representing—and thus inviting comparison to—some legendary and beloved musicals. The shows that constituted *Prince of Broadway* had shaped musical theater as we know it, and their original productions burn brightly in the memories of many, including critics. Still . . . their response made me mad. Couldn't they let a ninety-year-old theatrical legend take his victory lap without being snide?

The plays we do are literature, they remain on the page long after the show has closed. But the art of staging those shows is ephemeral: it exists for a moment in time and then it's gone. The work of actors, designers, and directors is written on air. *Prince of Broadway* wasn't groundbreaking. It wasn't trying to be. It was a compilation of Hal's long and varied approach to the theater. It was an opportunity, before he left us, for a final visit to the imagination of a director who reshaped the American musical theater.

EIGHT

Prince's Tower

A Conversation with Harold Prince

Setting: *Hal Prince's office on the eleventh floor of a Rockefeller Center office building. The windows look over the plaza, the ice rink, the Christmas tree. Until the early 2010s, the name plate on the front door still read "George Abbott," Hal's own famous mentor with whom he shared the office until Abbott's death in 1995 at age 101. When you walk into the reception area you're greeted by posters of* West Side Story, Cabaret, Company, Evita, Phantom of the Opera, A Little Night Music . . . *followed by what feels like every significant twentieth-century production stretching on down the hall. It's more than a little overwhelming. The walls of Hal's office are covered with memorabilia as well: an original three-sheet from* Follies, *a Hirschfeld drawing of Hal, original signed sheet music from Sondheim, Kander and Ebb, and Lloyd Webber, photos of Hal with every president from Ford to Clinton, and hundreds of framed candids covering the director's seventy-year career. In short, it's everything you'd imagine—minus the twenty-one Tony awards he's received. He keeps those at home.*

BEOWULF BORITT: Hal, I want to talk about how a designer works with a director. Set design books don't focus on that, and as a designer, I think it's the most important part of the job.

HAL PRINCE: It's important for the director too. The reason that you and I work so closely when we're doing a show together—and that I work so closely with all designers—is I don't know how to direct a show until I see the set. I proved that once, with *Merrily We Roll Along*. I couldn't *see* it, so I couldn't *direct* it.

BB: Tell me about *Merrily*. How did that production unfold?

Merrily We Roll Along, by Stephen Sondheim and George Furth, based on a play by George S. Kaufman and Moss Hart, relates the story of three friends—Frank, Charley, and Mary—and how the challenges of being an artist test their idealism and ultimately destroy their friendship. After a prologue set at a high school graduation, the story jumps to its end, when Frank is a successful but alienated Hollywood producer. Scene by scene, the narrative then moves back in time, until the three young dreamers are found on the rooftop of their New York apartment, imagining the future. Hal Prince directed the Broadway production with choreography by Larry Fuller, sets by Eugene Lee, costumes by Judith Dolan, lighting by David Hersey, and sound by Jack Mann.

HP: Well, it started with my own very bad idea. [My wife] Judy said to me, "I wish you'd do a show about kids." I liked that idea, so I repeated it to Steve [Sondheim] and said, "I have this favorite play called *Merrily We Roll Along*." I was crazy about the structure of it, which has older people getting younger through the course of the story. Anyway, Steve liked it, so we went to George Furth, with whom we'd done *Company*, to write the book, and we embarked. My thought was to do it with kids. We follow what happened to them—backward—until they're back to their young selves.

The problem for me was that I had no vision for it. I had Eugene Lee designing, whom I worked with a lot, and he had no vision for it either. None. He's really a terrific designer, but he did a very bad set, very complicated, very unlike him. It was like a false gymnasium or something—really not right.

I called a meeting of my staff, which, in those days, was about eight people. I said, "The only way I know how to do this show visually is on an empty stage with a ghost light. The kids pull in a lot of costumes on racks and rifle through them for each new scene." The thing is, tickets cost twelve dollars! We had to give audiences something more than an empty stage.

BB: Twelve dollars?!

HP: Or whatever the price was; I can't tell you exactly. (*He buzzes the intercom answered by his assistant, Dan Kutner.*) Dan, can you tell me what a theater ticket cost in 1980?

So anyway, my staff said, "You do what you want to do! Do it exactly that way. It doesn't matter what tickets cost." Had I listened to them and done it that way, it might have worked. (*The intercom buzzes and Hal mutters for a moment.*) The average was thirty dollars a ticket.

BB: Still . . . cheap compared to now.

HP: The point is, we ended up planning a big production. Judy Dolan did the costumes, and she let her imagination fly. They were farcical—which was not a good idea. In the end, we threw them all out. I said, "Let's put sweatshirts on them and label them with who they are: 'Mistress,' 'First Wife,' and so on. In a way, that was approaching what I'd originally wanted to do.

BB: At what point did you decide on the sweatshirts?

HP: We were probably in tech. We didn't have an out-of-town tryout for *Merrily*.

BB: Really?

HP: Yes. Same with *Sweeney*. Fewer shows were going out of town in those days. My instinct was, it's working, the show is perfect, so why go out of town? It costs too much. I can see now that opening cold in New York was arrogant. Between my ineptitude and Eugene Lee's contribution, the whole production was too complicated. *Time* magazine ran a picture of Steve and me captioned, *The hope of the theater*. That spelled death right away. We'd had ten great years changing the theater, but the minute they say you're the hope of something—

BB: Everybody turns on you.

HP: That's what happened. First preview, everybody hated it. The audience did not come back for the second act. So we rolled up our sleeves and went to work. We did terrific work. I have a sneaky feeling that if we had come in with the show we ended up with four weeks later, when we opened, it would have gotten mixed but basically good reviews. The score was brilliant—one of Steve's best. The cast mostly was swell; Lonny Price was fantastic. It might never have been one of our biggest hits, but it could have been a hit. But after that first preview, every single gossip columnist immediately wrote about it and said it was a disaster. You can never get past that. I had flop-sweat every single night. It was like an incipient nervous breakdown. Daisy [Prince, Hal's daughter] was in it, and she'd come home at night and say to me, "Well, Daddy, we played the whole second act to an empty house."

BB: Rough.

HP: But the show still gets done today.

BB: I designed it once, a very small production. I've always loved the show. When people say this or that doesn't work about it, it always mystifies me. It's always worked for me.

HP: There is something in it that people really care about.

Boris Aronson was born in Kiev, in czarist Russia, in 1898. His first Broadway show was *Walk a Little Faster*, in 1932. His final Broadway design was *Pacific Overtures*, for Hal Prince in 1976. His seventy-six Broadway designs include the original productions of *Awake and Sing*, *Love Life*, *The Rose Tattoo*, *The Crucible*, *Bus Stop*, *A View from the Bridge*, *The Diary of Anne Frank*, *Fiddler on the Roof*, *Cabaret*, *Zorba*, *Company*, and *Follies*.

BB: We'll get back to Eugene Lee, but first I want to talk about Boris Aronson. Whenever you and I work together, I feel as if Boris is in the room.

HP: Boris was as much fun as anyone I've ever worked with. Him and Steve. Boris was flinty and difficult, and without Lisa [his wife], he would've been very difficult to work with. But with Lisa, everything was perfect. She interpreted for him, she scolded him in front of me. What I learned from Boris was to talk a lot. For six months before he did a design, I never knew whether he was working on anything. We rarely talked about architecture or visual things. We'd talk and talk about sensory things—smells and sounds of locations. I figured out that he was designing the whole time. Finally, he'd say, "OK, I'm ready to show it to you," and his design would always include a surprise. The mirror in *Cabaret*, for example.

BB: When we designed the *Cabaret* section of *Prince of Broadway*, Lisa asked me if we could have the mirror.

HP: I did *Cabaret* right after *Fiddler on the Roof*, which I produced and he designed. Jerry [Robbins] made his life hell during *Fiddler*. He was a great choreographer and an excellent director, but he was never articulate. He was besotted with pretentious things like the Actor's Studio, so he would direct by making the actors throw a baseball while they were doing a love scene, that sort of thing—to *free* them. When we'd all had enough, we pounced on him and said, "Stop all this now! Direct like you're a choreographer." And then he was brilliant. He knew what he liked, but he didn't know how to describe what he *didn't* like, so he'd drive designers insane. I don't know how many times Boris redesigned Tevye's house and that *roof.*

BB: Robbins had to see it, see the set onstage, before he knew if he liked it?

HP: Often. And as for costumes, he drove Florence Klotz insane too. Most of the time, he ended up with leotards of various colors.

BB: It's amazing how many directors are like that. It's not so uncommon.

HP: I didn't realize that.

BB: I want to talk about *Cabaret* because it seems to contain the root of a lot of ideas that you and Boris would develop. There's the abstracted cabaret with the weird mirror, but then there are realistic sets that slide in and out of it.

HP: The realistic sets disappeared from our later work together. We used them in *Cabaret* because I wanted it to be a success. I had never had a long-run success on Broadway. *She Loves Me* was as well directed as anything I'd ever do, but it didn't pay off its investment. I lost money. And I kept not having hits. By 1966, I decided I better have a hit or stop directing. I figured I better not abstract the stage too much, so we created two stages in one: the "real" one and the abstract "limbo" one. I could live with that.

Cabaret by Joe Masteroff, John Kander, and Fred Ebb takes place in and around a seedy cabaret in 1930s Berlin, where Sally Bowles, a performer, and Cliff Bradshaw pursue an erratic love affair. Outside the confines of the decadent club, the Nazis inexorably rise to power. Hal Prince directed the original Broadway production, with choreography by Ronald Field, sets by Boris Aronson, costumes by Patricia Zipprodt, and lighting by Jean Rosenthal.

BB: You and I have talked about limbo—essentially an empty stage—a lot. It's part of musical theater vocabulary now.

HP: *Cabaret* had two spiral staircases where the showgirls sat all evening and watched the show. That hadn't been done before.

Boris Aronson and Lisa Jalowetz's model for *Cabaret*: the club with its mirror and one of the realistic sets
Top: Boris Aronson and Lisa Jalowetz © Billy Rose Theatre Division, The New York Public Library for the Performing Arts;
Bottom: The collection of Douglas Colby

BB: Did you get a sense that people were aware of the innovation when they were watching it?

HP: I don't think people analyze; I think things come in subliminally. The apex of that whole experience had to do with the gorilla song. The emcee character waltzes lovingly with a gorilla in a dress, singing this love song, and the last line is, "If you could see her through my eyes, she wouldn't look *Jewish* at all." After the first preview, the audience stayed in the Broadhurst and argued about it. There must have been a hundred people arguing with a hundred others about that line. A lot of them were offended; they were not smart enough to realize what it really meant. So I said to Fred, "You're gonna change it! You're gonna change it because this show's gonna run." Fred was furious, but he changed it. The realistic wagons coming on and Cliff singing love songs to Sally, I felt we had to do all that conventional stuff. None of it was at the heart of the show, but we had to have that stuff as a safeguard.

BB: And it worked, I guess.

HP: By the time the movie was made, they could say, "wouldn't look Jewish at all"—so that went back in.

BB: A few years after *Cabaret*, Boris designed *Company* for you. That design feels current even today, and you left any vestiges of traditional box sets behind you. Was the design he first showed you for it—after all the usual talking—very close to what you ended up doing?

HP: Not *very close*; it was *exactly* what we ended up doing. Boris's surprise in *Company* was the elevator. That elevator, the feeling of a sleek glass skyscraper, was his metaphor for both the glamour and the dislocation of modern urban life.

BB: He designed *Follies* for you next.

HP: Yes. That stage pointing into the audience and the odd angle was just brilliant. All those levels.

BB: I used to look at pictures of Boris's set before I knew *Follies* well. I always thought, *It's a ghost story set in an old theater. Why didn't they just make a realistic empty theater?* Then I saw a production done just that way and realized that it doesn't work at all. Somehow the abstraction of your set allowed the ghosts and the real people to exist in the same space in a theatrical way.

Follies, by Stephen Sondheim and James Goldman, tells the story of two former Follies girls who, with their husbands, return to the decrepit Weismann Theatre for a reunion the night before the theater is to be destroyed. Old jealousies and old loves are rekindled, conjuring the "ghosts" of the four characters' younger selves. Ultimately, the action spirals into a mad reimag-ining of a Follies show—the "Loveland" sequence—as truth and high emotions surface. Hal Prince codirected the original production with Michael Bennett, who also choreographed, with sets by Boris Aronson, costumes by Florence Klotz, and lighting by Tharon Musser.

HP: The whole thing was informed by a photograph that I found of Gloria Swanson in the Roxy Theater. She had opened the Roxy in a movie called *The Love of Sunya* in 1927, and when they tore it down, she was still alive, still very glamorous. So *Life* magazine took her there, dressed in an evening gown, and she stood in the rubble.

BB: Like the musical, it's got both the crumbling present and the memory of a glam-orous past.

HP: When I agreed to do the show, it was called *The Girls Upstairs*. I renamed it *Follies* and put in the ghosts.

BB: They were not part of the original?

HP: No. The whole thing was a realistic party with a bunch of people who'd met in a theater that was going to be torn down the next day. They got drunk and started to fight. Then everybody sobered up and went home. It was a very different show. There was no "Loveland" section. The big change was when I said, "Let's have the four alter egos—the kids—and the four older people they've turned into suddenly come onstage and yell at one another, circle one another—and then go into the 'Loveland' Follies section."

BB: When I was researching *Prince of Broadway*, Lisa Aronson told me that the first version of the "Loveland" set was Art Nouveau, but at the last minute you said, "That's wrong, it should be a valentine!"

HP: I don't remember that, but we worked very well together.

BB: Let's move on to *Evita*. It had relatively little scenery, but you once told me it was the best piece of directing you ever did.

HP: For sure. My best directing. Andrew [Lloyd Webber] and Tim [Rice] brought me the initial idea. I listened to just the opening and I said *yes* right away. A scene with two hundred thousand people at a funeral? I thought, *I don't know how to do that, but I gotta do it.* A year and a half later, they brought me the concept album. I pulled out the lyrics, which were on four pieces of slick paper inside the album cover. I asked Arty [Masella, Hal's assistant at the time] to come in and I dictated a script, probably no more than twenty pages. I specified how each scene should be done with each lyric. That suggested each new set to me.

One of the first things I thought of was for the song "Goodnight and Thank You." I came up with the idea of a revolving door. Eva is in a crappy dressing gown, and then she's in a lot of feathers, and so on, getting fancier. She keeps turning the door, and guys keep coming out: sergeants, then generals . . . she's sleeping her way to the top.

Evita is Andrew Lloyd Webber and Tim Rice's dramatic political musical of the charismatic Eva Perón (Evita) and her husband, Argentine president Juan Perón. It charts Eva's rise from the slums to the halls of power and culminates in her death. The story is narrated by a man named Che, an everyday Argentinian. Hal directed the original Broadway production with choreography by Larry Fuller; sets, costumes, and projections by Timothy O'Brien and Tazeena Firth; lighting by David Hersey; and sound by Abe Jacob.

BB: I'm too young to have seen it, though I've seen snippets on YouTube. Was there an actual revolving door onstage?

HP: Yes. It was . . . what do you call it when furniture is puffy?

BB: Tufted?

HP: It was a tufted door. Anyway, I went through the lyrics figuring out, "How do we do this scene? How do we do the next scene?" And when I'd gotten all twenty pages together, I looked at the whole thing and saw that there was a scene missing. We hadn't given Perón the stage. We hadn't made it as clear as we should that Evita is looking around for who to hitch her star to. Who is her *Donald Trump*?

BB: Ouch.

HP: She sees this colonel and thinks, "He's gonna run this country someday." So she arranges to meet him "by chance" in a theater.

BB: Right.

HP: Next question was, what's the setting for this new number? I thought about it and said, "Why don't we have musical chairs? Write me a number where there are five rocking chairs and five colonels, generals, whatever. Chairs keep being taken away

Evita: "The Art of the Possible." Set design by Timothy O'Brien and Tazeena Firth
Martha Swope, ©Billy Rose Theatre Division, The New York Public Library for the Performing Arts

until finally there's only one left. One person. He tips his hat back, puffs some smoke out, and you see that it's Perón. To go with the sequence, the guys wrote "The Art of the Possible"—a wonderful lyric to go with a wonderful idea.

BB: It stemmed from a staging and furniture idea?

HP: Yes. The whole show was abstracted from the get-go. But when Timothy O'Brien and Tazeena Firth had finished the *Evita* design, I still thought it was missing something. Around that time, I was in Mexico with Judy, on vacation. We went to the palace in Mexico City, where the Siqueiros collection is, along with the work of a lot of other painters, including Diego Rivera. I bought a huge book of images from the collection and brought it back and gave it to the designers. "This is what the proscenium should look like," I told them. "It should be masses of oligarchs and peasants, brutality, banality, happiness—everything." They created it, and the set was finished.

BB: It was basically empty inside that, right? Things came and went as needed for the scenes but there was no "set" filling the space?

HP: Empty.

BB: I didn't know *Evita* until I saw a recent revival. To be honest, I didn't understand what I was watching. It seemed like a weird costume drama with a big, heavy, architectural set. I was so confused that I went on YouTube that night and found clips of your production. Then I understood what the show could be: theatrical and political.

HP: That revival was the worst. Terrible.

BB: People often do these big, heavy, realistic productions of musicals. I guess sometimes it can work, but usually it just kills the piece.

HP: You want a lot of air. You want a lot of blank spaces. You want the audience to be complicit in the production—to fill in the blank spots. No two people will imagine the same wallpaper or furniture, but they'll be participating. That's key to what I do.

BB: That's a good segue into *Phantom of the Opera*. You've described it to me as a "black box show," and I used to think that was ridiculous. But conceptually it is. Even scenes that seem very full of scenery are, for example, just a big staircase full of costumed characters set against black. But I don't think anyone watching it sees it that way.

Maria Björnson's set model for *Phantom of the Opera*
Maria Björnson (Photo used by kind permission of The Maria Bjornson Archive and Redcase Limited)

HP: Never. They think they're seeing so much scenery, they can't believe it. If they realized how little scenery it was, they'd be shocked.

BB: Yes.

Maria Björnson was born in Paris in 1949 and died tragically young in 2002. She worked primarily in London and internationally, designing 120 projects. Among her shows were many operas and ballets, including a skewed-perspective *Sleeping Beauty* for London's Royal Ballet, which inspired me personally as a graduate student. Her three Broadway designs included two shows by Andrew Lloyd Webber—*Phantom of the Opera* and *Aspects of Love*—and a production *of Cat on a Hot Tin Roof* that opened posthumously.

HP: One thing that influenced the design was knowing that we were going into Her Majesty's Theatre in London. It was the only theater there that still had its Victorian stage machinery. They oiled it up and so on, and we used it to make the candles come up from the basement. When we came to Broadway, everything was mechanized at the push of a button. I looked at the candles coming up and said, "That's very unexciting. What the hell's going on?" In London, the candles were in three rows, cranked individually, and they didn't come up exactly in sync. So we purposely mistimed them in New York.

BB: It's amazing when you have to make a machine intentionally less precise to make it feel more human—but it happens all the time.

HP: Maria Björnson was a terrific designer.

BB: You hadn't worked with her before, had you?

HP: Never, and never again either. Cameron had sent me the work of lots of designers and I picked her based on a set design she'd done for Ibsen—*The Wild Duck*, I think. She'd done it with spare wooden walls and glass windows and I thought, *She could do this show.*

We worked together on it for a year. I flew to London regularly, and she flew to New York a couple of times. Once I went all the way over there just to see a mock-up of one segment of the proscenium. I wanted the proscenium to be fiercely erotic. I wanted sexual mayhem on that proscenium. I knew the audience would never notice it but that it would register in some weird way.

BB: There's incredible craft in it.

HP: You know . . . a lot of people hate *Phantom*. They hate it because it's banal to them; because Andrew Lloyd Webber wrote it, so it can't be that good. And, you know, I don't prize it myself, as I do so much of my work, including Andrew's *Evita*. I don't prize it that way. What I see when I look at it is the apex of experience. I admire Andrew for doing three operas inside the show for an audience that doesn't know what the fuck they're looking at. They don't know they're seeing *Aida*, seeing Mozart . . . and God knows they don't know they're seeing Stockhausen. I think there are holes all over the place in *Phantom*, but I don't dwell on them. It all ends with a mask on a throne and a little girl holding it up, and I think that's right.

BB: Ultimately, this is the magic of what we do. Even when the most accomplished people put a show together, there's no guarantee that the recipe's going to work. Things that should work don't and, and things that shouldn't work do.

HP: Exactly right. I had no idea when we opened *Phantom* in London that it would be a success. I knew the day after *Evita* first previewed that it would be historic. But, guess what? *Phantom* is the one that's been running thirty years—and that's kind of amazing.

BB: Obviously, it touches something in people.

HP: Every once in a while, someone says, "I really love *Phantom*," and I'm shocked. I think a lot of people don't even know I directed it. But I'm proud of the stagecraft that went into *Phantom*. The audience doesn't get that, though. They get that when she kisses him, it's very romantic. But you know what actually informs it? *The Elephant Man*. The whole show works for me based on the fact that every time we see a person who's deformed, we recoil. Then we hate ourselves for recoiling. That's the nuts and bolts of why *Phantom* works.

BB: It's *Beauty and the Beast*.

HP: It is, and talk about homage. I couldn't forget those arms with the candelabra in Jean Cocteau's *Beauty and the Beast*. I didn't use them, but I certainly kept thinking of them.

BB: That must have informed all the writhing bodies in the proscenium, the demons grabbing the girls' breasts?

HP: Yes.

BB: Speaking of demons grabbing girls, I read recently that Donald Trump considers *Phantom of the Opera* his second-favorite show. *Evita* is his favorite.

HP: I didn't know that. But I'll tell you a Donald Trump story. On the third night of previews, before *Phantom* opened on Broadway, the audience was pouring out and Donald and Ivana Trump went by and I heard this voice say, "Hal, Hal! It's Donald!" I'd never met the man before in my life. Then he said, "Ivana, this is Hal!" I said, "Is this the first time you're seeing the show?" He made a big deal of it. "Is this the first?! No, we saw it in London! And we saw it last night!" "Really?" I said. "Well . . . that's wonderful. Now I must be going." As I walked away, he called out, "Hal! Ivana and I are so proud of you."

BB: Since we're talking about demons . . . let me jump to *Sweeney Todd*. That's an iconic set.

HP: Very simple.

Eugene Lee was born in 1939 in Beloit, Wisconsin. His first Broadway design was for *Wilson in the Promise Land* at the ANTA Playhouse in 1970. His twenty-seven Broadway designs include Hal Prince's productions of *Candide*, *Sweeney Todd*, *Merrily We Roll Along*, and *Show Boat*. He also designed the original productions of *Ragtime*, *Wicked*, and *Bright Star*. He has been the production designer of *Saturday Night Live* since the show's 1975 premiere.

BB: In its way. But it was enormous! Eugene Lee carted a real factory into the theater and reassembled it!

HP: I'm not a vengeful person. I don't understand vengeance exactly. I know it's the most theatrical thing in the world, but it's creepy to me. The show had a vengeful central character and a lot of chorus. But what are the chorus members doing? Very little. They sing "City on Fire." They sing "Attend the Tale of Sweeney Todd." But what joins them all? Eugene and I were talking about this, and I thought, *Maybe they're joined together by working in a factory*. Maybe they're vengeful, too, because they have to work eighteen hours on an assembly line. It's the beginning of the Industrial Age, and there's too much smoke in the air. It gets in their lungs. They're all suffocating from whatever comes out of the chimneys. They never see grass. The factory has filthy windows, so they never see the sky. So they're all vengeful. They share a sense of revenge that Sweeney feels because of the way he lost his wife.

Sweeney Todd, a Stephen Sondheim/Hugh Wheeler musical, tells the story of a Victorian barber who returns home to London after many years in a penal colony. Sweeney seeks revenge on Judge Turpin, who falsely convicted him and caused the death of his young wife, the object of Turpin's lust. Sweeney opens a barbershop over a pie shop owned by Mrs. Lovett, and the two commence a spree of murdering local citizens and baking them into meat pies—which develop an enthusiastic following. Sweeney ultimately exacts his revenge . . . and then the tragic truth comes to light. Hal directed the original production, with choreography by Larry Fuller, sets by Eugene Lee, costumes by Franne Lee, and lighting by Ken Billington.

BB: As you describe it, it's the same idea you had for your *Evita* proscenium. You were pointing out the hierarchy within the society. I often try to do that in a design. Whether there are six actors onstage or twenty, the physical space around them can further populate the story, imply a wider world. It's exciting when you can make it work.

HP: Exactly.

BB: It was such a smart idea. My absolute best ideas come in a flash of lightning—a eureka moment. I'm pondering something, my mind moves on to something else, and suddenly the answer is there. It feels like God provided it, but I guess it's really the power of the subconscious.

HP: Over my lifetime, I've learned that if I envision the problem in my head when I go to sleep, it's solved in the morning when I wake up. I've come to rely on that.

BB: It's magical when it happens and frustrating when it doesn't.

HP: Steve gave me a very Steve-like moment in *Sweeney* when he wrote "More Hot Pies" for the opening of the second act. He said, "There are twenty tables all over the set and everybody is singing a different lyric that is personal to them." "They're all singing at the same time?" I asked, and he nodded. I thought, *We can't do that. Nobody's going to hear what they're singing about.* It was a brilliant puzzle that only Steve could create. I went to bed thinking about it, and in the morning, I had it. There would be one long table with everyone sitting around it. Toby would keep bringing the pies out. That long table organized the number. I solved that problem in my sleep.

BB: That long table created a structure for you to stage within. My experience, in working with you, is that once we get the set right, it seems to answer a lot of the questions you have about how you're going to direct the show.

HP: The set determines how the scenes will move. It becomes the motor of the show. We should talk about the work you and I have done together.

BB: I owe a lot of my career to having met you at Lincoln Center twenty years ago.

Ming Cho Lee was born in 1930 in Shanghai, China. His first Broadway design was for *The Moon Besieged* in 1962 at the Lyceum Theater, and his final Broadway design was for Emily Mann's *Execution of Justice* at the Virginia Theater in 1986. His twenty-four Broadway sets include the original productions of *K2*, *for colored girls who have considered suicide / when the rainbow is enuf*, and *All God's Chillun Got Wings*. He designed productions of *King Lear*, *Two Gentlemen of Verona*, *Much Ado about Nothing*, *Caesar and Cleopatra*, and *Romeo and Juliet*. However, his most lasting impact on the theater may be that he taught design at Yale Drama School from 1969 to 2017 and influenced generations of young designers.

HP: I think we should talk about that. Ming's Clambake. They don't do it anymore, but the Clambake was the best place in the world to find a brilliant designer. And guess what? I never saw many directors there. I'd see designers there, all wanting to tell the next generation what they were doing wrong. I'm sure you spoke with some of them. But I never saw many directors or producers.

BB: You're the only director I met there—at least the only one who ever hired me! You gave a young designer a chance. I guess George Abbott did that for you when you were young?

HP: Yes. George Abbott taught me discipline right away. You're very disciplined. Abbott taught me that the theater is a job, and that I should be disciplined and listen. He didn't teach me his taste, though. Our taste wasn't remotely the same.

BB: No?

HP: I learned the profession from him. I learned to express myself from Lyubimov and Meyerhold, and then Boris: to have the guts to put on the stage what may seem disconnected.

BB: You made a great disconnected moment when we did *LoveMusik*. Late in the show, Kurt Weill's suitcase fell open, the contents spilled out, and he walked away, leaving it all on the stage. Somehow, we understood that meant he had died.

HP: That's Judy's favorite moment that I ever directed. Ever.

BB: As I recall, you came up with it early in the process. I kept thinking, "Hal's crazy. That doesn't make any sense. Why is that suitcase going to suddenly fall open?" But I was smart enough to keep my mouth shut and make you a suitcase rigged to burst open magically. The first time I saw the moment staged, I thought, *That's brilliant.* Where did that idea come from?

HP: It came from thinking about what happens when a person dies. I'm eighty-eight now. I feel about forty, but who knows how long I'll feel like that? Every once in a while, I walk into my home office, with the Tonys and all the letters and design renderings, everything. It's macabre, but I think, *When I go, the kids are gonna take what they want. The letters are worth something because of the signatures; maybe·they'll sell them. But certainly, my stuff won't be kept together.* What do you do with it all? Do you send it to the Performing Arts Library? Do you send it to the Library of Congress? What do you do with all this shit that meant so much to a person? I've always thought, *It'll just dissolve out into the world.*

BB: So . . . that's the stuff falling out of the suitcase—it was really wonderful. It's so simple. It's not realistic, yet it completely defines what's happening.

HP: I loved everything in that show. The only thing I would change is that I'd cut back even more—make it even simpler. I loved your red stage.

BB: I was terrified the day I showed you the red set for *LoveMusik*. It was one of those flash-of-inspiration moments. I saw that red in some Weimar art and painted the set all red. I figured, *Either Hal's going to love this or he's going to fire me today.*

HP: I more than loved it.

BB: It pushed us into a less real, more theatrical space.

HP: You know, I think I'm a good director. I don't think anybody knows more about the empty space than I do. I'll tell you something that happened when I went to Moscow three weeks ago. I've never experienced it in this country or even in England. They knew all about everything I've ever done, every production I've ever directed. Every director there, every manager, came and made a fuss over me. It was shocking.

BB: I worked in Russia once. Their cultural reverence for art—theater, painting, dance, all art—I've never experienced anything like it. I've traveled a fair amount of the world at this point and it amazed me how Russians revere art in an almost religious way.

HP: For a week I felt like an important director; an international director. I went to the Meyerhold Museum while I was there. His granddaughter wrote to me years ago, saying, "I understand you work like my grandfather. Could I beseech you to send a few dollars? We're trying to make their apartment into a museum." I sent a couple hundred dollars. When I got to the Meyerhold Museum, they treated me like I was family, and I thought, *This is the place where I feel I made a historical contribution*. But . . . when I die, I can tell you what the headline will say: *Twenty-One Tony Awards!*

BB: We want to quantify things in this country, to measure them in some way. The show that's run the longest or made the most money or won the most Tony Awards is what makes you the king.

HP: That's bullshit.

BB: Says the guy with twenty-one Tonys! But you're right, Americans don't seem to have the same reverence for the theater's history.

HP: It shows such an absence of appreciation for the history of the art form you work in. Everybody wants to work in the theater, but they don't want to learn about it. As a kid, I haunted the library on Forty-Second Street. I'd go in and say, "I want the Norman Bel Geddes," and the sweet lady would bring me all the Norman Bel Geddes books. I'd say, "I'd like the Barrymore family," and she'd bring me all the scrapbooks. I knew who Ina Claire was. I knew who Rouben Mamoulian was—one of the most brilliant directors who ever lived. You say the name "Rouben Mamoulian" to a class of directors now, they don't know who you're talking about.

BB: Theater is an ephemeral art form. It exists for a moment in time; then it's gone, except for the literature, the texts.

HP: Why are people not infatuated with the history of it? Steve Sondheim studied with Milton Babbitt. He knows every bit of the history of music. Boris studied with

Aleksandra Ekster in Moscow, and one of his great strengths was painting. He was a wonderful painter. I learned from the best. I read all their books: Meyerhold, Lyubimov, Brecht. Brecht didn't influence me as much—I never quite got him, but I certainly respected him. I've been as influenced by some films as by stage. German film, the Weimar films: *Dr. Mabuse* and Fritz Lang's *M*. Murnau was a great, great director who influenced me a lot. So did Orson Welles. Everybody wants to be successful and famous, and nobody wants to figure out what the building blocks were to create a career.

BB: I don't know how you make something new if you don't know what you're building on. Even if you then want to throw out the old stuff, it's good to understand what it was before you throw it out. Speaking of early influences, do you have a memory of when you first became aware of stage design?

HP: When I saw *Julius Caesar* done by the Mercury Theater, I was besotted by that Norman Bel Geddes set. Then I saw Bel Geddes's set for *The Eternal Road*. I also thought Jo Mielziner was a spectacular designer. What he did for *Streetcar* was incredible. I love design.

BB: Did you ever work with Mielziner? He's my biggest design hero. His renderings are so beautifully evocative.

HP: I never worked with him—he was the generation before me. I was in the same room with him though, when I went to the Rodgers' holiday parties. They always included a few kids: me, Steve Sondheim, and Burt Shevelove. In that living room were John Steinbeck, Rouben Mamoulian, Josh Logan, Moss Hart, and Kitty Carlisle.

Jo Mielziner's design for *A Streetcar Named Desire*

Jo Mielziner: courtesy of the estate of Jo Mielziner/ © Billy Rose Theatre Division, The New York Public Library for the Performing Arts

BB: Wow. How did that feel? I vividly remember the first time I went to *your* Christmas party. I was thrilled and terrified.

HP: That's exactly how I felt.

BB: I hid in the corner most of the time and watched!

HP: Our Christmas party is a result of who I married. Judy had experienced the Hollywood version of it. Her folks were very intellectual, way over on the left politically. Their living room was always full of great composers, great artists, writers—a lot of people who got blacklisted. When Judy and I married, we resurrected that at Christmastime. Every time we have the party, I feel like it's part of a continuum.

BB: I feel so lucky to be included.

HP: I can't wait for you to write this book. I love that you're doing it. You might want to consider making your last chapter a prediction of what might happen in the theater. I'm so damn curious about what the future will bring.

NINE

Plumbing and Poetry

Designing *Meteor Shower* for Jerry Zaks

Does the Plumber Care What the Faucet Means?

I was at Hudson Scenic checking in on the scenery build for *Prince of Broadway* when my phone rang. The caller ID said Jerry Zaks.

"Moishe," he said. Jerry calls everyone *Moishe*—his equivalent of "buddy" or "pal." "Moishe, I know you're busy, but I've got a new Broadway play going up in October. Are you available?"

A Broadway play with Jerry Zaks? Even if I wasn't available, I'd be available.

When I was in college in the 1990s, Jerry—J.Z.—was the toast of Broadway. In the span of a few years, I saw his original productions of *Lend Me a Tenor,* one of the funniest plays I've ever seen; *Six Degrees of Separation*, one of the most compelling dramas I've ever seen; and *Guys and Dolls,* a stunning revival of an almost perfect musical comedy. After seeing my set for *Act One*, J.Z. asked me to design *A Bronx Tale* for him. It was a great experience, and I was eager for another.

"It's a new play," he explained. "It's got some challenges scenically, but I think you can figure them out. I'm still working out my deal so it could still fall through—but there are worse things than working with Steve Martin and Amy Schumer."

It didn't fall through, and I signed on happily. The play was *Meteor Shower*, an absurdist comedy by Steve Martin. As a child I'd loved Steve's *Saturday Night Live* shtick, and as an adult I loved his thoughtful plays and novels. I was excited by the opportunity to work with him, but—J.Z. was right—the play had its distinct challenges.

The story unfolds in and around an upscale home in Ojai, California, during a meteor shower. The action moves rapidly—cinematically—from one place to another around the house and yard and, in the play's climactic moment (spoiler alert), a meteor slams into a character sitting on an outdoor lounge chair.

J.Z. and I both felt this cataclysmic act was better imagined than seen. Blood and gore onstage can easily devolve into unconvincing, embarrassing special effects. That meant the exterior scene had to disappear seconds before the meteor strike. This quick cut and others throughout the evening necessitated a set that could shift swiftly and elegantly. J.Z. also made it clear that he didn't want a conventional star backdrop for the night sky; he wanted something more magical.

The play was set in 1993, exactly twenty-five years prior to when we were producing it. The home in question was meant to be very fashionable; a character refers to it as worthy of *Architectural Digest*. This, in itself, was tricky. Anything that was fashionable twenty-five years ago is likely to seem outmoded, even ridiculous, in the present. (In fifty years, it might seem iconic—as "midcentury" pieces do today.)

J.Z. and I met with Steve to explore whether that 1993 date was important to him. As his hair has been white since he was a young man, Steve looked very much as he had in his *Saturday Night Live* days—but in person he was anything but "wild and crazy." In fact, he was so utterly shy and polite that I began to wonder how he managed to access that famously antic persona. As for the 1993 time frame of the story, he made it clear that it *was* important; apparently, there had been an actual meteor shower in California that year, and he liked that point of accuracy. That's a playwright's prerogative, and we didn't question it further.

I set to work. The space had to transform from interior to exterior over a short span of time, and it had to represent period style over an inconvenient span of time.

J.Z., with his (almost) eternally smiling face and full head of snow-white hair, has a quality of a vaudeville performer: he's always "on," always in motion and ready with a joke. For our first design meeting, I didn't bring any materials. We just chatted about the play, which begins as a seemingly conventional domestic comedy about a dinner party and then veers into the absurd via several surreal twists. We quickly agreed that the style of the physical production had to be conventional, almost "sitcom," so that the surreal elements would be genuinely surprising. "But," J.Z. added, "I want a little hint in the design that something unconventional is coming."

I like abstract scenery but pride myself on being able to do realism when it's called for—as any designer should. (That's one reason I selected this production for inclusion here.) One challenge of realistic stage design is proper scaling of the spaces. The setting, be it a living room or house exterior, must appear to be the right size as its inhabitants move around in it. An average Broadway stage is about forty feet

Designing an exterior and an interior to fill the same proscenium area can lead to a very grand interior and fairly modest exterior.

wide, which can make for a pretty grand living room but a pretty small house. I'm sure you've seen your share of overlarge interiors and dollhouse-seeming exteriors. And keep in mind that human-sized doors and windows—through which the actors move and can be seen—must be incorporated, whatever the overall scale. It's easy for the proportions to fall out of balance, and unhappy compromises between the needs of the actors and the look of their surroundings can turn everything ugly fast. For that reason, I keep matters of scale constantly in mind as I develop my models. Even a 10 percent increase or decrease in size can throw off the overall proportions and make a set look clumsy.

Once J.Z. and I had discussed some of these challenges, we turned our attention to the meteor shower of the title and the night sky that featured prominently in the script. I spoke conceptually about the cosmos as a metaphor for marriage, musing that maybe the husband and wife are like two celestial bodies locked in a gravitational dance. Before I could wax on about attraction and repulsion, J.Z. stopped me and said, "Save all that nonsense for your interview with the *New York Times*, Moishe. I'm a plumber, not a poet."

I laughed but took his meaning. Metaphors and metaphysics could wait while we figured out how to make this quirky play flow swiftly and effectively from start to finish. And what J.Z. said about himself really isn't true. He creates wonderfully poetic productions precisely because he keeps his laser focus on the physical particulars, making sure every moment leads to the next like clockwork. The mechanics of putting a play together—the craft that results in seamless, consistent storytelling—is less glamorous than the artistic ideas behind a production, but these nuts and bolts are essential. Art and craft must be present in equal measure. So bear with me as this chapter focuses more on the plumbing than the poetry.

Reinventing the Faucet

I was intrigued by J.Z.'s request for a nontraditional star wall. A frequent challenge for a set designer is how to make a confined space—the stage—feel like an infinite one. Nothing seems more artificial than seeing an actor's shadow fall across your "sky." I spend a lot of time attempting to create the illusion of depth onstage.

Years before I tackled *Meteor Shower*, while working on a show, I visited the Milwaukee Art Museum and saw an installation called *Walk-In Infinity Chamber* (1968) by Stanley Landsman. It consisted of a small room lined with black mirrors. Tiny points of light reflected infinitely in every direction, resulting in the same effect you get when you stand between two mirrors and see your reflection repeated endlessly into the distance. I was struck by the image and filed it away in my brain for possible use onstage one day. Maybe this was the day.

I got a piece of two-way mirror, the kind you can see through but that is reflective on one side. I put some tiny light bulbs under it, put a mirror behind the lights, and boxed in the sides so no other light could get in. My little contraption worked just as I wanted it to: the lights were reflected infinitely in the back mirror, creating the illusion of great depth. It was rough, but a good approximation of the idea I was after.

I quickly made a quarter-inch scale model and put the infinity box behind it to show J.Z. I like beginning in quarter-inch scale because I can make a model very quickly when it's so small. It's like a quick sketch of an idea that I can later refine, without the kind of details that can bog me down.

I prefaced my presentation by telling J.Z. I'd never done anything like it and that we'd probably need to make several mock-ups in full size to see if it would really work. He thought the infinity wall was weird, wonderful, and worth pursuing.

As I began to build a more refined, half-inch scale model, I realized that the "stars" all reflected in a straight line, making it look a bit like the view from a *Star Wars* spaceship going into light speed. I tried angling the back mirror so that the infinity effect could tilt up or down, but that didn't quite solve it. Next, I broke the back mirror into multiple smaller ones and placed them at a variety of angles, sort of like a corrugated roof. The lights still reflected in lines, but because each one hit the mirror at a different angle, the effect felt more like a starry sky.

Stanley Landsman (American, 1930–1984).
Walk-In Infinity Chamber, 1968
Courtesy the Milwaukee Art Museum

Infinity mirror effect

Initial rough model for *Meteor Shower*

It was time to ask a shop to build a portion of my "infinity chamber" at full scale. As I understood physics, scaling the thing up wouldn't alter the overall effect—but I wasn't sure how it would look and feel at full size.

Model with the back reflective surface broken into pieces so the lights hit it at a variety of angles

Bill Mensching and ShowMotion, who'd built *Act One*, had been hired to build the set. Our producer, Joey Parnes, liked them, and their price was reasonable, so they got the gig without having to go through a competitive bidding process. Bill always seems to know—or is curious enough to figure out—just the right technical solution to any weird artistic challenge.

The shop quickly made a mock-up. The cost to build the whole infinity wall, which would be twenty-five feet tall and fifty feet wide, would eat up about half of my set budget, so I had to make sure it would be worth it. I saw immediately that it would. Even with the angled mirrors, there was a bit of a *Star Wars* effect—but the illusion of depth was stunning. Joey's reaction was, "I've never seen anything like this. It's great! Dammit, now I have to pay for it!"

The shop had also come up with a clever idea for the meteors that had to fly across the sky. I had asked for single LEDs hung on weights and released down a zipline in front of the two-way mirror. (If it were upstage of the mirror, the meteors would reflect infinitely, which we didn't want.) A black scrim downstage of the meteors would hide the ziplines. This old-school mechanical approach would work, but it would be cumbersome. Resetting the weights and lights back at the top of the ziplines for each performance would be labor-intensive, and on Broadway that means expensive.

ShowMotion came up with an alternative involving very high-resolution LED tape (144 LEDs per meter, RBG) that could be programmed to create convincing shooting stars with fading "tails." I was delighted! Instead of a finite number of lights on weights, we could create as many meteors as we wanted. It looked great in action, and when it was turned off, the scrim effectively hid the LED tape. In fact, we discovered that as long as it was black, almost any object could be hidden inside the infinity box. The structure of the final set was composed of two-inch by two-inch steel, but inside the mirrors and behind the scrim, it was invisible to the audience. It was "smoke and mirrors" at its best!

Another improvement Bill proposed was to fracture the upstage mirror even more than I'd suggested. I'd asked for a series of four-foot-tall mirrors fashioned into a corrugated wall stretching the length of the stage. Instead, the shop proposed a tiled wall of seventy-two mirrored pyramids with their apexes pointing toward the audience. Each pyramid would fracture the reflection into four separate planes. The lines receded in so many directions that the effect was of a random, infinite starry sky. After much experimentation and tinkering, we really achieved something poetic.

Finally, I paired a full-stage voile drop with the scrim. The double layer of fabrics—black scrim and black voile—helped keep objects downstage from being reflected in

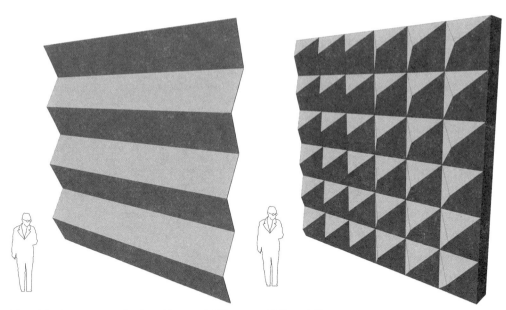

My original "corrugated" mirror idea and Bill's pyramid tile solution

the mirrors. When two scrims are placed one on top of the other, tiny air movements can make the weaves "ripple," creating a moiré effect. People can find this disconcerting—it can even make some feel seasick—so it's not something you want onstage. But scrim hung against voile, a fabric with a much finer weave, minimizes the moiré effect while doubling the density of the masking.

We were ready to build the full-size infinity wall and bring it to the theater.

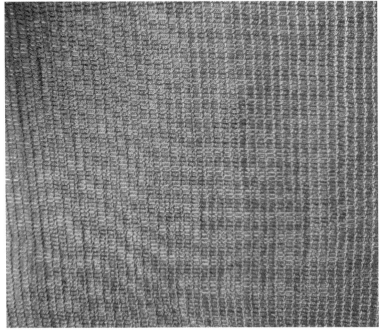

Two similar weaves causing a moiré effect

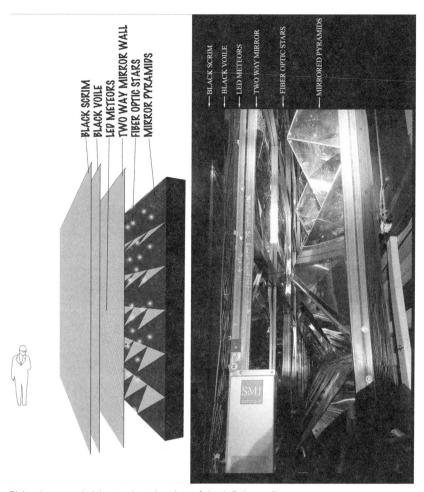

Side photo and side section drawing of the infinity wall

Is the Faucet Passé?

The play's time period continued to worry me. It's easy to make twenty-five years ago look silly. It's hard to make it look elegant.

I've written elsewhere in the book about the fact that it's more important to me that a set have the correct emotional feel than perfect historical accuracy—if I have to choose. I try not to shackle myself slavishly to precise visual history. But in this case, I understood that evoking the specific year was important to Steve, so I did more thorough research than I might ordinarily, hoping I'd find a 1993 look that could feel elegant in 2017. On eBay, I found a year's worth of 1993 *Architectural Digests* as well as a 1992 book called *Showcase of Interior Design: Pacific Edition.* Jackpot! It's rare to find a book that so exactly matches what you're looking for.

Much of what I saw in the book and magazines felt embarrassingly unfashionable—but some of it didn't. I love 1920s architecture, and there was a lot of Spanish Colonial design that predated our period but had been attractively updated for the '90s. A classic look like that might crack the twenty-five-year curse. J.Z. liked the idea, which felt very "California" to us East Coasters. But Steve thought Spanish Colonial was too old-fashioned for his style-conscious characters.

Back to the books.

My next find was a very spare modernist home built in LA in the early '90s, all clean white walls, sleek stone floor, and beautiful stained-wood accents. It looked elegant and it could have been 1960 or 2017 as easily as 1993. Steve liked it. I had a winner.

The difficulty of putting sleek modernism onstage is that the craftsmanship must be meticulous. Busy wallpaper, textured stucco, and molding can hide the seams of flats, joints, and other sins, but the look I'd chosen involved sleek, textureless plaster walls and a minimum of detail. Nothing would be camouflaged, so the construction had to be perfect.

There wouldn't be a lot of set dressing in our sleek, simple room either—and that is often what cements the sense of realism. Clutter implies a lived-in, *real*

1990s style that didn't age well
Patti McConville/Alamy Stock Photo

Spanish Colonial
Patti McConville/Alamy Stock Photo

space, and that provides a sense of drama inside the proscenium. Oddly, in real life the converse is true. A simple, modern, empty living space is inherently dramatic, precisely because it *is* lived in but doesn't feel like it. Sparseness in real life feels like a set, while sleek, empty sets feel like scenery, undermining the reality one is attempting to suggest.

To address the challenge, I broke things up as much as I could. Instead of erecting three simple walls to define the room, I broke the set into many smaller facets. I pierced the walls with doors, windows, and stairs. I added carefully selected artwork and every kind of hardware that might plausibly adorn a living room. I continued to add things all the way through tech: light switches, electrical outlets, a phone jack, a thermostat, a smoke detector, several wall sconces, several heating vents, and a stainless-steel banister. None of this stuff was earth-shattering; much of it probably went unnoticed; but it all added up to enough detail to make the room feel real.

I still faced the problem of making sure that both the interior and exterior sets filled the proscenium space while remaining in proportion. I played with how the elements I needed (sofa, chair, lounge chairs, front door, back door, exits to the kitchen and the upstairs) might fit onto one or more turntables and, after a lot of false starts,

Meteor Shower interior model

Meteor Shower exterior model

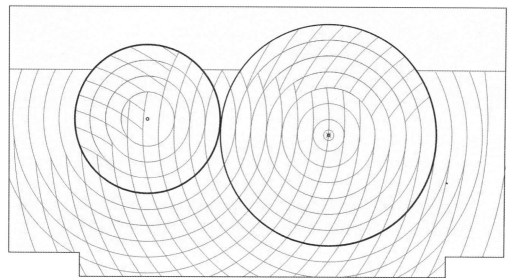

Black arboron deck painted gloss black with very fine grey overspray.
Lines routed with 1/16" V-groove. Grooves painted white.

Meteor Shower deck pattern

I had the basic layout of the set. The interior, appropriately scaled for a room, would have empty black space around it. But when the turntables revolved to the exterior scene, the set would fill more of the proscenium and skew toward stage right, where it would trail into darkness—implying that there was more house in that direction.

I planned an elegant, black stone floor that would work for both sets and was polished enough to reflect the stars and meteors. To disguise the edges of the turntables, I came up with a complicated stone pattern consisting of two sets of concentric rings. More important—to me, anyway—the design evoked the intersecting orbits of celestial objects. Plumbing be damned; I was going to sneak in a nod to my metaphor of married people as planets orbiting each other!

Sadly, the orbit pattern didn't make it into the final design. It wasn't that expensive, but it did cost money, and my infinity wall had gobbled up a lot of the budget. On top of that, as we'd worked out the details of the house, J.Z. had thrown me an expensive curveball. He wanted the entire set to exit the stage in the final moments of the show, leaving the actors alone in front of the magnificent star wall. Another major challenge.

To strike the entire set, the furniture would have to move with the walls, not just revolve with the turntables. We couldn't have stagehands carry it off during the final emotional moment of the play; that would be clumsy, to say the least. I could build platforms on wheels—wagons—attached to the walls to carry the furniture.

But neither wagon could be larger than the turntable that carried it, or the two wagons would crash when the turntables revolved. Restricting the wagons to the diameter of the turntables would mean there would be a step down at the edge of the turntables, and I didn't want architecturally random steps in the middle of my elegant living room. What I came up with instead was a sumptuous shag rug that would sit under the living-room furniture. Under that, hidden by the thickness of the shag, would be an oval, inch-thick steel plate attached to the walls of the set. My steel-reinforced rug would be able to carry the furniture off as the walls moved. Or . . . I hoped it would.

After multiple revolving transitions from interior to exterior throughout the evening, the turntables would be positioned so that two tracks lined up: one running under the house walls and one in the surrounding stage. Motors hidden in the walls would then push the set off the turntables into the wings. The guide tracks would twist the stage-left portion ninety degrees as it moved, so it would fit into its respective wing.

With that solved, I refined the exterior set as I had the interior. In addition to ficus trees and myrtle vines, both of which grow in Southern California, I added exterior outlets, floodlights, porch lights, a dryer vent, a garden hose and spigot, and a large gas meter. The pebbled stucco I'd chosen for the exterior walls helped hide seams while providing a nice contrast with the smooth interior—necessary since both were fundamentally flat white surfaces. Steve was concerned that the stucco might seem tacky and cheap ("My stucco expertise is vast," he insisted, "having lived in Orange County and Los Angeles all my life") and suggested we use a nonswirled variety instead.

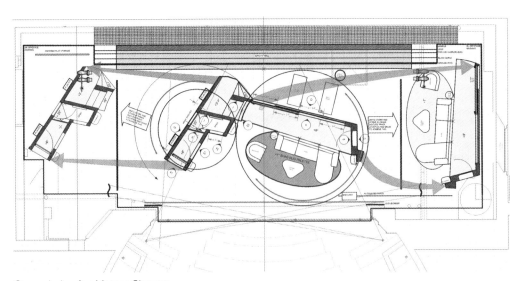

Ground plan for *Meteor Shower*

I ended up making the exterior stucco a very pale gray, which would read as white but be a better background for the actors than the white-white of the interior. Many of my favorite sets are white. I love how it looks onstage. But I understand the strong sentiment against it. True white is brighter than even the palest skin tones, making it a challenge to pop actors out of their surroundings. I never make a white set without discussing it with my lighting designer, but most good lighting designers are up to the challenge.

To avoid an unlightable white set, I attempt to keep white walls a little removed from the main playing areas. Then the light hitting the actors can be different, and brighter, than the light hitting the set. I also try to break up the white surface. In the case of *Meteor Shower*, I placed artwork at face height and several black cabinets along the base of the walls, so the surfaces against which the actors played were not relentlessly white. I also asked my painters for a fine overspray of pale gray—so fine that you could barely see it up close—to break the white up a little and add the tiniest bit of variety to the surface. Natasha Katz, our lighting designer, handled the white— and everything else—beautifully.

The "period" furniture posed the same style challenge as the architecture. I've already spoiled the big (offstage) moment in the play, when a meteor smashes through a character reclining in an outdoor lounge chair. That lounge chair—first intact and later with a big, smoking, cartoony hole through its cushion—would be a central prop and needed to look great.

I found images of high-end patio furniture in my copies of *Architectural Digest*. My excellent props-supervisor, the perky and cheerful Christine Goldman, found the exact lounges I'd flagged for sale on Craigslist at a bargain price. Because they were over-sized and luxurious, they were perfect for the seduction scenes that would be played on them. We sent them to rehearsal and then had to send them to a shop to reduce the size of the arms slightly (they interfered with Amy Schumer's seduction blocking!) and shorten their length by nine inches so they'd fit on the turntable. Even so, in tech, one of the lounges got moved a few inches during a scene and when the turntable revolved— *crunch*. The smashed lounge went back to the shop to get straightened out, and we took a few more inches off for safety. (It's not unusual to allot just a few inches of clearance for moving scenery, but, of course, more is better if you've got the room.)

The interior furniture was trickier, and I built some of it from scratch. My research included a sectional sofa with a small extended chaise/footrest. This felt "California" but was also practical; actors could sit on it from either side, or lounge on it. In a living-room set featuring a sofa, making that sofa actor-friendly and blocking-friendly is important. I wanted the seating to feel luxe but be firm enough that actors wouldn't disappear into it, and the backs had to be low enough that actors standing behind the pieces wouldn't disappear. In general, for this reason, I tend to make sofa backs, along with things such as counters and bars, a bit lower than they would be in reality. When an actor's lower half is obscured by furniture, the actor can seem remote from the audience.

I also found a photo of an odd arm detail from 1993 that I incorporated. It somehow felt period but not dated.

I wanted to pair the sectional with a swiveling armchair that would sit close to center stage. Swivel chairs are a great choice for a realistic interior, because they allow so many staging options. They become their own little, actor-controlled turntable in the midst of a larger set.

Somewhat bizarrely, the color of the furniture turned into a nagging problem. First, I made it cream with moss-green throw pillows, inspired by the image above. Then Alexis mentioned that in 1993, her parents' home had been all gray and pink.

Research collage of '90s style

I remembered that color combination well, so we tried it—but felt it looked dated in the wrong way.

Finally, I made the sofa red. Red is a dramatic color with lots of associations in Western culture, and that can be a cop-out—an easy design solution without much nuance. But J.Z. and I liked the way it looked, and the producers did too. The pop of red at the middle of the set was just the kind of heightened visual J.Z. had alluded to when we first spoke: a clue that perhaps this wasn't a straightforward sitcom after all. I topped it off with a zebra throw that had come up often in my research and helped unify the sofa with the rest of the set. Problem solved, or so I thought.

I turned my attention to the final detail that would establish the main characters as aspiring culturati: their art collection. It was not directly referenced in the script, but we spent a long time picking it. Steve Martin is a knowledgeable art collector, and I had great fun learning from him as we "curated" what might be appropriate. We decided on pieces that were modern and abstract and that seemed significant without being recognizable. I found an image I dubbed "hashtag art" that felt period yet interesting—if a tad pretentious—and Christine made a version of it that lit up. It became the anchor for all the other art choices.

Keegan-Michael Key, Laura Benanti, and Jeremy Shamos in *Meteor Shower*

Indigenous Australian art from Steve Martin's collection

Indigenous Australian art (with Steve Martin to indicate scale)

Steve has a large collection of Indigenous art from Australia, and we initially planned to use copies of some of these pieces. I went to his apartment, which is practically an art museum in its own right, and took high-resolution photos of the artworks. Then we had them printed on canvas and mounted onto stretchers.

Finally, Steve chose a few small Picasso prints, and once everything was hung, I added some picture lights—a good excuse for more practical light fixtures and yet more realistic touches on the set.

If the Faucet Leaks

The set looked good and worked well, but even with all the careful planning in the world, issues always arise in tech. Something doesn't work right or feel right or tell the story as it should. In this case, the process was complicated for me by the fact that my little dog, Hermione, died just before tech began. The show must go on, and I soldiered forward, but in retrospect I can see that I really wasn't firing on all cylinders. I was heartbroken.

With automated scenery, there is always the fear that it will malfunction. When directors ask what we can do to ensure this won't happen, I reply, "Don't use

Hermione
Jessica Fallon Gordon

automation." Almost all stage machinery is custom-built to do the specific job at hand; it's a complicated prototype made with off-the-shelf motors and custom software. Our automation problem on *Meteor Shower* came at the end of the show: We couldn't get the house to leave the stage. As I explained, the guide tracks in the surface turntables had to line up perfectly with those in the rest of the deck and then the two heavy, awkwardly shaped house halves had to move along those tracks powered by separate internal motors. If something was a little off balance, the guide knives (steel plates that guide the set along a groove in the deck) would catch against the grooves and the house wouldn't budge. If one half worked and exited and the other didn't, the error was painfully obvious.

The apparatus had worked fine in the shop and when we tested it before tech, but I guess one half of the set developed a taste for the limelight; it just refused to exit during run-throughs. The first night it was irritating. The second night it was alarming.

Sometimes when things aren't working, and I'm concerned that the crew isn't taking the problem seriously enough, I throw a calculated temper tantrum. I get no pleasure from screaming at people, but in the end, I'm the one responsible for making sure everything functions. A bit of designer fireworks can make people work harder to fix a thorny problem. But this wasn't an option on *Meteor Shower*. Early on, both J.Z. and Joey had made a point of telling us all to treat one another kindly—that there was no problem we couldn't solve if we worked together. It's a good sentiment, but after the second time the set failed, I grabbed Joey at the stage door and said I was starting to lose it. He laughed and said, "Beowulf, the set always breaks. Don't worry, they'll get it fixed."

The next morning, the carpenters worked on balancing the set and adjusting the speeds to keep it moving properly. No dice. Once again, half the set remained onstage at the end. Ordinarily, I'd have been on my feet, angrily demanding a solution from our production manager, Larry Morley. The truth is, my reticence wasn't just due to the dictum to "be nice." I think I was a bit paralyzed with grief over Hermione, so instead of raising hell I slumped in my seat and put my face in my hands.

After that night's production meeting, Joey asked the scenery team to stay behind, and he let us have it with both barrels. "You guys are competent professionals! You have to focus and get the goddamned set working!" Really, I think he was yelling at Larry, and the rest of us were there to help diffuse the attack. But it was my design, my department, and my responsibility—and he was absolutely right.

Larry asked the shop to come in the next morning to solve the problem, and they succeeded. They extended the knives so the set wobbled less, and added a tiny cue to the automation that would test each unit imperceptibly before it moved. That way, the operator would know if it was responding and if not, he could keep both halves of the house onstage so the problem wouldn't be obvious to the audience. From then on, the set left the stage successfully at the end of every performance.

My next battle was over the red sofa I thought we'd settled on months before. Joey and his producing partners decided it made too strong a statement, and I had to admit, the jump from a half-inch painted model to a twelve-foot-long swath of red upholstery was dramatic. J.Z. and I defended it, but the producers were adamant: rather than hinting at the surreal events to come, the thing simply called too much attention to itself on the otherwise monochrome set.

Christine brought in stacks of new fabric swatches, and we looked at them under the lights. I repainted the model sofa in a neutral shade and added a darker gray stripe to make it feel more like a custom-made piece chosen by characters straining for "taste." Finally, everyone agreed on the new look and, at significant expense, we had the offending sofa driven back to the shop to be reupholstered two days before the first preview. I would always miss that red sofa, but the final choice was fine: it was appropriately pretentious. There is usually more than one good solution to a problem onstage.

A final, odd problem arose in previews, during a comic bit when the guests (Laura Benanti and Keegan-Michael Key) attempt to abscond with some valuable silverware. As they shake hands goodnight with their hosts (Amy Schumer and Jeremy Shamos), the stolen goods are meant to fall out of Laura's sleeve. The problem was that the silver didn't fall reliably.

Ann Roth had designed the costumes and had faced a similar problem to mine: making 1990s clothes seem chic, not ridiculous. She had succeeded brilliantly, only to face this vexing little issue—which she decided to deflect. Was the silverware real sterling, she asked, or was the problem that it was cheap and didn't make the proper sound when it hit the floor?

I'm fond of Ann and deeply admire her talent, so this shocked me a little. I didn't respond in the moment, because, of course, we hadn't bought real sterling silver. We also hadn't laid a real stone floor, which probably affected the sound of it falling more than the alloy of the flatware. But neither the alloy, nor the sound it made, affected the release mechanism in the sleeve one way or the other.

Boris Aronson was once asked about how to succeed in the theater, and his response is well known (and best quoted in the man's signature Russian accent): "On every show there is a wictim. Don't be the wictim." Well, I wasn't going to be the "wictim" even in this minor controversy. The next morning, I brought in an assortment of sterling pieces I'd inherited from my grandmother and made J.Z. listen to the difference between them and our prop silverware hitting the floor. He agreed that there was no meaningful distinction, and I was off the hook. The costume was altered slightly, and the gag worked every time.

It wasn't all problems, of course. J.Z. has a mischievous teenage boy buried not terribly deeply inside him, and his iPad has a fart-sound effect. Despite the best efforts of his wonderful associate director, Steve Edlund, to keep him in line, at least once during every tech J.Z. aimed his God mic at his iPad and let one rip. To be fair, this bit of sophomoric silliness did serve a purpose; it instantly broke the tension that inevitably arises during a long, exhausting tech.

Amy Schumer, from whom you might expect an endless stream of prurient humor, was the epitome of kindness. At one point during tech, she hired her personal masseuse to come in and provide shoulder and neck massages for all. I'm pretty sure my muscles have never been so relaxed.

As much as I try to plan out all the set dressing ahead of time, there are always changes up until the last moment. In this case, I continued to move the artwork around the set throughout previews. A final, melancholy addition to the collection was a Keith Haring *Radiant Dog*. I own an original chalk graffiti version, so I made a copy and placed it as a little memorial to my Hermione.

With the problems solved and details attended to, the show ran smoothly in front of preview audiences. The set's repeated transformations established the pace, and J.Z. found ways for the actors to move from inside to outside during the changes in a kind of stage version of a cinematic tracking shot. This is one of my favorite stage tricks, and turntables are especially good for creating the effect. The actors can appear to be moving through space while remaining center stage as the set moves under and around them, allowing the story to seamlessly continue from one scene to the next.

Twice in *Meteor Shower*, the exterior set spun out of sight as a character sitting on a chaise longue described an incoming meteor. But as we'd planned, the moment of the meteor strike was left to the audience's imagination. As the doomed character was obscured from view, an LED meteor streaked across the sky and disappeared behind the house. What followed was a deafening crash, an enormous flash of light, an explosion of CO_2 smoke, and a blast of ashy-gray confetti over the top of the house. It was very effective, weird, and surprisingly funny within the context of this absurdist play.

Keith Haring's *Radiant Dog*
Keith Haring/collection of Beowulf Boritt

The star wall remained my most ambitious and innovative effect. First in the shop and then in the theater, I was stunned by the illusion of infinite depth it created. The fractured reflections caused the starfield to morph and appear differently from different vantage points around the theater, adding to the magic. As technical as its creation had been, the result was lyrically beautiful—definitely more poetic than a traditional fiber-optic star drop would have been. But if I'm honest, I have to wonder if it was worth its huge cost.

When you're trying a new idea, you can't know ahead of time exactly how it will be perceived. Even in a play where there's a lot of discussion of the sky, I suspect 90 percent of the audience wouldn't have noticed if we'd gone the cheaper, traditional route. It's worth noting that because of the star power of the playwright and cast, we had a pretty good idea going in that the show would be successful at the box office. Without that expectation, we probably couldn't have attempted such a pricey stage effect. I'm happy to say the show recouped its budget and ended up in the black.

Every other project I've written about in this book (with the exception of *The Scottsboro Boys*' brief Broadway run) was at a not-for-profit theater, where the budgets are smaller but the appetite for risky, unproven ideas is larger. I remain deeply grateful that on *Meteor Shower*, we had commercial producers willing to invest in a new and interesting technique.

I don't consider realistic sets my strong suit but, as previously noted, I believe a set designer should be able to create a credible one when asked. Establishing a realistic space onstage involves quite a few rules; it takes solid craft to follow them. It's neither the most glamorous nor the most exciting part of creating a show but, from the splashiest musical to kitchen-sink dramas, a clear understanding of the plumbing is crucial to allowing poetry to flow.

TEN

Nomad's Camp

A Conversation with Jerry Zaks

Setting: *Jerry Zaks's kitchen on the Upper West Side of Manhattan. Jerry doesn't keep an office; instead, he holds design meetings all over the city: in a producer's conference room, a private meeting space in Robert De Niro's apartment building, at Steve Martin's dining-room table—you name it. His own kitchen has a table, meaning it's spacious for New York. The rest of the apartment, receding into gloom down a hall, looks big too. Stacked along one wall are piles of framed memorabilia, including a series of painted renderings of Tony Walton's set for Jerry's production of* Guys and Dolls. *It looks like they've just come back from the framers. There's a sense of impermanence about the place, although Jerry has lived there for a long time. It all suggests a man who harbors a nomadic restlessness even after five decades in the theater.*

BEOWULF BORITT: J.Z., I'm talking with directors about how they work with designers.

JERRY ZAKS: My relationship to my designers has evolved over time from being totally unimportant to me to becoming critically important. When I started directing, it was with just two to three actors and a sofa. That was it. That was all I needed. That was all I cared about. My sense of what a set could contribute, the extraordinary importance of it, has evolved as I've gotten older.

BB: One of those shows with an extraordinary design was your 1992 revival of *Guys and Dolls.* When I was in college, I saw several of your shows, and I remember them vividly. Whenever I am doing a light musical comedy, I compare it to *Guys and Dolls* because I think it's the perfect representation of the form. It is so brilliantly constructed.

JZ: It's a solid structure. If you mess with it, if you try to put your own stamp on it at the expense of the structure, it will bite you.

BB: The writing of the scenes interlocks one with the next to make the show function like a machine.

JZ: Like a machine. Right down to the scenery changes. It's written to allow for a drop to come in behind a short in-one scene, sealing off the upstage area so the set can be changed behind it.

Tony Walton was born in 1934 in Walton-on-Thames, England. His first Broadway design was for *Once There Was a Russian* in 1961. His fifty-four Broadway designs include Jerry Zaks's productions of *The House of Blue Leaves, The Front Page, Anything Goes, Lend Me a Tenor, Six Degrees of Separation, Guys and Dolls, Laughter on the 23rd Floor, A Funny Thing Happened on the Way to the Forum,* and *The Man Who Came to Dinner.* He also designed the original Broadway productions of *Forum, Golden Boy, Pippin, Chicago, The Real Thing, Hurly Burly, The Will Rogers Follies, Steel Pier,* and *A Tale of Two Cities.* His notable film designs include *Mary Poppins, Murder on the Orient Express, The Wiz,* and *All That Jazz.*

BB: I've read that you and Tony Walton were consciously trying to recall Jo Mielziner's original set.

JZ: I had had the pleasure of collaborating with Tony several times, but I was not familiar with *Guys and Dolls* when I agreed to do it. I listened to it and read it and was thrilled and intrigued. The challenge was how to do it in a way that felt fresh, as though it were written yesterday as opposed to many years ago.

One of the reasons I hate the word "revival" is that it suggests resuscitation. I thought, *I'm going to figure out a way to get around the alternating shallow in-one scene, full stage scene, in-one, full stage. I'm going to figure out a way to do it differently. I don't know how, but. . . .* So I began exploring that in my head. Then I had a critical phone conversation with Cy Feuer, who was one of the original producers. He said, "Be careful. I tried to do the same thing you're talking about, and it bit me in the ass." I may be paraphrasing a little, but I got the message and dedicated myself to it, because it's hard to get around the fact that the show was constructed that way.

BB: You decided not to reinvent the wheel?

JZ: I thought, *Dammit, we're going to do the best possible version of an in-one show that we can.* I was visiting with Tony in Sag Harbor and I noticed a book of his

Guys and Dolls, by Frank Loesser, Jo Swerling, and Abe Burrows is set in a seedy but almost fairy-tale version of Times Square. Nathan Detroit is trying to avoid marriage to his longtime girlfriend, a burlesque dancer named Adelaide, while attempting to arrange an illegal craps game that will make him rich. He makes a bet with a high-rolling gambler named Sky Masterson that gets complicated when Sky falls for an uptight Salvation Army sergeant named Sarah Brown. After a drunken night in Cuba and a choreographed craps game in the sewers beneath New York, the couples are happily united for the finale. The original 1950 production was directed by George S. Kaufman, with choreography by Michael Kidd, sets and lighting by Jo Mielziner, and costumes by Alvin Colt. Jerry's 1992 revival was choreographed by Christopher Chadman, with sets by Tony Walton, costumes by William Ivey Long, lighting by Paul Gallo, and sound by Tony Meola.

illustrations. Thumbing through it, it struck me that his colors were so vivid and so bold—the boldest colors imaginable. I said, "That's what we have to do! That's the palette! That's what it should feel like!" That was the beginning of *Guys and Dolls*.

Tony and I went through the show endlessly. He would sketch and draw, and the process culminated in these pictures that were thrilling to look at. I knew his work would help us tell the story the way the story needed to be told: relentlessly.

BB: So the intense color was the starting point?

JZ: Yes. Beautiful color, and the fact that I was determined not to screw with the structure of the show. Once those things were established and we had some drawings, we showed them to [costume designer] William Ivy Long, who went berserk with color as well. Intellectually, you'd never want to use the colors William chose against the colors that Tony chose, but—

BB: William still talks about it. He said he was terrified when he first saw Tony's set, thinking, *There're no colors left for me!*

JZ: Yes. The result was make-believe—a fantasy world—because it's a fable. It was never meant to be realistic.

BB: Realism would kill it. I saw a production that made it heavier and more real once. It didn't work. It pops the balloon.

JZ: It gets in the way of the actors. I'm very sensitive to that.

BB: Speaking of reality versus theatricality, in "Luck, Be a Lady Tonight," the actors mime throwing the dice in the craps game. As much as I love abstraction, I always find mimed dice unsatisfying. I feel like nothing else is mimed, why are the dice? I always wish they were real.

JZ: It would be a nightmare. I mean, to control them, to confine them, to make the audience able to see what's on them? Leave it to the audience's imagination, and let everyone onstage be seeing the same thing and reacting. Of course, if I could cut to a close-up of dice bouncing off a wall and landing on whatever side they were supposed to, we'd do it in a second.

BB: You did manage to create at least one "close-up" in that production, an image I remember very specifically. It was during "Marry the Man Today," when Nathan and Sky appeared through the scrim in a tight circle of light, almost like a thought bubble. Adelaide and Sarah were imagining them.

JZ: Yes, yes, yes.

BB: One of them was up on a ladder clipping a hedge with a big grin, if I remember right.

JZ: That's right. I have never forgotten the first time I saw a scrim—you know, a wall that suddenly becomes translucent. It always makes the audience gasp. They don't expect a wall to melt and become transparent. In that particular case, I got the idea by going back to the script and asking, *What does this script demand?*

BB: So you wanted the two women to be imagining their perfect husbands in that moment?

JZ: Yes. Whenever I'm lost, the only thing I can do is go back to the script and wait for something to happen.

BB: Let's move on to a show where the script demands that *lots* of things happen: *Lend Me a Tenor.*

JZ: *Lend Me a Tenor*, oh my God! You're assuming I can remember these things!

Tony Walton's set model for the original Broadway production of *Lend Me a Tenor*. A dark patch on the floor, back wall, and a floating header imply the missing wall dividing the rooms.
Tony Walton

BB: I remember two things. One, I thought it was the funniest play I'd ever seen—I was dying laughing through the entire thing. And two, it was essentially a very realistic set with the center wall missing for sightlines.

JZ: That's right.

BB: You could see what was going on in two rooms at the same time. Was it obvious from the script that that was the way to go, or was it something you guys came up with as you started talking about it?

JZ: It was obvious from the script that two rooms were needed with X number of doors that could all be slammed. People don't understand that when they say, "Louder, faster, funnier," they're really talking about life-or-death stakes. What really translates into louder, faster, funnier is actors acting as though their characters' lives depend on what they are doing. The actors we had were able to do that, and it's part of what made the show as funny as it was. When people think their lives are at stake, they will do the most absurd things. Really absurd.

Lend Me a Tenor, Ken Ludwig's rollicking farce, tells the story of an Italian tenor named Tito, an opera impresario; and his hapless assistant Max, an aspiring singer. The dense plot plays out in a hotel suite and includes Tito's apparent death from an overdose and Max donning an Othello costume to impersonate Tito. When Tito wakes up, the mistaken identities and madcap events escalate to hilarious effect. Jerry Zaks's production had a set by Tony Walton, costumes by William Ivey Long, lighting by Paul Gallo, and sound by Aural Fixation.

BB: Tony Walton designed it.

JZ: We knew that at a minimum we'd need a set with those two rooms and all the doors: the hotel suite. At our second meeting, Tony showed me two drawings and said, "It either wants to be this or wants to be that." One was a traditional hotel, old-fashioned, realistic, with the two rooms split in cross-section. It felt like the Plaza or the Fairmont in San Francisco, traditional. Then he showed me an Art Deco version with white walls, and I thought, *God, the only person who might be unhappy with this is the lighting designer.* I mean seriously, it was so beautiful, we *had* to go with it. There's nothing like a beautiful setting for mayhem to take place in. It just seems like you're in danger of breaking something, you know? Messing up the walls or breaking something valuable. I just fell in love with it. And in the execution, Tony did an ingenious thing that I remember to this day. Knowing that the doors had to be slammed, he built in a quarter-inch space between the doors and the walls.

BB: So the walls wouldn't shake?!

JZ: That's right!

BB: That's brilliant.

JZ: You couldn't see the space—I couldn't believe it. But if the doors and walls had been connected, it would have been awful. This way, the actors didn't have to hold back when they slammed; they could show their anger or determination to keep someone out or whatever.

BB: That's brilliant. I've never done that. Honestly, every set designer should know that trick.

JZ: In retrospect, it seems so obvious.

BB: So . . . back to that white set. Paul Gallo, the lighting designer, did he worry about the white?

JZ: What I remember is his reflex, "Oh my God." But I loved the idea of the actors being silhouetted in front of a white wall. I loved it.

BB: I bounce back and forth. I love how a white set looks, but then I'll work with a lighting designer who screams bloody murder: "I can't light that thing!" So I get gun-shy and don't do a white set for a while.

JZ: I think when it's right, it's really right. What we came up with for *Meteor* Shower was just perfect. That was *white*!

BB: At the time, you told me the *Lend Me a Tenor* story and I thought, *I bet that set wasn't really white. I bet it was gray.* So I asked Tony about it, and he said, "No, it was white. True white!"

JZ: What is the problem with white? Keeping light on the actors and not overlighting the walls?

BB: Yes, trying to keep the actors' faces brighter than the walls behind them. Because even the palest skin is darker than a white wall. Some lighting designers can handle it, and some can't, but you sure don't want to give an all-white set to one who can't!

JZ: Of course.

BB: In a farce like *Lend Me A Tenor*, door placement can be crucial to timing. If a door is two feet closer to an actor or two feet farther away, it changes how you stage the scene. Did you have to change the door layout at all as a result of rehearsals?

JZ: No. Tony laid it out, and I went through the play so I knew it would work. As far as door choreography goes, it was perfect; we didn't have to change the door positions at all. Not that I remember, anyway. Tony might say, "No, dammit, we did!"

BB: Those changes can be traumatic for designers.

JZ: For the curtain call, I mapped out a sequence re-creating the high points of the show, using the doors as punctuation. Percussive punctuation.

BB: The set helped you establish that breakneck rhythm.

JZ: There was one sequence where people were running after one another, and two of them paused—so I figured out a way to use the invisible wall in the middle. They were chasing each other and finally came to rest in exactly the same place in the two rooms. They both went, "Ahhhhh," and "leaned" against the imaginary wall opposite each other. It was a perfect way to cap that sequence.

BB: More punctuation.

JZ: And the furniture was really well planned, so there weren't too many moments of, *Oh, my God, I didn't figure this out.*

BB: You're always great about that. For *Meteor Shower*, we talked it all through extensively. I don't think we changed any furniture placement once we got into rehearsal. The best directors I work with do really careful preproduction, and it pays dividends down the road.

JZ: It does. And that thoughtfulness translates into being able to visualize every moment of the play in a way that is not going to be hindered by the furniture.

BB: If you carefully play out the whole show in your head, or with the set model, you have a plan for every moment. You'll probably change some of it in rehearsal, but the physical world you've created will be right for the story that's inhabiting it.

JZ: I can't imagine a director not doing that. First of all, it's fun. Second of all, it arms you and contributes to making the actors feel taken care of. That's something all actors need. The idea of trying to move furniture in tech rehearsals: I'm not talking about an inch here or there, but completely rethinking something? No. You better have figured all that out well before.

BB: About those two guys leaning on the imaginary wall: Did you find other comic bits like that inherent in the script?

JZ: Yeah, of course. All directing goes back to the script. Ken Ludwig wrote a really superfunny play. The essential sequence of events was brilliantly conceived and constructed. That's inspiring. What's great about theater, as opposed to film, is that you can go home from a rehearsal and get in the shower, be inspired, and come back the next day and implement your brainstorm. There was one sequence with Max, played by Victor Garber; the impresario, played by Phil Bosco; and the tenor, played by Ron Holgate. It was critically important that Max render the tenor unconscious, so he slipped a mickey into the tenor's drink when he wasn't looking. He gave him the drink and then poured one for himself and they toasted. I watched it and said to Victor, "Wait a minute. You've just poured this sleeping medicine into his drink. Don't you think you'd want to make sure that it's dissolved, that he won't taste it? Because that would ruin everything you've lived for. What do you think your character would do?" Victor lit up! And what he did was stuck his finger in the guy's drink and stirred it—while Ron was watching. It was hysterical, because Ron's character was Italian, from a different culture, so he interpreted the gesture as a local custom—and stuck his finger into Victor's drink and stirred it! It got a huge laugh from the audience. That's a little microcosmic example of a prop-driven joke that was not in the script but that the script demanded.

BB: The show is things like that over and over and over again until your sides are hurting from laughing.

JZ: Most of the comedy was thanks to the brilliant structure of the playwright. The new ideas and plot development just keep coming at you, taking you by surprise. You fall in love with these characters.

BB: Let's move on to a play where you don't love the characters so much: *Six Degrees of Separation*. That one was done on a nearly bare stage, and there was the two-sided Kandinsky painting that spun around.

JZ: We had two two-seater sofas. We started downstairs at the Newhouse [the smaller space at Lincoln Center]. The reason I remember that is they became three-seaters when we moved to Broadway and had more space.

BB: Move to Broadway, and you get an extra cushion!

JZ: But the idea was still the two sofas and the Kandinsky painting and an opening here and an opening there for phone calls and limbo scenes. The back wall was translucent, which of course the audience didn't know until well into the show, when it dissolved to reveal the two guys fucking.

I was like a pig in shit. Two sofas on an empty stage and a good group of actors.

BB: Put the bare minimum onstage that you need to tell the story.

Six Degrees of Separation is John Guare's play—based loosely on a true New York story—about a young hustler named Paul who charms his way into the homes of two different Manhattan couples for the purpose of scamming them for money. He first appears at the Kittredges' elegant Central Park West home, falsely claiming to know their children. When his deception is revealed, he goes on to pretend that the Kittredges are his estranged parents in order to con a second couple—with deadly results. Jerry Zaks's production had a set by Tony Walton, costumes by William Ivey Long, lighting by Paul Gallo, and sound by Aural Fixation.

JZ: [The playwright] John Guare gave me *Six Degrees*, and I started to read it in a cab. You have no idea what's going on in the first twenty pages. Then, on page twenty-one, you realize that the whole thing was a flashback and you figure out what's happening. Unfortunately, I'd only gotten through page twenty when I had to get out of the cab. On the way upstairs I was thinking, "How am I going to tell John I don't know what in God's name this is about?" Then I finished the play and I thought, *Holy crap, this is great!*

When Tony Walton and I sat down to talk about it, I said, "The first part takes place in this apartment, which suggests we create an apartment; but the rest of the play moves from place to place to place." I knew the show had to feel as if eighteen John Guares ran into a room at the same time and simultaneously said, "I've got a story to tell you! You go—No, you go—No, you go!" That was the relationship of the play to the audience. Which meant there would be no time for scenery to move. *No time*. The play needed to move as fast as it read.

BB: This is one of the points I'm trying to make in this book: that the pacing of the scenery is absolutely crucial.

JZ: Crucial.

BB: You can do a long scene change if you've only got one or two and if they have some dramatic weight to them.

JZ: You have to give the audience something to listen to or look at or think about.

BB: Right. Or the change has to drive the narrative in some way.

JZ: If you make the rules clear to the audience at the beginning, they will go with you. Some plays require that new ideas be delivered instantly. For *Six Degrees*, Tony kept pushing me to consider an abstract solution: an emptiness that becomes *everyplace*.

As it turned out, all we needed was a disk of carpet, two sofas, and the two-sided Kandinsky revolving around. I knew I could create the phone calls that took place between father and child by having the two actors face front and play off a common focus on the back wall. I didn't want to waste time with conventional entrances until the rate of new ideas had been established.

One thing that helped was that I convinced the producers to give me six seats in the first row.

BB: They gave up sellable seats?

JZ: Yes! At the five-minute call, the actors would wander in and take their seats in the audience.

The opening cue was a spot center stage on an actor who had entered in the dark. We popped the lights on, and boom! The play was off and running. The first entrance was someone standing up in the front row and saying, "I knew it was this way," and then making his way onto the disk. I got a lot of mileage out of those instantaneous entrances.

Tony and I talked through the play and came up with this sequence of uses for the sofas and the Kandinsky. We had the limbo spaces and an entrance center that went off to the bedroom or any other place it needed to be. One day, I went into Central Park and played through the entire show in my head, imagining it on that set—and it worked. It worked really well. If it hadn't come from Tony, I don't know that I would have trusted the idea. But he kept saying, "If you tell the audience where they are, you don't have to show them. They'll be very happy to imagine it."

BB: The way Hal Prince puts it is, "You make the audience complicit." If you can engage them that way, it keeps them more interested. If you give them just enough so they can imagine a mansion, it'll be a mansion that's right for them—and probably more elegant than anything a designer could put onstage.

JZ: Giving the audience room to use their imaginations is such a critical part of live theater. Making them part of it. The audience loves being asked to believe that Central Park is two sofas with a moonlit gobo playing on them.

BB: I remember a tiny thing in the costume design for *Six Degrees*. Paul, the hustler, was having sex with a guy he'd picked up. They got caught, and the guy ran onstage naked—except he had socks on. Nothing but socks. I remember thinking, *He looks so much more naked because he has socks on!*

JZ: That's very funny. I don't remember how we got to that, but it's really funny. William [Ivey Long] would remember. Ask him if we talked about it.*

BB: All three of the shows we've talked about so far, you did with Tony. Obviously, you developed real trust in him. That kind of trust goes both ways. The first time I work with a director I tend to be scared to do something simple—like the abstract set for *Six Degrees*. Because I don't know yet if the director can use that kind of space well. But as I get more comfortable with someone—and vice versa—I dare to suggest things that might make a play more difficult to stage but potentially more interesting.

JZ: Yes. I totally get that.

BB: With trust, you believe your collaborator will be able to fill in the blanks.

JZ: Or say, "You know, that's not a good idea," without embarrassment.

BB: You gain the freedom to toss out ideas that might not be great.

JZ: It's really hard at the beginning.

BB: The beginning for you and me was *A Bronx Tale*. We did a bunch of workshops and talked about it, and I had the idea to make the set all red because the world of the story, the small neighborhood it takes place in, is such a pressure cooker.
    There were a lot of details to deal with, but that red defined the design.

JZ: It really seemed so right and so inspired—exactly the right visual metaphor for the story. I think you played with the red so it wasn't as bright and bold in the end?

---

*I did ask William about the socks. He laughed and said, "When I first moved to New York and lived at the Chelsea Hotel, I brought a man home who hung up his soaking wet red-striped gym socks to dry. I gave him a dry pair of mine when he left. When I was designing *Six Degrees*, I remembered those red-striped socks with holes in the toes and heels and re-created them. When I told Jerry the story, he turned beet red all the way back to his ears! That's why he's pretending he doesn't remember the socks!"

BB: Yeah, it was very bold originally, and we dialed it down a bit. Originally, the masking was red as well. We were well along when you called me up about it, nervous that it would make it hard to focus on the actors. So I changed the masking to black with a little red crackling along the edges.

JZ: That's right.

BB: It helped the focus and was also more visually energetic.

JZ: Then we added little stair units and the fire escape towers. But the inspiration was there in the first red sketches. Boy, did that turn out great. It's all about making the actors the most important thing. There's a script, and there are actors saying words. Everything else needs to serve and support them or enhance them somehow.

BB: Absolutely. When I'm making a model, the first thing I do is put a little figure in it to try to get the proportions of the set to complement the human figure—to pop it out.

JZ: That's critically important.

A Bronx Tale, Chazz Palminteri's autobiographical one-man play, was first made into a film by Robert De Niro and then a musical with songs by Glenn Slater and Alan Menken. It's the story of Calogero, a teenager in the Little Italy section of the Bronx in the 1960s who feels pulled between his honest working-class father, and his glamorous friend and mentor, a murderous gangster named Sonny. His life is further complicated when he falls for Jane, a Black girl he meets at school, whom his racist family and friends will not accept. Jerry Zaks codirected with De Niro, with choreography by Sergio Trujillo, my set design, costumes by William Ivey Long, lighting by Howell Binkley, and sound by Gareth Owen.

BB: Seeing the actors has to be the first priority for all of us. We use a lot of video onstage these days. One of my big issues with that is seeing the actors. It gets hard to see people against video.

JZ: The biggest mistake that I ever made was with video. On *Capeman*, by Paul Simon, I couldn't be talked out of using it. Talk about having a terrible effect on the audience! The show was about a real-life gang member in Hell's Kitchen who committed a murder. The idea was to turn him into a mythic figure, and we succeeded at times. Then, at one point, we moved from the fantastic, compelling, charismatic, actor playing the Capeman—Marc Anthony—to documentary footage of the actual guy being arrested and taken out in handcuffs. It was so vivid, so bold, so real that when we went back to the actor, he didn't have a chance of living up to it.

BB: Video can be used really well, but it's hard. I did a show in Vegas where the producer insisted on a big LCD wall, a movie playing constantly behind the action. We ran a number in tech, and I leaned over to Alexis and said, "This has to be the worst show we have ever done." Right at that moment, the video wall died for some reason—just went completely black. The number was so much better without the damn video stealing focus. Not that the video content was bad—it wasn't. It was created by a really good designer. But that giant LCD wall was so overpowering that real people couldn't compete.

JZ: Did they learn and change it?

BB: No . . . that producer was adamant about keeping it. But I have since discussed it with the director, who agrees with me.

JZ: Some people can see the stage; some people can't. I mean see it in terms of what a microsecond means in stage time. There is no such thing as someone just casually crossing from point A to point B. Everything makes a statement. Everything. The worst feeling in the world is to be in a room working with someone who you realize can't see or hear the stage.

BB: Some people naturally have the instinct; others learn to feel it.

JZ: I've run into some writers who haven't.

BB: When you work in both film and theater, you run into people who have made wonderful movies and want to put cinematic images onstage. Ideas can be great cinematically but unworkable onstage. In *A Bronx Tale*, I think we got stuck in that moment where Jane pops the button of the car door to let Calogero in. It's a beautiful cinematic moment and it's beautiful when Chazz [Palminteri] describes it in his one-man version of the show. It's quite literary. But we had to deliver it in a musical, and we couldn't make it climactic in the same way. . . .

JZ: You can't cut back to his face, you know? It's a little gesture. You can enhance it by exaggerating it. You can try to force focus on it and that's good, but it's not the same.

BB: It's tricky to translate those things. The other element in the show I want to touch on is the funeral wreaths. The wreaths for Sonny's funeral were all white at first because I'd designed the show in a very tight color palette: black, white, and red. In the middle of previews, Bob De Niro said, "That's not what they should look like. Italian funerals are really colorful."

JZ: I was skeptical. We all were. But Bob felt we should go over the top with the color, mass, and size of those flowers, and he was right.

BB: I was terrified that it would look ridiculous, but he was insistent. I was worried about my color palette, but I think you were worried we were going to lose the actors.

JZ: Right.

BB: But Bob made us do it and—

JZ: He was right. Which just goes to show that you can get imprisoned by an idea. The rules of the show were broken a bit by that visual, and it got a huge, appropriate laugh.

   The first time the curtain came up on those wreaths and everyone laughed the way they hadn't previously, we knew we were doing something right. I was elated.

BB: There was a laugh in there that we'd missed.

JZ: We hadn't done enough.

BB: Our next show together was *Meteor Shower*. When I read it, I thought, *This is an absurdist play*, but one of the first things you said to me was, "The real things need to be very real in order to make the weird things feel weird."

JZ: Right. Same as on *Lend Me a Tenor*, where the more beautiful the hotel suite, the more the mayhem resonated within it. In this case, the more normal the house . . . you know? Steve [Martin, the author] had said the home should be straight out of *Architectural Digest*, and you got it. Your set made it seem as if the characters had great taste. We made them very sophisticated, visually acute people into whose house madness comes. I seem to recall our process being straightforward, no?

BB: We went through a lot of steps, but it was linear. We kept developing the same idea.

JZ: Once we both embraced the turntables as a way to get us from inside to outside, and vice versa.

BB: That was the essential transformation of space over time. We decided that at the big moment—the meteor strike—the audience should see the guy seconds before he got hit but not the moment of impact.

JZ: You've only got so many seconds of goodwill, where the audience is willing to be confused, before you have to do something that brings clarity. I love the way that sequence evolved. We changed that sequence based on Steve's insistence on something that I didn't think was important—but he was right.

BB: Yeah. When the guy got hit by the meteor, we had three beats. First, the flash of the meteor strike as the actor was hidden by the moving set; then a few seconds of blackness; and then the reveal of the next scene. We connected the explosion to the scene before it; then paused. But Steve wanted the pause of the blackout *before* the meteor strike, not after. He wanted to change the rhythm so that the explosion was instantly followed by the comic reveal.

JZ: The reveal of Keegan-Michael Key standing there with his chest smoking after being hit!

BB: It was like a rim shot, but the way we were doing it, the last beat was coming too late. Steve kept pushing us to make the explosion and the reveal time out more comically.

JZ: That's exactly right. It was one of those moments where you go, *Aw, fuck. I'll try this because you're the writer, so I have to at least try it.*

BB: I suppose we should have known better than to question Steve Martin's comic timing! He was right all along.

JZ: He was. That's the kind of adjustment I can make much more easily these days than I might have when I was less secure.

BB: At a certain point, it no longer hurts your pride to realize you were wrong about something. It's exciting to realize there might be a better way of doing something. If it's a really good idea, who cares who thought of it? In my case, if something makes the set better, I'm going to get credit for it whether it was my idea or not!

JZ: Exactly. That set served us well. Give me two sofas, a bunch of actors, and one little pouf off to the side so I can get this angle and that angle. I can make the audience all look at the same place at the same time. That's all I want to be able to control.

BB: You started as an actor. Did you know you wanted to be a director?

JZ: No, I didn't. I think each director's sensibility or aesthetic or priorities stem from how he got into directing in the first place. Hal Prince, one of the greatest, started as a stage manager. I was an actor for ten years, and I loved it. That's all I wanted to do. I accidentally directed a workshop at the Ensemble Studio Theater of a play called *The Soft Touch*, by Neil Cuthbert. I loved the experience. Then I directed another of Neil's plays, *Buddy-Pals,* for E.S.T.'s one-act-play marathon. It was a single set, a sofa, and three high school–age kids having their last evening together before they headed off to college. It was fantastic. I got to choreograph life amongst three people. It was precision. I discovered the joy of doing that, causing that to happen. Standing in the back of the theater, I thought, *Wow, I could do this.*

At E.S.T., you couldn't do much set anyway—which is probably why it took me a while to appreciate design. Early on, my reaction to, "What is the set going to look like?" was, "I don't know; I don't care." Over time, I came to realize how critically important the set is if you want the audience to enjoy the story and get as involved as possible.

BB: Do you have a first memory of seeing a show and being aware of the design as an element?

JZ: Yes, it was the first musical I saw in college—a production of *Wonderful Town*. When the curtain went up, the combination of the set, the colors, the lights, the costumes was overwhelming. It was the beginning of my love affair with the theater.

But the moment when a set made me gasp came in the late sixties or early seventies. It was in a revival of *The Glass Menagerie* on Broadway, with George Grizzard and Jo Van Fleet. As you know, the character of Tom opens the play with a monologue. In this case, he delivered it in an alley outside the house, in front of what appeared to be a brick wall. When he finished and went inside, the lights bled through the brick wall. It was a scrim. The brick wall just disappeared. I remember thinking, "This is magic." That's the first moment when a set took my breath away.

BB: You use scrims all the time as a tool to get your laser focus on the actors: Nathan and Sky appearing in Adelaide and Sarah's "imaginations," Paul having sex with the hustler in a back bedroom, and even Calogero conjuring his Bronx neighborhood out of the darkness as he sings about it. It's theater spectacle. It surprises and delights the audience but always in service of the actors and the story they are telling.

ELEVEN

Puzzle

Designing *Sondheim on Sondheim* for James Lapine

Infinite Possible Combinations

I don't remember when James Lapine asked me to design *Sondheim on Sondheim*—which is odd, since I have vivid memories of being asked to design every other show featured in this book. I'm so flattered when someone asks me to design something that it tends to stick in my mind. But not this one.

Most of the designs I've written about, I cracked on my first or second attempt. This one took a long time. I'm hesitant to pick a favorite design experience because I have loved many of them ... but when someone does insist, I choose *Sondheim on Sondheim*.

I do remember the first time James mentioned the project to me. We were rehearsing a segment of *The 25th Annual Putnam County Spelling Bee* for the 2005 Macy's Thanksgiving Day Parade. I was schmoozing and trying to ferret out James's upcoming projects in hopes I could convince him to let me design one of them. He mentioned that he wanted to do a revival of *Merrily We Roll Along* and that he was developing a new revue of Stephen Sondheim's music.

I've always loved *Merrily*. I designed a small production once and have wanted to try it on a larger scale. I don't tend to like revues. I'm too story-oriented to enjoy compilations of songs where the only connection is that they were written by the same person, even if that person is Stephen Sondheim. So I launched a campaign to convince James to let me design *Merrily*. There was no firm plan for a production, and while he never said yes, he never said no, so I kept hoping. I've come to realize that James has never—literally never—asked me to design a project that I pushed for—only those I didn't. I don't know if that's coincidence or a consequence of James's contrarian nature, but it's true. True to form, sometime in late 2007 or early 2008, he asked me to design the Sondheim revue, to be called *Opening Doors*. "Just be brilliant please," he concluded as we sealed the deal.

No pressure.

The show would be a combination of live performances and video of Sondheim talking about the songs. Much of it would be filmed specifically for this production, but James also intended to use existing interviews and footage from years past. There wasn't a script when we started working on the design, though James had some idea of what songs he wanted to include. The first dated script I have is from over a year later.

I knew Sondheim's musicals well enough to guess at some of the general looks we might be shooting for. I loved the shows, so it was exciting to think about designing snippets of them, but designing without a text or even an outline was challenging. Some designers dream of creating while free of the constraints of script and staging, but I'm not that designer. Parameters help focus me. Infinite possibilities, though they may sound appealing, can be paralyzing. But I was getting to design a Stephen Sondheim show for James Lapine, so I was damn well going to figure it out.

The show would be produced by the team of Steven Baruch, Tom Viertel, Marc Routh, and Richard Frankel (I alluded to them in chapter 7—they were the second group who briefly attempted to produce *Prince of Broadway*). They were fresh off their successes with *The Producers* and *Hairspray*, so this show was bound to land on Broadway eventually, though we didn't know when or which theater. I'd have to design it for a generic Broadway-sized house.

The only other person who'd been hired then was the projection designer, Peter Flaherty. Peter is a tall, quiet gentleman about my age, meaning we were both a generation younger than James. Peter had designed the video for a one-night benefit performance at the Public Theater in 2007 that James had directed and I had designed. He was an artsy, downtown guy with a distinct disdain for musical theater, which he once described to me as "a guy in sequins running up some stairs with a shit-eating grin and going like this," at which point he flashed me some "jazz hands." But I liked him, and James did as well—enough to hire him for this video-heavy piece of musical theater.

I didn't get many specifics from James at first, but it was clear we would need video surfaces. "Levels would be good for staging," he noted, but it doesn't get much more generic than that, and my first attempts were correspondingly generic. I made some sketches of a set with scaffolding levels that could fill the proscenium or swing upstage to create more open space. There was a video screen upstage and a wall of picture frames designed to fly in front of it with more video imagery filling each frame. I suggested some angled sliders that could frame slices of the video wall. In retrospect, my first attempts were just another version of the set from that benefit for the Public—but you've got to start somewhere.

First renderings for *Opening Doors*

James wasn't impressed, and he wasn't wrong. But getting some ideas on paper triggered more discussion. "What if the set was a cube or a grid or something?" James offered. I wasn't sure how a grid would be useful, until James, Peter, and I visited Sondheim at his Turtle Bay town house.

Like Hal Prince, Steve has had a similar "look" since the 1970s. His rumpled, casual clothes give him the air of an absent-minded college professor, and his hair and beard have changed little over the years except to lighten with age. I knew him very slightly from Hal's Christmas parties. The first time I'd dared introduce myself to him, he'd said, "Oh, *you're* the one with the name!" cementing forever my gratitude to my creative parents for this ridiculous name. Sitting with him in his living room was overwhelming, but luckily, I didn't have to stammer awkwardly for too long. He and James disappeared upstairs to the study to talk about the show, while Peter and I settled in the conservatory overlooking the back garden to go through boxes of visual memorabilia. Among the wealth of research, I found a series of photos of my friend Daisy Prince and her brother Charlie at about ten years old, performing their kids' version of *Follies* for the adults who had created it!

More directly useful to the design was Steve's puzzle collection. He is well known for his love of puzzles, and his home is filled with a wide variety of uniquely beautiful ones, any one of which could be a style reference for a set.

Some of Sondheim's many antique games and puzzles including a framed deck of antique pornographic playing cards. When backlit as shown, the face cards' genitals faintly appear and a variety of erotic scenes play out on the numbered cards. There was no place for this particular novelty in the design, but it still amuses me.

I returned to my studio and played with ideas inspired by the grid of the first puzzle above, keeping in mind the practical needs of the show. The playing space would be the inside of a forced-perspective cube with a grid drawn on it, and the whole thing would be white, to serve as a blank projection surface. Side panels could slide away for access to traditional theater wings and to allow scenery to slide in and out. Upstage, a rear projection screen or video wall would continue the grid motif but also carry video content.

James didn't like it. No specifics, just *no*. Something about the grid and cubes stuck with me, though, and I spent the next few weeks trying to figure out different ways a cube might break apart onstage. I made a model of a cube that could rotate and unfold inside a larger cube of video walls.

Again, James said, "Nope," and I went back to my studio, still thinking about cubes.

I thought, *Sondheim took an existing form, musical theater, and radically reinvented it.* Instead of a perfectly square cube in a square box, I made a cube hurtling through space toward the audience that could burst open to reveal what was hidden within: scattered pages.

Second model and renderings for *Opening Doors*

Third model and renderings for *Opening Doors*, including some ideas for the *Company* sequence

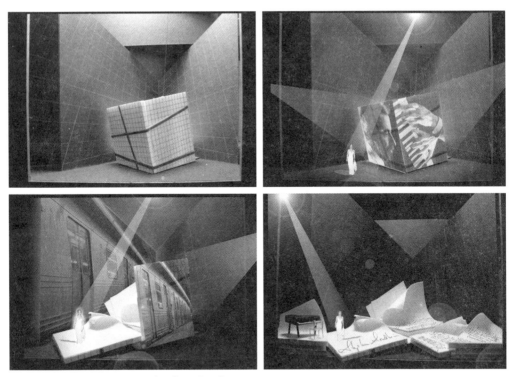

Fourth model and renderings for *Opening Doors*

And again, James hated it. He felt it was too static, that we needed something that could transform more. He had a point. Versions two and three offered an exciting reveal as the cube opened, but after that, the set couldn't change much. I understand now that the show was so nebulous in James's mind in those early days that it was hard for him to guide me. Maybe he was hoping that whatever I came up with would help define things. The show was also so unformed that I couldn't identify a theme to express visually, which left me floundering stylistically. As Peter and I walked away from yet another unsatisfying meeting, I said, "I'm really beginning to understand the phrase 'back to the drawing board.'"

It was time to jettison the cube/grid idea. I was still thinking about the curved "paper" panels in my most recently rejected design when I read an article about Frank Gehry and how he developed some of his architectural ideas by crumpling paper to create interesting forms. The piece went on to say that his buildings could be so unconventional that they were hard to build—and often leaked.

Anything new is likely to be difficult and leaky. I started twisting and folding paper, coming up with curved, abstract forms that might work for our set. These, in turn, reminded me of Richard Serra's monumental steel sculptures, which I'd first seen at the Dia Beacon museum in upstate New York.

Frank Gehry's Walt Disney concert hall
Chad J. Smith

Richard Serra's steel sculpture in Guggenheim Bilbao Museum
Sérgio Nogueira/Alamy Stock Photo

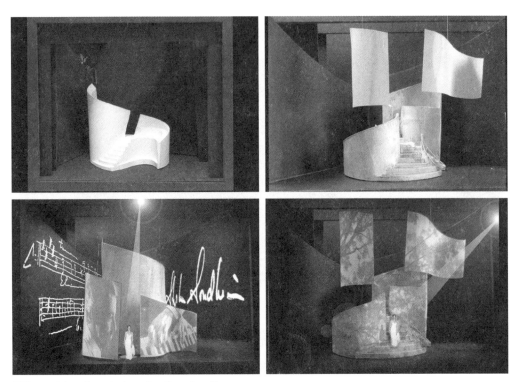

Fifth model and renderings for *Opening Doors*

After another week, I had a new set—a series of curved walls that could accommodate projections and rotate to create the effect of a fluid, ever-changing space. A few more curved panels could fly in front of the main unit or float above it and also receive projection. Stairs curving through the main unit would provide levels for actors to stand and sit on.

James liked it! There were a lot of details to sort out, but we had a basic approach as we entered the summer of 2008 and were ready to develop the projection ideas. How would they look against dynamic, curved, asymmetrical surfaces? What should the surfaces be? Might they have the texture of paper that's been crumpled and then smoothed out? Might they be angular metal plates similar to the skin of Gehry's buildings?

Peter thought that the ideal way to develop the video was to build a large model of the set—a quarter the size of the real thing, so seven feet tall—and experiment with real projections. I had never approached video design that way, but both James and I were excited at the thought of playing with the video in three-dimensional space before tech rather than relying on renderings or virtual 3D simulations.

Our next step was to begin creating some of that video. In early June, we spent a day shooting interviews with Sondheim at his house. Peter and his team handled all the logistics, and James conducted the interviews. I was extraneous, but it was fun to tag along as part of the creative team.

Later in the month, James wanted me to show our small, rough model to the producers, to get them excited about where we were going and convince them to fund the big quarter-scale model. I was in Pennsylvania directing and designing a musical version of *Rapunzel* for a little summer theater in my hometown of Gettysburg. It was the theater where I'd interned in high school and first realized that "set designer" was an actual job. My wife Mimi was playing the title role, and it was a nice break from our New York routine.

Directing was something I'd done occasionally and always enjoyed. I found that flexing different creative muscles made me a better designer, and I wasn't a terrible director. But as it turned out, *Rapunzel* was the last thing I'd direct—at least as of this writing!

The meeting James planned with the producers was right in the middle of my rehearsals. Broadway commitments have a way of plowing everything else out of their path, so I arranged to be away from Gettysburg for a day and took Amtrak back to New York with my model for *Opening Doors*. As the train crossed New Jersey, it suddenly slowed down and then stopped altogether. Ten minutes passed, then twenty. Finally, a conductor came on the intercom and said, "Some unfortunate person has jumped in front of the train. We won't be moving until the police arrive and complete their preliminary investigation into the death."

I called James in a panic saying that I'd be late for the meeting with our producers. Surely I'd be fired on the spot! But both James and the producers were understanding. When I finally made it to New York, hours late, we met at Richard Frankel's offices in Times Square. The producers looked at the set and liked it, and I returned to Pennsylvania on an evening train.

Scattered Pieces

James spent the rest of the summer at his place on Martha's Vineyard. By late August, when we started work again, our producers had plans for an out-of-town production, at Atlanta's Alliance Theater in April 2009.

On September 29, 2008—Black Monday—the stock market crashed, causing what would eventually be called the Great Recession. But our show was driving forward unaffected, or so we thought. James asked me to send Sondheim some renderings, and soon we had his approval of the design. Neil Mazella and Sam

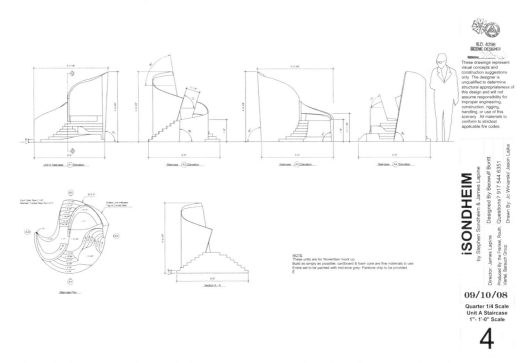

Jo Winiarski and Jason Lajka's drafting of quarter-scale set model (with a human figure to make the odd scale clear).

Ellis, one of Neil's lieutenants, joined us as production managers, and the project felt more and more real.

I hired Jo Winiarski, a cranky old man hidden in the body of a downtown-cool New York woman who had been my design associate on my three previous Broadway shows, and she began drafting the design so we could make the quarter-scale model of it.

James decided to change the name of the show to *iSondheim*. We were in the early days of iPhones and iPads. James was a recent convert to Mac, and it felt current to him. I was still figuring out what I thought of the title when Jo, who has always been edgier than I, emailed me to say, "It is a terrible name. It makes everyone seem old and lame." I laughed and kept her opinion to myself. Until now!

The model was much too large for me to build in my studio, but the cost of having it built at Hudson Scenic, Neil's shop, was three times what the producers were willing to spend. Since it was a mock-up, we could use a nonunion shop, so I reached out to a small Brooklyn outfit called Daddy-O that had built off-Broadway sets for me. Even their bid was higher than the production had budgeted.

As we debated how to proceed, Sam told me that the producers wanted to tour the show around the country before bringing it to Broadway. Suddenly, the cost of our workshop model was the least of our problems; I would have to reconceive the set so it could travel!

Almost all big scenery is designed to break down into pieces, but a touring set presents its own engineering challenges. On Broadway, we frequently spend many weeks installing a production. On a tour, a set must be able to be assembled in a new theater in eight to twelve hours once every week for many months. My *iSondheim* design, with its ever-shifting assembly of curved projection surfaces, was complicated. Furthermore, the distance of the various projectors from the set would vary vastly from theater to theater, leading to excessive installation time. If this production was going to tour, our design simply wouldn't work.

While I spiraled into mourning for a design I was proud of, Peter began researching LED or LCD panels that could travel easily so we wouldn't have to rely on projectors. He sent me options he thought could work as the building blocks of a set. There was no getting around it: I'd have to return to the drawing board yet again—but this time, the clock was ticking.

In October, James did a short workshop. Actors sang the songs, and we played early edits of the Sondheim interviews on TV monitors. The whole thing was very rough, but it was the first time any of us had gotten a glimpse of what the show would be. Perhaps I should have realized it long before, but watching that workshop made me see that Sondheim—who, via video, logged considerably more stage time than any of the actors—was the show's protagonist. The live performers were supporting players. We were making a documentary in musical-revue form. The story of Sondheim's life was the plot of the show. His artistic development and effect upon the American theater was the theme. Suddenly I had an intellectual framework to support a set design.

In a eureka moment that had taken nine months to hit me, the set magically reassembled itself in my head. Sitting in the back of the rehearsal studio while the performance was still going on, I scribbled down my new idea.

Looking over my shoulder, Jo said, "That's cool. It's very Nam June Paik."

That's why a smart associate is so important. I probably should have known who that contemporary-ish video artist was, but Jo led me to his work. His style didn't radically affect my final design for the show, but, as I tried to translate my initial rough sketch into a more finished idea, having some research to look at clarified my thinking.

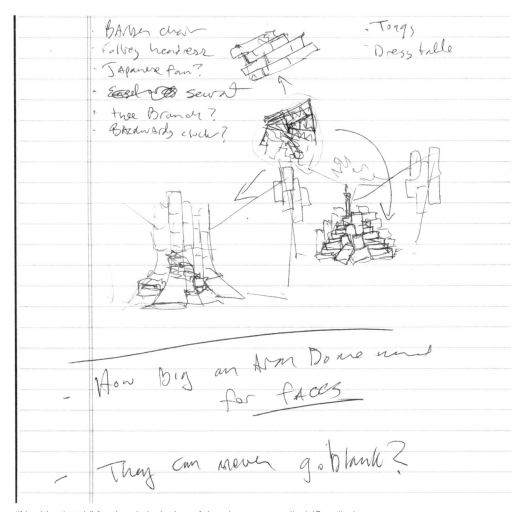

"Napkin sketch" for the sixth design of the show, now called *iSondheim*

The artist's juxtaposition of organized grids of television sets with disordered piles of them was exactly the aesthetic I had in mind. I could create a set that would transform from an ordered world to a reimagined, deconstructed one, and the disordered version could become stairs and levels for the performers. The set would physically reinvent itself during the show as Sondheim reinvented the musical theater. James understood the touring concern, was open to switching to video panels, and liked my doodles and the Nam June Paik research.

Peter had concluded that flat-panel LCD televisions, with their plasma screens, would give us the best resolution we could afford. The downside of the LCDs was that they were individual television sets. (While LED panels have no frames, making a seamless video surface, in 2008 the resolution we wanted was too expensive.) Peter

Rendering of *Meteor Shower*

Jeremy Shamos with the new, gray sofa

Meteor Shower: Laura Benanti and Jeremy Shamos on the exterior set

Meteor Shower: Amy Schumer and Jeremy Shamos as the meteors fly past

A Tony Walton rendering for the finale of *Guys and Dolls*
Tony Walton

A Bronx Tale (clockwise) First sketch, Broadway set, Colorful funeral wreaths, White wreaths, Set model.

Jo Mielziner's original 1945 set for *The Glass Menagerie* featuring the scrim wall which is frequently recreated in revivals.
Jo Mielziner

Rendering of *Sondheim on Sondheim*

Painted renderings for *Sondheim on Sondheim*

Leslie Kritzer, Vanessa Williams, Norm Lewis, Barbara Cook, Matt Scott, Euan Morton, Erin Mackey, and Tom Wopat in front of the full-screen look

Euan Morton, Leslie Kritzer, Erin Mackey, and Matt Scott sing "Something's Coming" as the screens break for the first time

Tom Wopat sings "Epiphany," from *Sweeney Todd*

The company sings "The Gun Song," from *Assassins*

Peter Flaherty's Saul Bass-inspired animation of 1950's New York, playing on a constantly moving set as the cast performs "Opening Doors," from *Merrily We Roll Along*

Vanessa Williams sings "Smile Girls," from *Gypsy*

Nam June Paik's *TV Garden 1974–7*, Tate Modern
Guy Bell/Alamy Stock Photo

found an LCD model with a very thin bezel (the frame, which James always called the "bevel"). As thin as they were, the borders around each set were visible, so that any wall of them would include a grid of bezels breaking up the image displayed on them.

Sam arranged several field trips for James and me and Ken Billington, who had just joined the team as our lighting designer, to look at both LCD and LED panels. (I've written about Ken in previous chapters, but this was the first time I actually worked with him.) We all agreed with Peter that LCDs looked better, and I felt strongly that the bezel grid wouldn't be a problem; in fact, it was a good thing. Like the breakup of the Nam June Paik televisions, it would make the technology more visibly present, adding a self-consciously performative aspect to the show. That felt appropriate for a documentary-revue.

With the specific hardware chosen, in November I started to translate my rough sketch into a model. I wanted to incorporate the flexibility and abstract mobility of my previous design with the building blocks of the LCD panels. I broke quarter-inch-scale LCDs into groupings to see what looked interesting. Over the course of a week, I met with James and Peter every morning and translated our conversations into refinements to the model each afternoon.

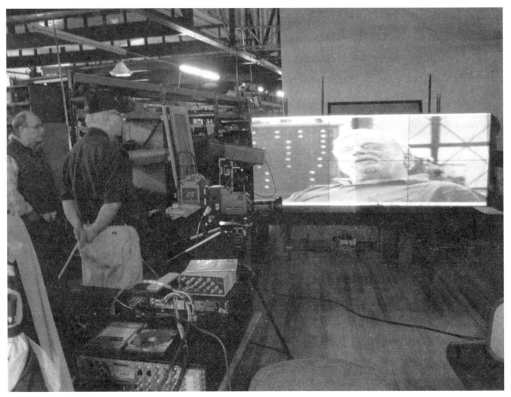

James Lapine and Sam Ellis looking at six ultra-thin-bezel LCD panels at Sound Associates, an audio-video shop.

Sixth model and renderings for the show now called *iSondheim*

By the end of the week, we'd broken the panels into more groupings of fewer televisions to allow for more flexibility and create more complicated, interesting shapes. We continued to refine the idea for several more weeks, and by the end of November, we'd conceived what I hoped was the final set. James looked at it and said, "You've made a puzzle. It's like those 3D puzzles in Steve's living room. It keeps reassembling itself in different ways. It's perfect. Steve's a puzzle."

We presented the new set to the producers as a solution to the touring issue. This set was much more modular and easier to break down. The screens would carry the video content so we wouldn't have to worry about hanging and focusing projectors in each venue. Employing a popular catchphrase of the day, I confidently asserted that the whole thing was "plug and play." This was a case of not knowing what I didn't know; I was woefully ignorant about the kind of technology required to drive all that video—but that would be a problem for another day.

The producers signed off, Jo did the technical drawings, and Hudson priced the set—we were well over budget. The design called for the steps and platforms to be lightboxes built to look like the LCD screens. We didn't need them to play video, but they had to light up so that the entire construct seemed to be made of the same objects. In the struggle to get costs down, I finally agreed to cut the lightbox component, with the understanding that we could add it back in when we went to

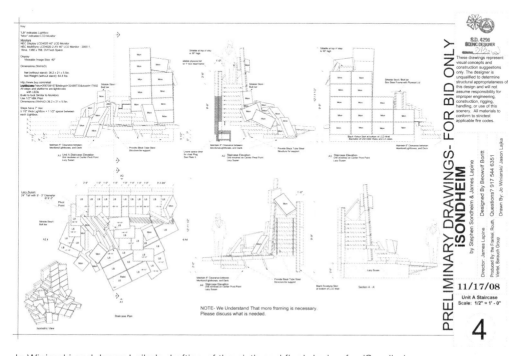

Jo Winiarski and Jason Lajka's drafting of the sixth and final design for *iSondheim*

Broadway. The tryout might have to include "dead televisions," but for Broadway, I'd fight to bring them to life.

Because the new set was made almost entirely of screens, the video content had to be constant, or it would look like a pile of turned-off televisions. James, Peter, and I started working on what that content would be, beyond the Sondheim interviews.

Sometimes my involvement in the projection design is minimal. Sometimes directors and projection designers want a lot of input from the set designer. Sometimes I have such a strong opinion of what the design should be that I want to be in charge of the projections myself, as on *Prince of Broadway*. Although Peter was the projection designer, James asked that I actively be involved. This is a balancing act: projection designers can be irritated by set designers with strong opinions, but fortunately, Peter was happily collaborative.

Beyond the straightforward interviews, the video imagery used during the songs would evoke some representation of the shows they came from. I wanted that video to be more emotional and textural, not literal. I almost never want video content to be literal. Projecting a realistic background always feels clumsy to me, much as a realistic scene painted on a canvas backdrop feels like an old-fashioned, two-dimensional substitute for three-dimensional reality. We began gathering images to inform the video design.

We made steady progress sketching out the sequences through December 2008 and January 2009. I made a rough digital model of the set, and Peter and his team began putting the video looks into their own digital model.

On Wednesday, February 4, 2009, I got the following email from James:

> I just got a call from Richard Frankel. They don't have enough money for Atlanta. I am meeting tomorrow at 4 to go over budgets. Beowulf and Peter, if you could come at 4:45 that would be great. I have no idea where this is headed. To say that I am angry about the situation does not do the sentiment justice. I will email back whenever I have more information to share. Sorry

It wasn't a Monday, but our show's Black Monday had arrived.

For a month after that, James and Steve tried to keep our show on track for an April bow in Atlanta. James's ongoing emails tell the story:

> Saturday, February 7, 2009: There is no news, but SS and I are on the case. I have a morning chat with a big player who I think will jump in, but not sure for how much. We have to get a million more! Yikes! (No, Peter, this is not how it usually

works. I've never had to raise money for a show—ever.) As we have decided that we are not going to do the concert version, no way, I think we should make sure we don't fall behind. So please let me know your schedules and let's meet up next week and get a game plan. Thanks, JL

I am too bummed out to work but would like to go over our options with you guys and plan for the future, whether the show goes as planned or farther down the line. JL

Sunday, February 22, 2009: Yeah, I am way deep in depression—but it will lift. Trying not to be angry, but it's hard.

Wednesday, February 25, 2009: Sorry, no taker for iSondheim. It was just too quick for them to make that kind of commitment. Can't say we didn't try to the bitter end. JL

The show was dead. I was shocked and massively disappointed. How could a new show by Stephen Sondheim and James Lapine not get produced? Yes, it was a revue and not a new musical, but I couldn't believe it. Despite the sense of optimism in the theater world that had accompanied the 2009 inauguration of Barack Obama, the world's economy was in shambles. Many of the people who had been investing in theater through the previous boom years had lost a lot of money in the crash. Those who hadn't were suddenly a lot tighter with it. It was a harsh reality check about life in show business: There is no level of fame that can guarantee the success or financing of your next project.

Handmade

The show was dead. And then it wasn't. Unbeknown to me, James had been discussing *Merrily We Roll Along* with Todd Haimes, the artistic director of New York's Roundabout Theatre. The financial disaster had made funding the twenty-seven-plus company needed for *Merrily* problematic. But *iSondheim*, with its cast of eight, was more manageable and would allow the Roundabout to offer a Sondheim/Lapine collaboration after all.

Just a month after James had declared the show dead, the Roundabout was on board. The show wouldn't go on until the spring of 2010—a full year later than planned—but it would be going straight to Broadway. The Roundabout had converted

Studio 54, the famed 1970s club, into a theater a few years earlier. It would be our home and the salvation of our project.

And the show's title changed again! James emailed me: "No one seems to like *iSondheim*. What do you think of *Simply Sondheim* or *Sondheim: Off the Wall*?"

My suggestion was that it be called *Stephen Joshua Sondheim*. He was our protagonist and the inclusion of his middle name promised illumination of unfamiliar aspects of his life and career.

There's a reason I'm a set designer and not a title writer. In the end, James settled on *Sondheim on Sondheim*.

I met with two people with whom I would work closely on the production. The first was Sydney Beers, the Roundabout's general manager. At some theaters, the GM has little to do with the physical production, but Sydney is very hands-on, and we would spend a lot of time together. I once introduced her to a friend who afterward asked, "Was she drunk?" I laughed. Sydney has a very big personality—but if she has your back, she will move heaven and earth to get you the resources you need. The Roundabout had rescued our project, but it was Sydney who stepped in over and over to say, "No, that can't be cut. The show needs it. Let me try to find the money." More often than not, she'd find it.

The second person was Steve Beers, Sydney's husband. He was the production manager for Studio 54 and is as silent as Sydney is loud. He looks like a linebacker, and I was initially wary of him. But I soon found that he valued preparation and appreciated my carefully detailed design. Any time an issue arose, he'd say, "Don't worry. You did your homework; we'll figure it out." He is a brilliant technical director as well. As I mentioned, I hadn't fully grasped the intricacies of the technology needed to fling and spin all those LCD screens around the stage in the way I'd envisioned. Luckily for me, Steve understood it and would figure out how to make it all work.

The summer and autumn of 2009 felt like a repeat of the previous ones as we dealt with budgets and fitting the show into the theater. One advantage of the lag was that a new generation of LCDs had come to market—lighter, thinner, and with better resolution. They were slightly larger than the previous model, so Jo had to redraft the entire show. By the end of the year, we had settled on PRG Scenic Technologies to build most of the set, while some of the surround would be built by my friend Warren Katz, at Global Scenic Services.

James's diminutive, whip-smart niece, Sarna Lapine, joined the team as his associate director. Any suspicions of nepotism disappeared quickly, as Sarna proved herself invaluable. She had been Broadway director Bartlett Sher's associate director for years and had a film background to boot. Over the next six months, she and I developed a digital storyboard showing the physical changes in the set as the script and story morphed.

The digital version of the scenery for these storyboards was clear and communicated the set's movement, but it wasn't very evocative. I did some Photoshop renderings but they also were a bit unexpressive. James was afraid the renderings made for the show could come across as emotionless and dry. He didn't want the renderings to feel digitally generated; he wanted me to do paintings. After some particularly vigorous coaxing, I spent a sleepless night doing just that.

When I told James the renderings were a product of "Lapine-induced insomnia," he replied, "Welcome to my world. I have that every night." But he liked them, and many of the looks I rendered ended up in the final show. More important than that, we came to see that a handmade element created a nice juxtaposition to the intense technological feel of the LCD monitors and interview footage. Peter and I decided I would create painted backgrounds that he could manipulate digitally and use as part of the video content. James has amazing visual instincts, even when he can't articulate what he's after. His insistence on the hand-drawings proved a style breakthrough.

I had designed a curved cyclorama surrounding the set, with a deep curve cut into its opaque lower half. The upper half was scrim, which could disappear to reveal the band upstage of it. Initially I'd planned to make the cyc a deep, solid blue, but based on the hand-drawings, I changed it to a much more theatrical, swirling, water-color-style surround.

The new paint choices marked the completion of a design I'd started almost two years before. I would call the painterly treatment a *style choice* that enhanced the established *conceptual* one. A solid conceptual foundation for a design leads to the right style choices: the finishes that define what the set actually looks like. In this case, the painterly surround added a warmer, more human quality that balanced the technological feel of the LCDs. The two looks together—humanity and precision—came to define our conceptual representation of Sondheim and his art. We'd begin with a literal video of Sondheim on a conventional, monolithic video wall. But then it would change and reassemble throughout the show, offering a metaphor for the wide variety of Sondheim's work. The style juxtaposition would mirror the traditional musical knowledge that Sondheim employs in the service of a form he so thoroughly reinvented.

Half-inch-scale set model

Putting It Together

The late winter and spring of 2010 are a bit of a blur to me. I was working on *The Scottsboro Boys* for Susan Stroman and *Paradise Found* for Hal Prince, and they were scheduled to tech and open on either side of *Sondheim on Sondheim*. I was overwhelmed and excited to be working with so many theatrical legends but terrified I'd screw something up.

The months leading to the *Sondheim* tech were a flurry of logistics and details both big and small: the plumbing that would facilitate the poetry. I visited Barbara Cook at her Riverside Drive apartment to measure her favorite chair. We were building some LCD-inspired seating units, and James wanted them to be at the most comfortable height possible for the grande dame. Barbara was lovely and it turned out her favorite chair was eighteen inches tall, the standard chair height I would have chosen in any case. But it's never a bad idea to make sure your star is as comfortable as possible—and I got to enjoy the beautiful view of the Hudson River out her living room windows.

After several revisions, we ended up with fifty-four working LCDs (a nice coincidence since we were at Studio 54) along with the fake ones that made up the steps and platforms. (I'd had to let go of my insistence that they be lightboxes; we just couldn't afford it.) The system used to drive all the LCDs turned out to be much more complicated and expensive than Peter had estimated, and in early January we were bedeviled by the problem. James leaned on me to take charge of solving it, although I kept telling him I simply didn't understand the technology well enough. If he didn't trust Peter to solve it, I said, he should fire him, because no amount of pressure on me would give me the magical ability to fix things. In the end, Steve and Sydney Beers came to the rescue by finding the money to pay for the system we needed—and both Peter and I were out of the hot seat.

Sarna and I made tracking sheets that matched James's continually evolving script, and I made a variety of watercolor patterns Peter could digitize and use as neutral backgrounds for some songs. He called them "glue"—to this day, I have no idea why—but we all started referring to them that way.

Steve built a manual rehearsal turntable/LCD pile so that James could stage the actors on the various levels of the set as it was turned by our stage manager Peter Hanson and his team. As James rehearsed with the cast throughout February, the load-in and assembly commenced. Dan Hoffman, our head carpenter, has the quality of a really wise but really grumpy Keebler elf. To me, his kind of wisdom excuses almost any amount of grumpiness, and I found myself deeply grateful for him and Steve Beers at the helm of the tricky process. Aligning the flying, tracking LCD monitors perfectly with the deck-tracked and turntabled LCDs required great precision. At one point, Steve informed me that he'd ordered some elevator rails (which are

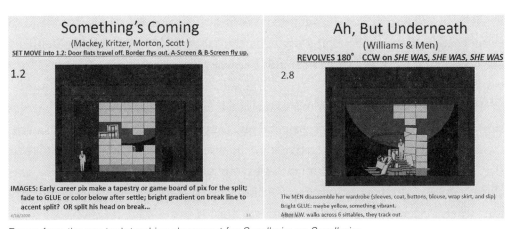

Pages from the pre-tech tracking document for *Sondheim on Sondheim*

exactly that—rails that guide working elevators) to help guide the flown screens in and out of position. I'd never used or even heard of such a thing being used onstage, but I was thrilled that he had thought of it. The kind of care Steve and Dan were taking, coupled with the precision of PRG's construction and automation systems, ensured the success of our extremely tricky design. In lesser hands, it could well have been a disaster.

As the set took shape, I saw that the "dead televisions" that made up the stairs and platforms looked even worse than I'd feared, especially when the real LCDs lit up. I proposed that we put Christmas lights inside them to make them glow. It wouldn't be ideal, but it wouldn't cost much either. We put a string of Christmas lights inside one panel and I asked Sydney to come look, hoping she'd approve the small expenditure.

After a quick look she said, "We can't just stuff Christmas lights in there! That'll be embarrassing. This is Broadway. I'm going to find the money for the color-changing lightboxes you really wanted." And she did. Then and all through the load-in, I kept pinching myself and thinking, *I can't believe they are letting me build this set!*

As we were finishing construction, we got a request from our press representative, Matt Polk: Anita Gates of the *New York Times* was writing a story about the use of projections in the theater and wanted to interview us. As much as I try not to take press coverage too seriously, I understand that if something is in the *Times,* a *lot* of people will see it—and that can have a big impact on a show and a career. So Peter and I spent a day being interviewed and having our photos taken on the set under construction.

For fifteen days, from February 24 until March 9, Peter and I were in the theater every day. He programmed the video into the system, and I stepped through the show move by move, setting the automation. There were about fifty automated moves when some or all of the set reconfigured. We frequently wanted set pieces to land so close together they were touching—which meant that any set piece could potentially crash into another if we weren't careful. Because they were all covered in LCDs, a crash could be catastrophic.

The process of setting each move so that it felt fast enough to be dramatic but was slow enough to avoid a crash was painstaking. Dan Hoffman spent hours with a tape measure as we parsed out the negative space between moving screens relative to their size. For example, a flown unit might sit exactly one or two or three screen heights above a deck unit. This organized the overall stage picture and heightened the contrast when we spun the set into its shattered, disordered-looking positions.

Dan Hoffman fine-tuning the set

On March 10, we started nine days of tech with the cast. As long and exhausting as this period was, because of all the careful planning, it went remarkably smoothly.

We played our first preview on March 19 to a full, loud, appreciative house of Sondheim fans. The next day, we dry-teched* in the morning and then spent the afternoon putting in changes with the cast. I was so tired at that point that I fell asleep in a seat in the audience. I woke up a little later, checked my email, and saw a new message with the heading, "From Steve Sondheim." Heart in my throat, I opened it.

> Beowulf—Just a note to tell you that I think your set is one of the most beautiful (and ingenious) I've ever seen in the theater. And, although you may not believe it, I've been around a long time. Thank you so much. —Steve

I burst into tears. I've had the colossal good fortune to work with some giants of the American theater, and of course, familiarity makes them a bit more human. Steve, by contrast, has retained his status as a deity. When someone you admire that much says something so kind, it is utterly overwhelming.

---

*Dry-tech: slowly working out the set moves, the video programming, the sound cues, and the lighting without making the actors stand onstage endlessly while we do it. Often we spend the morning slowly dry-teching a sequence and then teach it to the actors in the afternoon.

Solution

March 22 was Sondheim's eightieth birthday, and the Roundabout was holding a benefit to honor him and raise money: dinner and a performance of our show. Needless to say, we were all on edge during that afternoon's rehearsal. As we jumped through the show out of order, polishing up various scenes, we had an accident. The set had been carefully programmed to avoid collisions, but when we began skipping cues and jumping around, something got out of sync, and one of the flying screens smashed into a stack of deck screens, knocking them out of their track at a terrifying angle.

"*Stop!*" I screamed as I ran toward the stage and carpenters swarmed out from the wings. While Dan and his crew righted the screens, I paced the stage, terrified that the set wouldn't be working properly for the benefit that night. Luckily, after a half hour of fussing and running the two crashed pieces through their moves, it seemed we'd dodged the bullet. The edges of the LCDs were scratched up, but the screens were undamaged and the automation was working.

I was a nervous wreck, but Jo worked hard to calm me down—another reason a great associate designer is important! For the remainder of the preview period, the carpenters were doubly diligent about having someone onstage watching the units whenever we ran sequences out of order.

The benefit performance went well, and at the curtain call, Todd Haimes announced that one of Roundabout's Broadway houses was going to be renamed "the Stephen Sondheim"—quite the birthday present! At the dinner, the Roundabout donors at my table seemed interested in the set, so I proudly described how we had figured everything out over many months—years, really—of painstaking work. "Oh!" one of them exclaimed, genuinely surprised. "Is this playing for the public as well? I thought you guys just put it together for tonight."

I'm sure this person had no intention of being rude, but it certainly took me down a notch!

Now comes the flipside of a story I told in the *Prince of Broadway* chapter. Early in previews, Hal Prince came to see the show and left angrily at intermission. An interview where Steve reminisced about his collaborations with Hal played just before the song "Franklin Shepherd, Inc." from *Merrily We Roll Along*. The song is about the friendship between two theater collaborators and how it sours because one becomes artlessly commercial. *Merrily* was the last show Steve and Hal did together before that longtime collaboration ended and Steve began working with James. I wouldn't presume to psychoanalyze either of them, but the relationship between Hal and Steve, though very close, was complicated. Whatever the implication of the placement of the song and the interview one after the other, at Steve's request they were separated the next day and the implied connection severed. I was intrigued to be a fly on the wall for this and the parallel *Prince of Broadway* incident but kept out of both. When the mighty battle, the meek better stay out of the way!

The *New York Times* piece about projections had come out on the Sunday before our previews started and, although a half dozen other designers and directors were interviewed, the picture of Peter and me on our set was featured on the cover of the arts section. It's the only time in my career that has happened, and I was pleased—until I checked my Facebook feed and saw a comment by one of the other designers featured. The designer complained about Peter and me being the cover photo and that I got all the jobs that this designer *should* have gotten.

I'm often jealous of other designers, but I can't imagine posting it on social media—which is akin to shouting it in a crowded theater. To make it worse, someone else decided to chime in and make fun of my name (which, let's face it, is a weird name). I decided I'd message both the designer and the friend privately. Both were embarrassed, and that was the end of it. But it served as a warning not to take press coverage too seriously—and as a reminder, if one was needed, of the power of social media to sting!

Through a month of previews, we rehearsed three or four days a week, and James constantly tinkered with the show. The options for the running order of the songs were endless, and James was making adjustments based on the reactions of the audience. I watched in awe as a master director used his instincts, worked his alchemy, and made the show better and better.

About ten days into previews, James wanted to move two comic moments from act 2 to act 1. The first one was a rendition of "Send in the Clowns," Sondheim's best-known song and his only commercial "hit." Everyone has sung it, some well, some less so. Its mainstream appeal has made it a bit of a cliché, but in the context of *A Little Night Music*, it is a deeply moving song. Peter edited together a sequence of amateur YouTube versions of it—from the sublime to the ridiculous. It was a very funny tip-of-the-hat to the overexposure of the song. Later, in act 2, Barbara Cook sang a simple and beautiful rendition of it, so it ultimately got the reverence it deserved.

The second moment James decided to shift sprang from Sondheim's onscreen comments about his less-than-successful collaboration with Richard Rodgers on *Do I Hear a Waltz?* As Steve finished talking, Erin Mackey came on and began a pretty rendition of the title song—only to be cut off and shooed offstage by the video Sondheim. It always got a laugh.

Erin Mackey sings "Do I Hear a Waltz?"

To shorten act 2 and inject some levity into act 1, James made the two moves—which meant a lot of reprogramming of the scenery. We spent a long and busy Tuesday morning getting it done, spent the afternoon retching with the actors, and ran it in the new order that night. Inexplicably, the two repositioned sequences, which had gotten laughs in act 2, fell flat in their new positions. At the Wednesday matinee and evening shows, they still weren't funny.

Thursday morning, we did what we had to do to put them back where they'd been, and—presto—they were funny again. That's the alchemy of putting a show together.

My favorite moment in the show was when the monolithic screen suddenly cracked open for the first time, to reveal four cast members singing "Something's Coming" from *West Side Story*. A wave of reactions rippled through the audience every night at that moment, and I remember one man half jumped out of his seat, his hands raised in surprise and delight as he very audibly said, "Oh my God!" The preceding twenty minutes had lulled the audience into thinking they were watching a concert in front of a video wall. When that screen cracked and separated, they realized they were in for something much less conventional.

For the remainder of the evening, the set continued to fracture and reconfigure as Peter's video played across it. Most of the video accompanying the songs consisted of color and texture, but there were also some architectural details I'd drawn, such as a crumbling proscenium for the *Follies* sequence.

Euan Morton, Leslie Kritzer, Erin Mackey, and Matt Scott sing "The Girls Upstairs," from *Follies*

In some moments, we embraced our documentary format and used the video screens to carry literal imagery. And for other sequences, Peter created animated journeys to help tell the story of an individual song.

The flexibility of the set made it fun to tinker with. We kept finding new and interesting ways to recombine its parts. Opening night was to be April 22, and as it approached, I felt sad. I think it's the only time in my career I've experienced sadness about opening a show and no longer being able to play with my "toy."

Opening night was enjoyable. The reviews were less glowing than I'd expected, but they weren't bad. I guess I was so enamored of the project that anything short of raves would have felt disappointing. I was further disappointed when the season's Tony nominations were announced, and I wasn't recognized. I loved that set so much that I'd convinced myself I'd win for it. Over and over, I'm reminded that in the theater, it doesn't pay to place too much value on other people's opinions of your work.

No matter. If you want a satisfying life in the theater, you have to do your work for the love of doing it. All the other reasons—money, awards, fame—will fall short in the long run. And part of the love of doing it is the satisfaction of a great collaboration. Neither James nor Peter nor I could have envisioned or executed that production on our own—or, arguably, with anyone else. But together, the three of us created a unique production of a unique show. I was, and am, incredibly satisfied with what we created, and that's the really the solution to this very puzzling career.

TWELVE

Mecca

A Conversation with Stephen Sondheim

Setting: *Stephen Sondheim's Turtle Bay town house: the holiest of holies for several generations of theater artists. We're in a ground-floor living room, sprawling and cluttered, spreading from a small front entrance foyer through the main chamber to a back conservatory that opens into a community garden. The room's salient visual feature is Steve's collection of antique puzzles, displayed in frames and vitrines and arrayed on tables. Despite the room's large size, the proliferation of tchotchkes creates the air of a cozy Victorian drawing room.*

BEOWULF BORITT: I'm writing this book about how set designers work with directors. Among the directors I've worked with are James [Lapine] and Hal [Prince], so you come up in the conversations constantly. I thought I ought to talk to you about some of those designs as well.

STEPHEN SONDHEIM: I'm afraid I'll have very little to tell you.

BB: James warned me you'd say that!

SS: No, really. Directors deal with the designers; I don't.

BB: I'm sure you hear this from a lot of people, but your shows, more than any others, are what convinced me to pursue theater. I grew up thinking musicals were frilly and silly, but when I started being exposed to your shows—first *Sunday*, then *Into the Woods* and *Sweeney Todd*—I thought, *This is what I want to do.*

SS: So you're blaming me?

BB: Just placing blame where it's due, Steve! But seriously . . . I've talked to Hal and James extensively about shows you guys did together, so I wanted to ask you about them as well.

I asked various directors, "What productions made a strong impression on you when you were young?" Both James and Susan Stroman credited *Sweeney Todd* and its design as the show that made them think, *This is what theater can be.*

Of course, Hal directed it, and the set was famously a real, and enormous, Victorian factory reassembled onstage by Eugene Lee. But that set isn't inherent in the

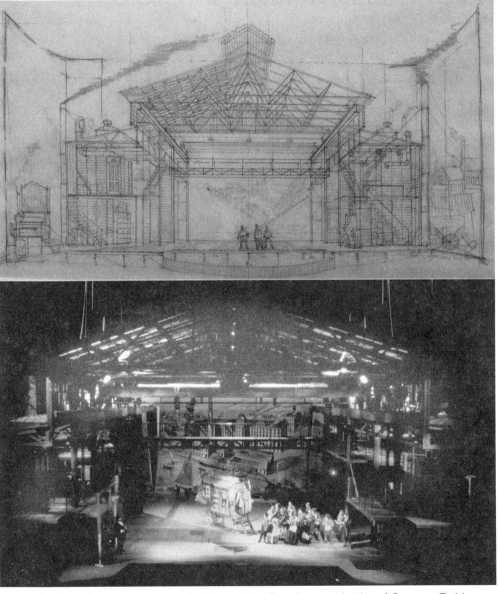

Eugene Lee's design, and a photograph of the original Broadway production of *Sweeney Todd*
Eugene Lee; Top: from the collection of Douglas Colby; Bottom: Martha Swope © Billy Rose Theatre Division, The New York Public Library for the Performing Arts of New York

writing; in fact, the action is never literally in a factory. When you were developing the show with Hugh Wheeler, it wasn't with a factory setting in mind, was it?

SS: No, no. That came afterward. That was Hal's idea. I don't know how he came to it. For me, *Sweeney Todd* is not really a story of how the Industrial Revolution manufactured vengeful Sweeney Todds. That had nothing to do with what I wrote at all—though I did ultimately put one line in the lyrics about machines, to make Hal happy.

I wanted to do it as a small, scary show. I told Hal that if we were going to do it at a big theater, I'd like to drape the entire place in black, have gaslit lampposts all around, and have the cast all around, too: on top of you, beside you, in the aisles, and so on. I wanted the whole theater to look like the inside of a coffin. I wanted an organ and an organist onstage for that opening prelude—a loud organ sound to start the show. Then Hal had the idea of the steam whistle. What led him to it was he saw this factory up in New England . . . but why he and Eugene Lee chose that setting, I don't know for sure.

BB: You said you have no part in designing the show, but that's a very clear visual image you just described—your initial thoughts about it.

SS: I have no visual imagination to say, "The costumes should be red." But of course I have some ideas about staging the numbers. The director can throw them out, but I do go on record with what I am thinking.

BB: That's a good segue to *Sunday in the Park*, because obviously that show is intensely visual, and you guys developed it with a very specific visual idea. James said he'd written a lot of the first act before you wrote the music for it.

SS: Well, I'd fiddled with it.

BB: He said you wanted a sense of what the skeleton was before you tried to sort out how to approach the music. That interested me, because that's how I approach design. I want the set to present a consistent idea through the duration of the evening. When, as inevitably happens, a scene gets cut and some piece of scenery goes along with it, it often feels to me like the whole thing is falling apart. Once you get into production, you must experience something similar—when a song gets cut for whatever reason.

SS: I learned from Oscar Hammerstein about a second-act ballad from *Oklahoma* that was a big selling point on the recording.* They cut it, and it didn't mess anything up.

BB: I guess I need to toughen up and not be so precious about my scenery!

SS: I've learned to be ruthless with my own material.

BB: With *Sunday in the Park*, you were starting from the painting, so that was the visual jumping-off point?

SS: We were going through various photographs looking for ideas. James had used that painting in another show, so he had a picture of it. I said, "One of the great things about that painting is there are about fifty people in it and nobody is looking at anybody else. That suggests that everybody is hiding from everybody." That suggested a framework. Then James said, "The main character is missing." And I said, "Who?" And he said, "The artist." Boom. We got the idea right there. After that, James put a transparency over the picture and drew arrows and wrote, "Artist's mother?" "Artist's model?" and so forth, and we began getting the main characters from the essential figures in that painting and assigning them parts in the story.

BB: Using the visual to figure out the structure of the show is fascinating. When you started *Into the Woods*, obviously there was some structure from the fairy tales; but did you have some visual ideas as well?

SS: No. The idea that I offered James was that we do a quest musical, like *The Wizard of Oz*. I love quest stories. "We can make up our own adventure characters," I told him. His response was, "The problem that leaves us is that we can pick from *anything*—and that's the hardest thing in the world to do." But then we had the idea of combining fairy tales. So that's how that happened. James felt the opening number ought to introduce all the fairy tales, and we could then move from one to the next in separate areas.

---

*"Boys and Girls Like You and Me" was cut from *Oklahoma!* Rodgers and Hammerstein sold it to MGM, and it was used in *Meet Me in St. Louis* but cut from that movie as well. However, you can hear Judy Garland sing it on the 1944 soundtrack, which was recorded before the scene landed on the cutting room floor.

BB: The three houses in the opening help separate the three fairy tales that begin the story. *Company* is spatially organized a little like that. There are scenes in the apartments of each of Bobby's friends.

SS: In the original discussions with Hal, the idea was that there would be five areas onstage, and all five couples would be on all evening long so that while you and I were having this scene, that couple was reading the newspaper in bed, that other couple was shopping, and so on. I'm not sure why it changed. I think Hal and Boris just decided it was unwieldy. But we wrote it that way, as if there were five separate areas and we could zero in on any one of them at any time.

The set we ended up with—the one you know—was determined by Hal and Boris. It was Boris's idea to do the elevator. As he explained it, "This show is about New York City and all its endless opportunities. Everybody's on top of everybody else." For Boris that elevator was the essence of the city.

BB: In *Side by Side*, the character of David says, "You know what comes to my mind when I see [Bobby]? The Seagram building."

SS: Yes.

BB: Typically, when I'm done with a day of tech in Times Square, I walk home across Midtown, and my route almost always takes me past the Seagram building on Park Avenue. It was one of the first of its style of modern New York skyscrapers, rising straight up with no terraced step-backs. They called them the flat-tops originally. I think of that line every time.

SS: It's beautiful and soulless. Gorgeous—but typical of an aspect of New York City life. Bobby's problem is that he's invulnerable. He's perfect. Good-looking. Nice. Heterosexual. He's everything you'd wish a young man would be, except that there's a hollowness in him. The story of the play is how he realizes that and goes about filling that hollowness. That was the idea.

Company, a musical by Stephen Sondheim and George Furth, tells the story of Bobby, a New York City man who can't commit to a relationship—much to the consternation of his married friends. The lack of a linear plot was groundbreaking, providing instead snapshots of moments in Bobby's life via songs and short scenes exploring contemporary relationships. The original production was directed by Hal Prince, with choreography by Michael Bennett, set and projections by Boris Aronson, costumes by D. D. Ryan, lighting by Robert Ornbo, and sound by Jack Mann.

Boris Aronson's concept sketch (showing the separate apartments) and final design for *Company*

Boris Aronson; Top: © Billy Rose Theatre Division, The New York Public Library for the Performing Arts; Bottom: from the collection of Douglas Colby

BB: Did you have some affinity for that specific building?

SS: No, it was just the first one that came to mind! And it's odd, because we had a lot of trouble substituting it for London, because no one there knows what it is. We tried the Statue of Liberty, but that didn't feel right. We had a couple of other candidates, but I found out the British have heard of the Chrysler building, so I think that's what we ended up with.

BB: After *Company*, you guys did *Follies*. You were working on it with James Goldman before you started working on it with Hal, yes?

SS: We'd done eleven drafts!

BB: When did the idea come up of setting it in the ruined theater? Was it always the ruined theater?

SS: Oh, yeah. That was always the notion—that all these old, lovely Follies girls were gathering in the abandoned theater. It came from a newspaper clipping about the annual meeting of the Ziegfeld club, and how all of Ziegfeld's surviving girls would meet. Our whole opening was about voices from the past in this decrepit and falling-down place. It was always that. Hal made a big deal about that Gloria Swanson photo, but it had always been our idea.

BB: When I was younger, I used to look at pictures of the Boris Aronson set and wonder why it was so abstract and not more realistic. At some point, I saw a mediocre production that used a more realistic set, and I realized that the ghosts, the memories, work so much better in the abstracted theatrical version of a ruined theater.

SS: Of course, of course. The great thing about the *Follies* set the way Boris did it was that, up until the last twenty minutes, it was almost nothing but three platforms.

BB: Just pure theatrical space.

SS: Our original idea, before we brought it to Hal, was that it would all take place at this party and then, at Sally's behest, they decide they're going to put on a little

Boris Aronson's design for *Follies*
©Billy Rose Theatre Division, The New York Public Library for the Performing Arts

Follies. The husbands are going to sit in the front row of the orchestra, and the girls are going to put on a Follies.

What happens is that while the show is going on, Sally and Ben go up to Ziegfeld's office at the top of the theater and start fucking—which is what they had done twenty-five years before. Then they get interrupted by Buddy and Phyllis—the way they had before—so it's déjà vu all over again.

We had thought that "Girls Upstairs" would take place by the stage door, and there would be a scene in a dressing room between Buddy and Sally. Hal said, "Do you really want a lot of wagons coming on and off with scenery on them? I'll just do it with lights. Lighting will define rooms. Don't worry about those locations." Then he said, "Why are you avoiding the ghosts from the past?" That was Hal's notion when he took over directing. He said, "Write in the ghosts intermittently through the whole show, and let me worry about how to show the different parts of the theater."

BB: It must be freeing for a writer not to have to worry so much about logistics. But you need a director of Hal's ability who you know *will* find a smart way to stage it! The two of you, and Hugh Wheeler, did *A Little Night Music* next, which also has a lot of locations. Did you have a visual in mind as you wrote?

SS: I think I just had Bergman's movie in mind! Hal and Boris's idea was that the whole thing would be in the forest. You'd see the bedroom in the forest, the salon in the forest. . . . When I worked with Hal, the best thing was he would say was, "Just write it, I'll figure out how to stage it." With Hal, less was almost always more.

BB: It was his great genius and the most important thing I learned from him: Try to start with an empty stage and figure out what the couple of things are that you actually need to tell the story.

SS: What's the important idea.

BB: Yes. There's a famous story that during *A Little Night Music*, Hal roughly staged "Weekend in the Country," and then you came in to see it?

SS: No, that's a showbiz myth! I wrote the scenario for him and said, "It's going to involve a lot of changes of venue from this scene to that scene." He said, "Don't worry about it; just write it." So, I did. I started it with Fredrick arriving on a bicycle to deliver the first invitation. I think we may have cut that because Hal couldn't find a way to get the bike through the whole sequence. That's my memory: we cut it for practical reasons. But otherwise, it was just what I wrote out.

A Little Night Music is a Stephen Sondheim/Hugh Wheeler musical set in early twentieth-century Sweden and based on the Ingmar Bergman film *Smiles of a Summer Night*. It centers on middle-aged Fredrick and his eighteen-year-old bride, Anne. When the girl is reluctant to consummate their marriage, Fredrick is drawn to an old flame, an actress named Desiree, who in turn is having an affair with a married soldier, Carl-Magnus. The romantic intrigues intertwine as the characters move about the city in the first act and converge for a weekend at a country estate in the second. Hal Prince directed, with choreography by Patricia Birch, sets by Boris Aronson, costumes by Florence Klotz, lighting by Tharon Musser, and sound by Jack Mann.

BB: And did you write the cars into that sequence too?

SS: No, that's the arrival at the estate. The cars arrive at the opening of the second act. Hal figured out how to get the cars onstage but not the bicycle! But I didn't point that out to him.

BB: After *Night Music*, you guys created *Pacific Overtures* with John Weidman, about Japan opening to the West in the nineteenth century. The writing is obviously influenced by Japanese music and theater, and the set had a very distinct Japanese aesthetic.

SS: Hal said he wanted it to be Noh theater—to have that ceremony and routine—and we looked at that. But when he actually went to see Noh theater, he was so bored by it that he left after a third of the play. Then we thought that Kabuki might have more of what we needed. Real Kabuki is all over the place, like American vaudeville—Buster Keaton followed by a dog act. Have you ever seen Kabuki? It has that vaudeville feeling of set-piece, set-piece, set-piece—but it also has the ceremony.

BB: Yes . . . when Mimi and I were in Tokyo, we went to the Kabuki expecting we wouldn't be able to last through the four hours of it—but we loved it, we were fascinated. Watching it, you feel the depth of the tradition; and the incredible skill of the performers just draws you in.

SS: I went to Japan with Hal and Judy to do research. It's amazing how cheap-looking Kabuki scenery is, like a high school play. At a performance I went to, just as the actor onstage finished a big speech, suddenly the Japanese man next to me leapt to his feet and started screaming. I was terrified! I had no idea what was going on. I found out later that he was just yelling, "Bravo! Bravo!" because he had loved the actor's rendition of the monologue.

BB: The dangers of not speaking the local language!

SS: Hal arranged for the two of us to visit one of the actors who played the female roles—the *onnagata*—so before the performance, we went backstage. The man allowed us to watch him prepare, which they never do, normally. He placed his mask in his lap, then bent forward and placed his face into the mask very ceremonially. When he straightened back up, he *was* the character. The ritual was astounding. That's what I had in mind when we developed *Pacific Overtures*.

BB: I'm going to rewind to early in your career, to one of my favorite musicals and one I have not yet had a chance to design. Did you have any visuals in mind as you wrote *West Side Story* with Arthur Laurents and Leonard Bernstein?

SS: Where is Puerto Rico? No, I don't think I had anything in mind, but I'll tell you an anecdote, one of those things that one never forgets. Oliver Smith, who designed it, wanted to show us the model of the set so we went out to his house in Brooklyn.

He showed it to us and there was concern over the scene with the highway bridge, for the rumble at the end of the first act. Jerry Robbins—or maybe it was Lenny or Arthur—turned to me and said, "What do you think?" I was twenty-five years old! "I agree," I said. "It just doesn't seem quite right." Oliver turned on me and said, "Who cares what you think? You don't know anything about the theater!" He was really ugly. He was upset that they didn't like it, but he couldn't lash out at Jerry, Lenny, or Arthur, so—

BB: And you were the new guy.

SS: Yes. You know, I understand why he did it.

BB: Did you ever work with him again?

SS: No.

BB: When you're the new kid, and an old hand lashes out at you, it's amazing how much it stings. You remember it forever. On my first Broadway show, *Spelling Bee*, that happened to me. Someone involved in the show, not James, really went after me because I was the new kid. To be honest, I had probably done something stupid—but it was unpleasant, and I will never forget it.

SS: And I don't forgive it! I'm sorry Oliver isn't around so I could kick him!

BB: You don't forget it.

Oliver Smith was born in Waupun, Wisconsin, in 1918. His first Broadway set was for *Rosalinda* (an adaptation of *Die Fledermaus*), in 1942, and his final one was for *The Golden Age*, in 1984. His 129 Broadway designs include the original productions of *On the Town*, *No Exit*, *Brigadoon*, *My Fair Lady*, *Candide*, *West Side Story*, *The Sound of Music*, *Camelot*, *The Night of the Iguana*, *Barefoot in the Park*, *110 in the Shade*, *Hello Dolly!*, *Baker Street*, and *Gigi*. He designed the movie versions of many Broadway musicals, including *Oklahoma!* and *Guys and Dolls*. Smith was a cofounder of the American Ballet Theater and taught design at New York University for many years. Two pieces of his wisdom were often repeated while I was there. He's said to have commented, "I design ten shows a year because I'm a working professional. If I'm lucky, I'll fall in love with one of them." And, "Draw tightly, paint loosely." I didn't really understand that second thing until very recently, as I stared at the rendering I mention in the next sidebar about Smith's contemporary, Jo Mielziner.

SS: My last set designer anecdote is about Jo Mielziner. He designed *Gypsy*, but I was fourteen when I first met him, through Oscar Hammerstein. He took my hand thus [puts out an extremely limp hand for a sad handshake], and I thought, *Oh my God,*

Jo Mielziner was born in 1901 in Paris. His first Broadway design was for *The Guardsman*, in 1924, and his final one was for *In Praise of Love*, exactly fifty years later. His 250 Broadway designs include the original productions of *The Glass Menagerie*, *A Streetcar Named Desire*, *Cat on a Hot Tin Roof*, *Summer and Smoke*, *Death of a Salesman*, *Street Scene*, *Of Thee I Sing*, *Annie Get Your Gun*, *Gypsy*, *Guys and Dolls*, *South Pacific*, *Carousel*, and *The King and I*. His 1956 text, *Designing for the Theater*, was recommended to me when I was in college, and his stunning renderings have been an inspiration—and unachievable model—for me ever since. His original painting for *Silent Night, Lonely Night* was hanging over my drafting table throughout the 2020 pandemic and, in one of those eureka moments, revealed to me how relatively simple his frequently monochromatic approach to scenic renderings actually is. It doesn't seem hyperbolic to say that forty-four years after his death, Jo Mielziner taught me how to paint. Many of my renderings in the photo spreads throughout this book are the result.

what's wrong with him? It felt like he'd put a herring in my hand, like I was holding a dead fish—like his hand had melted into a puddle in mine. I could never look at him without remembering that.

BB: What was he like? He's one of my heroes because his sketches are just exquisite.

SS: You know, I didn't know him very well. He seemed like a very nice man. His drawings *are* beautiful.

BB: They're so good they make me despair of ever being able to paint well enough.

SS: Jerry Robbins said, "Painting well is great. It's wonderful if a set designer can paint well, but that's not what it's about."

BB: Of course. Ultimately, it's a sculptural form.

SS: The painting is a skill, and Mielziner happened to be wonderful at it.

BB: He trained as a fine artist. His father was a painter.

SS: Boris always referred to himself as a painter, never as a set designer.

BB: Really?

SS: Sure. If anyone introduced him as, "Boris Aronson, the set designer," he'd say, "No, *painter*!" To him, set design was a way to make a living but a bit lower than being an artist.

BB: To go back further . . . you went to Williams College and majored in music?

SS: I did indeed, and nothing about it had anything to do with musical theater. It was all basic composition: theory, counterpoint, harmony, and the like. The closest I got to theater was my junior thesis, which was an analysis of Copland's *Music for the Theatre*.

BB: I could continue talking with you all evening, but I won't presume. I'll just ask you the same question I've been posing to all of the directors I've interviewed: Do you remember your first awareness of stage design as a specific element of a show?

SS: Hmm, yes. When I was seven years old, there was a place called the Center Theater. It was one block south of Radio City Music Hall on Fifth Avenue and it was like Radio City: a gigantic palace. The proscenium must have been a hundred feet tall. I saw a show—an operetta called *White Horse Inn*, with music by Ralph Benatzky and Robert Stolz. It starred Kitty Carlisle! The curtain went up, and there was a castle onstage! I thought, *Oh my God!* That castle filled the proscenium arch, filled the entire thing. It was all white and looked like an enormous wedding cake. As I remember it, a white horse came onstage. My father had taken me to Radio City before that, so I guess I'd seen other big sets. The real answer to your question is probably that I saw scenery at Radio City, but I remember that castle.

It was at Radio City that I saw my first movie, *Snow White and the Seven Dwarfs*, followed by a stage show. Every movie was followed by a stage show, and it wasn't just the Rockettes. They often had novel, spectacular sets and effects. I think that must have been the first time I was aware of the sets of a show.

A scene from *White Horse Inn*
Photo by Lucas Pritchard, Museum of the City of New York

BB: It's interesting what you remember from childhood about shows.

SS: The magic of the spectacle.

BB: Last question, and it isn't really a question. I'm going to shorten the quote, but you've said, "Lyric writing has to exist in time. . . . You have to lay the sentences out so there's enough air for the ear to take them in. . . . There's music, there's costumes, there's lighting. There's a lot of things to listen to and look at. And therefore, the lyric must be in that sense simple."

SS: The experience of a musical is so rich that it's like you're getting two kinds of dessert. You're getting the pecan cake *and* the caramel ice cream, so you don't want to overdo it with either one

BB: Well, that quote of yours is touchstone for me. I try to use only the elements I absolutely need.

SS: All art is about economy of means. It's about finding the part that is necessary and getting rid of the unnecessary. That's the hard part, but once you know it, if you're ruthless, you'll get rid of the extra and keep the great. In general, in art, less is more. Although . . . you must remember, there is also Tolstoy!

Epilogue—The Future

Advice for Young Designers

On November 26, 2021, as I was poring over the final copy-edits of this book, Stephen Sondheim died at the age of ninety-one. As of this writing, I'm still processing the loss.

I hope I honor him by continuing in my attempts to take his advice: cut away the extra and leave the essential.

Hal Prince died in the summer of 2019, also at ninety-one. Our last communication was about a new musical that he was developing: *How to Dance in Ohio*. Not long before his death, I wrote to him that even after years of friendship, whenever he offered me a new job, I still pinched myself and thought, *Hal Prince just asked me to design a set for him!*

His reply:

> Oh, Wulfie, your email is hilarious. I mean, pal, you're fast filling Norman Bel Geddes' shoes. Unfortunately, we won't get together until I return from Florida. I'll be at my desk from the 26th of the month and if you call Ben, he'll set up an appointment. I think we need an hour while I anguish, and you save my ass. Love, Hal

Even at ninety-one, he was always focused on the future. What was next? What was he going to do next?

He'd ended my interview with him for this book by suggesting that my final chapter be a prediction of the future of the theater. I've never had a talent for prediction.

Instead, I'll offer some advice to young theater artists. They are the theater's future and will determine what form it will take. My comments are aimed at young designers, specifically, because that's the world I know; but I suspect they apply to anyone starting out in the theater.

My first piece of wisdom is, *Don't listen to me*. Just because it worked for me, doesn't mean it will work for you. I have been colossally lucky in my career. You could do everything I did and yet be an abject failure in this business. Conversely, you could ignore my suggestions completely and have a triumphant career. There is no specific path to success in the theater, so all I can offer are the things that have worked for me. Do those things or ignore them, as you see fit.

I talk a lot about luck. Don't let that fool you into believing I don't have a high opinion of my own abilities—I have a very healthy ego! But I think anyone who has had a measure of success in the theater would agree that luck is a key ingredient. I was lucky that Tad Gesek, my set design professor at Vassar College, told me to go to New York University for graduate school, and lucky I was accepted there and granted the privilege of studying with an exceptional faculty. I was lucky to have met Hal Prince when I graduated and lucky that he introduced me to his daughter, Daisy, who hired me to design *The Last Five Years*. I was lucky that James Lapine loved the score of that show and decided to try me out on *The 25th Annual Putnam County Spelling Bee*. And I was lucky that show was a hit on Broadway and ran for three years. I could go on and on. Any one of those things might not have happened—and that's the scariest thing about a career in the theater. You can't decide, *I'm going to be lucky*; it's not in your control.

But of course, there are things you *can* control. You must do what you can to encourage the lightning of luck to strike and be prepared to deliver brilliantly when it does.

First, *you must network*. As a freelance artist, you probably don't know where your next gig will come from. For that reason, you must always be meeting people and making a favorable impression. Even after decades in the business, no matter how much work I have lined up, I anticipate that date in the not-too-distant future when I'll be facing unemployment. I am constantly aware of looking for my next job, and that means reaching out in every way possible.

I remember how hard this is when you are just starting out and don't know very many people in the field. So you need to meet some! Come to New York (or go to

Chicago, LA, London . . . anyplace with a thriving theater community). See shows. Be gregarious. (If you're not naturally outgoing, as I was not, you *must* learn how to be.) Contact people whose work you admire, and try to meet them for a coffee. Say you'd like a chance to work with them. Offer your services gratis or at a discount if you need to—call it an apprenticeship and get a day job to pay your bills—but get your foot in the door somehow.

When I began designing, I built my own scenery, sewed my own costumes, propped my own shows. I was a great carpenter, a good painter, an adequate stitcher, and a passable welder. Little theaters realized that if they hired me to design a set, for a little extra money I could build it for them too. That led to a lot of jobs. Building my own shows was effectively my day job for many years, though more enjoyable than waiting tables.

Early in my career, as I began to meet people, I kept a mailing list of everyone with whom I came in contact who might possibly give me a job. Eventually, I amassed over a hundred names. Every time I designed a show, no matter how obscure, I'd send out postcards to that list with handwritten invitations to attend. I was designing around thirty little shows a year in those days—and writing three thousand handwritten notes a year!

I realize that "snail-mailing" postcards sounds old-fashioned, and it's easier to use email or social media, but I still believe in paper and stamps. Emails are just so easy to just delete, while a personalized postcard—something you touched, with your real handwriting on it—is bound to get at least a moment of attention before it goes in the recycling bin.

I kept up my postcard practice until I had ten Broadway shows under my belt. Producers and directors often remarked on it and always favorably. If you send three thousand postcards and get two jobs because of it, that's time well spent. As a freelance artist, a significant part of your job is looking for your next job.

The second thing you can control is to *say yes to everything and love everything.* Early in your career, it's important to take on every job offered. (The exception would be a job that risks physical harm.) You cannot know which project will unexpectedly turn out to be brilliant or lead to an artistic relationship that thrives or be surprisingly beneficial financially. I've designed more than 450 shows, and I still don't know which ones will be big winners and which ones . . . the opposite.

This isn't to say that you should put yourself in a situation where you are constantly working yourself to exhaustion. You need to structure your time so that you are making a living without feeling overwhelmed or stretched so thin creatively that your work is devastated. Effective time management is a crucial part of your job.

Once you say yes to the show, make sure that you fall in love with it. *Love every show*. If you find yourself thinking a project is stupid or not worthy of you—or just plain bad—press on and give it your all. Make your contribution help compensate for inadequate storytelling, discover something fascinating about a topic that didn't interest you before, let a small budget drive you to unexpected creativity. Find *something* about it that excites you; it will make your work better.

While we're on the subject of "good," it's important to balance your desire to do good work with a drive to make it perfect. While establishing your career, it's better to do many projects well than a few perfectly. The more projects you do, the better the odds of one of them opening that life-changing door.

If you can't find work, make it. Don't bemoan that no one will give you a break. Find or create a group of people to make theater with. Become a producer or found a theater company—anything to get your work seen. Little theaters with tiny budgets have proved fertile ground for many long and fruitful careers. If you want a life doing this, do what it takes to put on shows that you love, over and over and over.

My third piece of advice is, *don't be an asshole*. Putting on a show is extremely difficult under any circumstances; the last thing a director wants is a designer who's a pain in the butt. That doesn't mean I am a pushover, but I try to pick my battles carefully, stand up for things I think really matter, and be generous about the rest. Never underestimate the importance of being a thoughtful collaborator, amenable to your fellow creators, and respectful of ideas, no matter where they originate. Being pleasant to be around buys you a lot. I can point to enormously charming people who have gone far in the theater on just a modicum of talent. Perhaps others would include me in that category!

The fourth, and most important, thing you can control is to *be ready to do the hard work once you have the opportunity*. As Susan Stroman said (see chapter 4), "You need to go in prepared. I don't think you can just knock on someone's door and say, 'Hey, it's me!' You have to have an idea and a plan." For my thoughts on how I approach the work once I've been given the opportunity, see chapters 1–12!

I want to address briefly the subject of financial and educational background, which certainly affect how you prepare for a career. My father is a Holocaust survivor who rebelled against, then fled from, Hungary's Soviet Communist rulers. He arrived as a refugee in New York with a dollar in his pocket. My mother's family, all descended from Swedes, rose to, then fell from, New England's industrial aristocracy—think *The Cherry Orchard* set in 1950s Boston. But they did well for themselves and I came into the theater a middle-class, heterosexual, white boy. My parents paid for my college education, and a graduate assistantship (which I earned by virtue of the carpentry skills I mentioned above) paid for most of my graduate studies. I finished school unburdened by debt. Although my parents didn't support me financially upon graduation, they provided an important emotional backstop: I knew that if I couldn't hack it in New York, I could always move "home" to Pennsylvania. The career I'd chosen was risky, but I knew I'd never end up homeless.

My point here is that I was lucky (that word again). My admiration for those who succeed without the kind of support I had is huge. And—back to the white boy thing—the theater community, while more progressive than some, is still heavily dominated by white men. Humans are attracted to those who are similar to them. No question I've benefited from that. Of the heavyweights I interviewed in this book, the people who gave me my opportunities, five of the six are white, five of the six are men, and five of the six are heterosexual. All but four of the fourteen set designers I briefly profile are men; all but one are white. Although there are many talented BIPOC designers, none designed the set for any of the seminal shows I discussed with these directors—and that says a lot about the realities of commercial theater. The theater may be more inclusive than some other professions, but it is inarguably subject to the biases of our society as a whole. I hope that is changing. It must.

It was also my good fortune to have received an excellent liberal arts education at Vassar. I majored in drama, but it was a heavily literature-based course of study, and I took as many classes in history and art history as I did in theater. My broad-based education has come into play consistently as I've worked with the accomplished people featured in this book. Hal Prince pursued liberal studies at the University of Pennsylvania; Jerry Zaks and Susan Stroman studied English at Dartmouth and the University of Delaware, respectively; Kenny Leon majored in political science at Clark College; James Lapine majored in history at Franklin and Marshall; and, while Stephen Sondheim majored in music at Williams, his training was classical, not focused on the theater. These artists were broadly educated before becoming laser focused on the theater. They are more interested in chatting with their designers about Weimar economics or Edgar Degas's Ukiyo-e prints than in knowing what Farrow & Ball paint swatch you're picking for the flats.

Of course, a liberal arts background isn't the only recipe for success. I have many friends who focused on their vocation early, earning BFAs from undergraduate conservatories. They certainly graduated college with more marketable skills than I had. The enormously successful and talented Jason Robert Brown never finished college at all, and he is one of the smartest, best educated people I know. But my liberal arts education has served me very well.

My final piece of advice about the theater is to *love it*. If you've gotten to this point in the book, you probably don't need to be convinced of how exciting the theater is. But a theater career will test your devotion to it. It will exhaust you and abuse you financially. It will break your artistic heart over and over and over. It will never make you famous enough to begin to compensate for the pain it causes. If you reach a point where you no longer love your life in the theater—and I don't mean a bad day or week, which we all have—it's probably time to do something else. There are many ways to make a better living working much shorter hours. There is really only one overriding reason to get up and go to work in the theater every day, and that's love.

I've tried to be honest throughout this book about the lows and highs of what I do. The highs have made the lows more than worth it. I love what I do, and that, more than anything, has animated my work and fueled my desire to share these stories.

—Beowulf Boritt, December 2021

Acknowledgments

I began this book while traveling on airplanes to design jobs all over the world. I completed it in the enforced solitude of the 2020 pandemic. I would never have finished without the help of many, many people. Below is an attempt to thank the key players for their encouragement and guidance—and an apology for any unintentional mistakes and omissions and slights; I'm sure there are many.

With that said, my deepest thanks to:

My theater agent Seth Glewen, at Gersh, for encouraging me to write it and for being a tireless and selfless cheerleader for this project.

Elizabeth Kaplan, my literary agent, for bringing the manuscript to Applause.

James Lapine, my mentor and friend for fifteen years, for encouraging and guiding me.

Laura Ross, for your painstaking work editing and sharpening my initial manuscript and for your kind patience teaching me about the publishing world.

David "Tommy" Thompson, Tom Schumacher, Sharon Washington, Michael Bradford, Jeff Sugg, and Alexis Distler, for reading early drafts and offering me your wisdom.

Dan Kutner and Ben Famigliatta, for your help and advice. Nate Bertone and Matthew S. Crane for transcribing early interviews. Steven Fine for audio editing and resuscitation

My mother, opera singer, jeweler, and carpenter, Liz Boritt, who taught me to build things. My father, historian Gabor Boritt, who taught me to write. My nana, gardener, painter, and set designer, Anita Marie Wilson Norseen Hooker, who showed me how to make things beautiful. My aunt, Judy Borit, for taking me to the theater. My cousin, Aaron McClennen, for being my co-conspirator during many years of creating childhood puppet shows. Ellen and Ed Bilinski, for welcoming me into your home and family and never even implying I really ought to consider getting a real job.

James Lapine, Susan Stroman, Kenny Leon, Hal Prince, Jerry Zaks, and Stephen Sondheim for participating in the interviews and for generously reading early drafts.

Stephen Sondheim, for the extraordinary experience of working through chapter 12 with you word by word, polishing and clarifying.

Steve Martin, for helping me chase permissions in the art world.

My publisher Rowman & Littlefield/Globe Pequot/Applause Books, John Cerullo, Chris Chappell, Jessica Thwaite, Jessica Kastner, Barbara Claire, and Laurel Myers for making this book a reality with grace and patience with a neophyte author.

The Billy Rose Theatre Division, The New York Public Library for the Performing Arts, especially Jennifer Schantz, Doug Reside, and Jeremy Megraw, for your generous help in finding and sharing images with me. Lauren Robinson, at the Museum of the City of New York, and Mark Horowitz and Catherine Rivers, at the Library of Congress, for the same.

Joan Marcus, Paul Kolnik, Matthew Murphy, Lucie Jansch, Monique Carboni, and Jessica Fallon Gordon for allowing me to use your photographs. Tony Straiges, Adrianne Lobel, Robin Wagner, Tony Walton, Eugene Lee, Santo Loquasto, Robert Wilson, David Gallo, Derek McLane, and the estates of Al Hirschfeld, Maria Björnson, Jo Mielziner, and Boris Aronson, for allowing me to use images of your designs. Douglas Colby, for access to your wonderful design collection.

Angela, Hermione, and Natasha—the little dogs who have brought me peace.

Mimi Bilinski, for holding me close, for reading me the riot act, for making me laugh, for making me think, for being my friend, and for being the extraordinary, brilliant person that you are.

Appendix

Production Credits

Original Broadway Production Credits for *Act One*

Vivian Beaumont Theater. Produced by Lincoln Center Theater (André Bishop, Producing Artistic Director; Adam Siegel, Managing Director; Hattie K. Jutagir, Executive Director of Development and Planning)

Written by James Lapine; From the autobiography by Moss Hart; Original Music by Louis Rosen

Directed by James Lapine; Choreographer: Mimi Lieber; Associate Director: Wes Grantom

Cast: Bob Ari, Bill Army, Will Brill, Laurel Casillo, Chuck Cooper, Santino Fontana, Steven Kaplan, Will LeBow, Mimi Lieber, Charlotte Maier, Noah Marlowe, Andrea Martin, Greg McFadden, Deborah Offner, Lance Roberts, Matthew Saldivar, Matthew Schechter, Tony Shalhoub, Jonathan Spivey, Wendy Rich Stetson, Bob Stillman, Amy Warren

Scenic Design by Beowulf Boritt; Costume Design by Jane Greenwood; Lighting Design by Ken Billington; Sound Design by Dan Moses Schreier; Hair and Wig Design by Tom Watson; Makeup Design by Jon Carter; Associate Scenic Design: Alexis Distler; Associate Costume Design: Daniel Urlie; Associate Lighting Design: John Demous; Associate Sound Design: Joshua Reid

General Manager: Jessica Niebanck; Company Manager: Matthew Markoff; Associate General Manager: Meghan Lantzy; Assistant Company Manager: Jessica Fried

Production Stage Manager: Rick Steiger; Production Manager: Jeff Hamlin; Associate Production Manager: Paul Smithyman; Assistant Stage Managers: Janet Takami and Christopher R. Munnell

General Press Representative: Philip Rinaldi; LCT Director of Casting: Daniel Swee; LCT Director of Marketing: Linda Mason Ross; Dialect and Vocal Coach: Deborah Hecht; Fight direction by Thomas Schall; Advertising: SPOTCo Inc.; Marketing: SPOTCo Inc.; Digital: SPOTCo Inc.; Photographer: Joan Marcus; Video Services: Fresh Produce Productions; Videographer: Frank Basile

Original Broadway Production Credits for *The Scottsboro Boys*

Lyceum Theater operated by the Shubert Organization (Philip J. Smith: Chairman; Robert E. Wankel: President)

Produced by Barry and Fran Weissler, Jacki Barlia Florin, Janet Pailet/Sharon A. Carr/Patricia R. Klausner, Nederlander Presentations Inc., the Shubert Organization (Philip J. Smith: Chairman; Robert E. Wankel: President), Beechwood Entertainment, Broadway across America, Mark Zimmerman, Adam Blanshay/R2D2 Productions, Rick Danzansky/Barry Tatelman, Bruce Robert Harris/Jack W. Batman, Allen Spivak/Jerry Frankel, Bard Theatricals/Probo Productions/Randy Donaldson, Catherine Schreiber/Michael Palitz/Patti Laskawy, and Vineyard Theater; Associate Producers: Carlos Arana, Ruth Eckerd Hall, and Brett England

Originally produced in New York City, February 2010, by Vineyard Theater; further developed at the Guthrie Theater

Book by David Thompson; Music by John Kander and Fred Ebb; Lyrics by John Kander and Fred Ebb; Music orchestrated by Larry Hochman; Music arranged by Glen Kelly; Music directed and vocal arrangements by David Loud

Directed by Susan Stroman; Choreographer: Susan Stroman; Associate Director: Jeff Whiting; Assistant Director: Eric Santagata; Associate Choreographer: Jeff Whiting; Assistant Choreographer: Eric Santagata

Cast: Josh Breckenridge, Derrick Cobey, John Cullum, Colman Domingo, Jeremy Gumbs, Joshua Henry, Rodney Hicks, Kendrick Jones, James T. Lane, Forrest McClendon, Julius Thomas III, Sharon Washington, Christian Dante White

Swings: E. Clayton Cornelious, J. C. Montgomery, and Clinton Roane

Understudy: Cherene Snow

Scenic Design by Beowulf Boritt; Costume Design by Toni-Leslie James; Lighting Design by Ken Billington; Sound Design by Peter Hylenski; Associate Scenic Design: Jo Winiarski; Assistant Scenic Design: Alexis Distler; Associate Lighting Design:

John Demous; Assistant Lighting Design: James Milkey; Associate Costume Design: Nicky Tobolski; Hair, Wig, and Makeup Design: Wendy Parson

General Manager: Richards/Climan Inc.; Executive Producer: Alecia Parker; Company Manager: Kathy Lowe; Associate Company Manager: Elizabeth M. Talmadge

Production Manager: Aurora Productions; Production Stage Manager: Joshua Halperin; Stage Manager: Alex Lyu Volckhausen; Assistant Stage Manager: Cherene Snow

Conducted by Paul Masse; Piano/Harmonium: Paul Masse; Trumpet/Cornet/Flugel Horn: Wayne duMaine; Tenor Trombone: Charles Gordon; Clarinet/Bass Clarinet/Flute/Piccolo: Andrew Sterman; Violin: Justin Smith; Upright Bass/Tuba: Ernie Collins; Drums/Percussion: Bruce Doctor; Banjo/Guitar/Mandolin/Ukulele/Harmonica: Greg Utzig; Orchestra Contractor: Charles Gordon; Music copying: Kaye-Houston Music; Additional drum and percussion arrangements: Bruce Doctor; Musical Coordinator: John Monaco

Dance Captain: Josh Breckenridge; Advertising: SPOTCo Inc.; General Press Representative: Boneau/Bryan-Brown; Casting: Jim Carnahan, C.S.A. and Stephen Kopel; Website Design/Online Marketing Strategy: SPOTCo Inc.; Photographer: CSI/Lance Castellana; Fight direction by Rick Sordelet; Press Associates: Jim Byk and Michael Strassheim

Original Off-Broadway Production Credits for *Much Ado about Nothing*

Executive Director: Patrick Willingham; Artistic Director: Oskar Eustis

Playwright: William Shakespeare; Composer: Jason Michael Webb

Director: Kenny Leon; Associate Director: Indira Etwaroo; Choreographer: Camille A. Brown; Associate Choreographer: Rickey Tripp; Dance Captain: Tiffany Denise Hobbs; Dance Captain: William Roberson; Fight Director: Thomas Schall; Fight Captain: Grantham Coleman

Set Design by Beowulf Boritt; Costume Design by ESosa; Lighting Design by Peter Kaczorowski; Sound Design by Jessica Paz; Wig, Hair, and Makeup Design: Mia Neal; Associate Set Designer: Alexis Distler; Associate Costume Designer: Annie Le; Associate Lighting Designer: Gina Scherr; Associate Sound Designer: Daniel Lundberg; Production Stage Manager: Kamra A. Jacobs; Stage Manager: Benjamin E. C. Pfister; Costume Supervisor: Amanda Roberge; Prop Master: Sydney Schatz; Hair, Wig, and

Makeup Supervisor: Stephanie Echevarria; Associate Music Supervisor: Andre Danek; Casting: Kate Murray; Casting: Jordan Thaler; Voice and Text Coach: Kate Wilson

Cast: Jamar Brathwaite, Danielle Brooks, Grantham Coleman, Chuck Cooper, Javen K. Crosby, Denzel DeAngelo Fields, Jeremie Harris, Tayler Harris, Erik Laray Harvey, Kai Heath, Daniel Croix Henderson, Tyrone Mitchell Henderson, Tiffany Denise Hobbs, Lateefah Holder, Lawanda Hopkins, Billy Eugene Jones, Margaret Odette, Hubert Point-Du Jour, William Roberson, Jaime Lincoln Smith, Jazmine Stewart, Khiry Walker, Olivia Washington, Latra A. Wilson

Original Broadway Production credits for *Prince of Broadway*

Samuel J. Friedman Theatre operated by Manhattan Theater Club (Lynne Meadow, Artistic Director; Barry Grove, Executive Producer)

Produced by Manhattan Theater Club (Lynne Meadow, Artistic Director; Barry Grove, Executive Producer); By Special Arrangement with Gorgeous Entertainment

The world premiere production was produced in Japan on October 23, 2015, by Umeda Arts Theater, Tokyo Broadcasting System Intl. Inc., and Amuse Inc.; Original New York stage production of *Fiddler on the Roof* directed and choreographed by Jerome Robbins; Original Broadway production of *West Side Story* directed and choreographed by Jerome Robbins

Book by David Thompson; New songs by Jason Robert Brown; Featuring songs by Richard Adler, Leonard Bernstein, Jerry Bock, Cy Coleman, John Kander, Jerome Kern, Andrew Lloyd Webber, Jerry Ross, Stephen Sondheim, and Charles Strouse; Featuring songs with lyrics by Lee Adams, Richard Adler, Mike Batt, Betty Comden, Fred Ebb, Adolph Green, Oscar Hammerstein II, Sheldon Harnick, Charles Hart, Tim Rice, Jerry Ross, Stephen Sondheim, and Richard Stilgoe; Book for *Damn Yankees* by George Abbott and Douglass Wallop; Book for *Flora the Red Menace* by George Abbott and Robert Russell Bennett; Book for *The Pajama Game* by Richard Pike Bissell and George Abbott; Book for *On the Twentieth Century* by Betty Comden and Adolph Green; Book for *Company* by George Furth; Book for *Merrily We Roll Along* by George Furth; Book for *Follies* by James Goldman; Book for *Show Boat* by Oscar Hammerstein II; Book for *West Side Story* by Arthur Laurents; Book for *She Loves Me* by Joe Masteroff; Book for *Cabaret* by Joe Masteroff; Book for *Kiss of the Spider Woman* by Terrence McNally; Book for *It's a Bird . . . It's a Plane . . . It's Superman* by David Newman and Robert Benton; Book for *Fiddler on the Roof* by

Joseph Stein; Book for *Zorba* by Joseph Stein; Book for *The Phantom of the Opera* by Richard Stilgoe and Andrew Lloyd Webber; Book for *Parade* by Alfred Uhry; Book for *A Little Night Music* by Hugh Wheeler; Book for *Sweeney Todd* by Hugh Wheeler; *Fiddler on the Roof* based on the stories of Sholem Aleichem; Sholem Aleichem's stories used by special permission of Arnold Perl; Book for *Flora the Red Menace* based on the novel *Love Is Just Around the Corner*, by Lester Atwell; *A Little Night Music* suggested by a film by Ingmar Bergman; *Sweeney Todd* from an adaptation by Christopher Bond; *Show Boat* based on the novel *Show Boat*, by Edna Ferber; *Merrily We Roll Along* from the play by George S. Kaufman and Moss Hart; Book for *Zorba* adapted from *Zorba the Greek*, by Nikos Kazantzakis; *She Loves Me* based on a play by Miklos Laszlo; *Parade* co-conceived by Harold Prince; *Kiss of the Spider Woman* based on the novel by Manuel Puig; *West Side Story* based on a conception of Jerome Robbins; *Superman* DC Comics created by Jerry Siegel and Joe Shuster; *Superman* DC Comics used by special arrangement with the Jerry Siegel Family; *Cabaret* based on the play by John Van Druten; *Cabaret* based on stories by Christopher Isherwood; *Damn Yankees* based on the novel *The Year the Yankees Lost the Pennant*, by Douglass Wallop; Music arranged by Jason Robert Brown; Music orchestrated by Jason Robert Brown; Associate Orchestrators: Charlie Rosen, Larry Blank, and Sam Davis; Additional Orchestrations: Jason Livesay, Nolan Livesay, Michael B. Nelson, and James Sampliner; Musical Director: Fred Lassen

Directed by Harold Prince and Susan Stroman; Choreographer: Susan Stroman; Associate Director: Daniel Kutner; Associate Choreographer: James Gray

Cast: Chuck Cooper, Janet Dacal, Bryonha Marie Parham, Emily Skinner, Brandon Uranowitz, Kaley Ann Voorhees, Michael Xavier, Tony Yazbeck, Karen Ziemba; Understudies: Rosena M. Hill Jackson, Quentin Oliver Lee, Eric Santagata, and Emma Stratton

Scenic Design by Beowulf Boritt; Costume Design by William Ivey Long; Lighting Design by Howell Binkley; Sound Design by Jon Weston; Projection Design by Beowulf Boritt; Hair and Wig Design by Paul Huntley; Makeup Design by Angelina Avallone; Associate Scenic Design: Alexis Distler; Associate Costume Design: Tom Beall; Associate Lighting Design: Joe Doran and Ryan O'Gara; Associate Projection Design: Christopher Ash; Associate Hair and Wig Design: Giovanna Calabretta; Assistant Scenic Design: Christopher Ash; Assistant Sound Design: Josh Millican; Assistant Makeup Design: Carole Barone; Lighting Programmer: David Arch

General Manager: Florie Seery; Company Manager: Robert Carroll

MTC Director of Production: Joshua Helman; Production Stage Manager: Gregory T. Livoti; Stage Managers: Libby Unsworth and David H. Lurie; Associate Production Manager: Celeste Lagrotteria; Assistant Production Manager: Sarah Pier

Musical Supervisor: Jason Robert Brown; Musical Coordinator: Michael Keller and Michael Aarons; Conducted by Fred Lassen; Associate Conductor: James Sampliner; Piano: James Sampliner; Drums/Percussion: Jamie Eblen; Bass: Randy Landau; Guitar: Hidayat Honari; Reed 1: Dustyn Richardson; Reed 2: Neil Johnson; Reed 3: Alex Hamlin; Trumpet 1: Dylan Schwab; Trumpet 2: Shawn Edmonds; Trombone: Karl Lyden; French Horn: Judy Yin-Chi Lee; Concertmaster: Hiroko Taguchi; Violin: Katherine Livolsi-Landau; Violin/Viola: Jason Mellow; Cello: Mairi Dorman-Phaneuf; Keyboard Programmer: Randy Cohen; Associate Keyboard Programmer: Taylor Williams; Assistant Keyboard Programmers: Enrico de Trizio and Jeremy King; Music Copyist: John Blane

Casting Director: Tara Rubin Casting; Creative Consultant: Jeffrey Seller; Press Representative: Boneau/Bryan-Brown; MTC Director of Artistic Operations: Amy Gilkes Loe; MTC Director of Marketing: Debra Waxman-Pilla; MTC Director of Casting: Nancy Piccione; MTC Associate Artistic Producer: Stephen M. Kaus; MTC Line Producer: Nicki Hunter; MTC Director of Play Development: Elizabeth Rothman; MTC Director of Development: Lynne Randall; Advertising: Serino Coyne; Website Design: AKA; Dance Captain: Eric Santagata; Photographer: Matthew Murphy

Original Broadway Production Credits for *Meteor Shower*

Booth Theater operated by the Shubert Organization (Philip J. Smith: Chairman; Robert E. Wankel: President)

Produced by Joey Parnes, Sue Wagner, John Johnson, James L. Nederlander, the John Gore Organization, Scott Rudin, Eli Bush, FG Productions, Jamie deRoy, Sally Horchow, Sharon Karmazin, Barbara Manocherian, JABS Theatricals, Ergo Entertainment, Seth A. Goldstein, Elm City Productions, Diana DiMenna, Jay Alix and Una Jackman, Jennifer Manocherian, Cricket Jiranek, Catherine Adler and Marc David Levine, and the Shubert Organization (Philip J. Smith: Chairman; Robert E. Wankel: President)

The World Premiere Production of *Meteor Shower* was produced by Old Globe Theater, San Diego, California (Barry Edelstein, Artistic Director; Michael G. Murphy,

Managing Director) and the Long Wharf Theater (Gordon Edelstein, Artistic Director; Joshua Borenstein, Managing Director)

Written by Steve Martin

Directed by Jerry Zaks; Associate Director: Stephen Edlund

Cast: Laura Benanti, Keegan-Michael Key, Jeremy Shamos, Amy Schumer. Standbys: Kate Reinders, Graham Rowat

Scenic Design by Beowulf Boritt; Costume Design by Ann Roth; Lighting Design by Natasha Katz; Sound Design by Fitz Patton; Associate Scenic Design: Alexis Distler; Associate Costume Design: Matthew Pachtman; Associate Lighting Design: Timothy Reed; Associate Sound Design: Shannon Slaton; Assistant Scenic Design: Sara Pisheh; Assistant Sound Design: John Sully; Moving Light Programmer: Alex Fogel

General Manager: Joey Parnes Productions; Associate Producer: Jillian Robbins; Company Manager: Jessica Fried; Assistant Company Manager: Celina Lam

Technical Supervisor: Larry Morley; Production Stage Manager: J. Jason Daunter; Assistant Stage Manager: Matthew Matulewicz

Casting: Caparelliotis Casting; Press Representative: DKC/O&M; Advertising: SPOTCo Inc.; Marketing: SPOTCo Inc.; Interactive: SPOTCo Inc.

Original Broadway Production Credits for *Sondheim on Sondheim*

Studio 54, operated by Roundabout Theatre Company (Todd Haimes: Artistic Director; Harold Wolpert: Managing Director; Julia C. Levy: Executive Director; Gene Feist: Founding Director)

Produced by Roundabout Theatre Company (Todd Haimes: Artistic Director; Harold Wolpert: Managing Director; Julia C. Levy: Executive Director; Gene Feist: Founding Director)

Music by Stephen Sondheim; Lyrics by Stephen Sondheim; Music orchestrated by Michael Starobin; Musical Director: David Loud; Music arranged by David Loud; Additional music by Leonard Bernstein, Jule Styne, and Richard Rodgers

Conceived and Directed by James Lapine; Musical Staging by Dan Knechtges; Assistant Director: Sarna Lapine; Assistant Musical Staging: DJ Gray

Cast: Barbara Cook, Leslie Kritzer, Norm Lewis, Erin Mackey, Euan Morton, Matthew Scott, Vanessa Williams, Tom Wopat. Understudies: Lewis Cleale, Kyle Harris, Dee Hoty, and N'Kenge

Scenic Design by Beowulf Boritt; Costume Design by Susan Hilferty; Lighting Design by Ken Billington; Sound Design by Dan Moses Schreier; Video and Projection Design by Peter Flaherty; Wig Design by Tom Watson; Hair Design by John Barrett; Associate Scenic Design: Jo Winiarski; Associate Costume Design: Tricia Barsamian; Associate Lighting Design: John Demous; Associate Sound Design: David Bullard; Associate Video Designer/Programmer: Austin Switser; Assistant Scenic Design: Jason Lajka and Maiko Chii; Assistant Lighting Design: Jeremy Cunningham; Assistant Video Design: Daniel Brodie

Executive Producer: Sydney Beers; Company Manager: Denise Cooper

Production Stage Manager: Peter Hanson; Roundabout Technical Supervisor: Steve Beers; Stage Manager: Shawn Pennington

Musical Coordinator: John Miller; Conducted by Andrew Einhorn; Assistant Conductor: Mark Hartman; Piano: Andrew Einhorn; Keyboard: Mark Hartman; Concert Master: Christian Hebel; Cello: Sarah Seiver; Woodwinds: Rick Heckman and Alden C. Banta; French Horn: R. J. Kelley; Bass: Bill Ellison; Synthesizer Programmer: Randy Cohen; Music copying: Emily Grishman Music Preparation/Emily Grishman, Katharine Edmonds

Casting: Jim Carnahan, C.S.A. and Stephen Kopel; General Press Representative: Boneau/Bryan-Brown; Roundabout Director of Marketing and Sales Promotion: David B. Steffen; Roundabout Associate Artistic Director: Scott Ellis; Advertising: SPOTCo Inc.; Interactive Marketing: Situation Interactive; Photographer: Joan Marcus

Index

Photos in photo spreads are indicated by *"p1, p2, p3, etc."*